Perspectives on Asian Tourism

Series Editors
Catheryn Khoo-Lattimore, Griffith University, Nathan, QLD, Australia
Paolo Mura, Zayed University, Abu Dhabi, United Arab Emirates

While a conspicuous body of knowledge about tourism in Asia is emerging, Western academic ontologies and epistemologies still represent the dominant voice within tourism circles. This series provides a platform to support Asian scholarly production and reveals the different aspects of Asian tourism and its intricate economic and socio-cultural trends.

The books in this series are aimed to pave the way for a more integrated and multifaceted body of knowledge about Asian tourism. By doing so, they contribute to the idea that tourism, as both phenomenon and field of studies, should be more inclusive and disentangled from dominant (mainly Western) ways of knowing.

More specifically, the series will fill gaps in knowledge with regard to:

- the ontological, epistemological, and methodological assumptions behind Asian tourism research;
- specific segments of the Asian tourist population, such as Asian women, Asian backpackers, Asian young tourists, Asian gay tourists, etc;
- specific types of tourism in Asia, such as film-induced tourism, adventure tourism, beauty tourism, religious tourism, etc;
- Asian tourists' experiences, patterns of behaviour, and constraints to travel;
- Asian values that underpin operational, management, and marketing decisions in and/or on Asia (travel);
- external factors that add to the complexities of Asian tourism studies.

More information about this series at https://link.springer.com/bookseries/15382

Ann Selvaranee Balasingam • Yue Ma
Editors

Asian Tourism Sustainability

Editors
Ann Selvaranee Balasingam
Nilai University
Seremban, Negeri Sembilan
Malaysia

Yue Ma
University of Tasmania
Sandy Bay, Tasmania, Australia

ISSN 2509-4203 ISSN 2509-4211 (electronic)
Perspectives on Asian Tourism
ISBN 978-981-16-5263-9 ISBN 978-981-16-5264-6 (eBook)
https://doi.org/10.1007/978-981-16-5264-6

© The Editor(s) (if applicable) and The Author(s), under exclusive license to Springer Nature Singapore Pte Ltd. 2022

This work is subject to copyright. All rights are solely and exclusively licensed by the Publisher, whether the whole or part of the material is concerned, specifically the rights of translation, reprinting, reuse of illustrations, recitation, broadcasting, reproduction on microfilms or in any other physical way, and transmission or information storage and retrieval, electronic adaptation, computer software, or by similar or dissimilar methodology now known or hereafter developed.

The use of general descriptive names, registered names, trademarks, service marks, etc. in this publication does not imply, even in the absence of a specific statement, that such names are exempt from the relevant protective laws and regulations and therefore free for general use.

The publisher, the authors, and the editors are safe to assume that the advice and information in this book are believed to be true and accurate at the date of publication. Neither the publisher nor the authors or the editors give a warranty, expressed or implied, with respect to the material contained herein or for any errors or omissions that may have been made. The publisher remains neutral with regard to jurisdictional claims in published maps and institutional affiliations.

This Springer imprint is published by the registered company Springer Nature Singapore Pte Ltd.
The registered company address is: 152 Beach Road, #21-01/04 Gateway East, Singapore 189721, Singapore

Foreword

In January 2020, the World Tourism Organization (UNWTO) published a boastful report that presented tourism as a champion sector in the global economy, with an uninterrupted growth for 10 consecutive years. The report exults sheer pride for the effectiveness of the global tourism system in managing 1.5 billion trips (the equivalent of 1/5th of world's population) and reinforces expectations that the bountiful growth will continue. *"A 4% increase on the previous year which is also forecast for 2020, confirms tourism as a leading and resilient economic sector, especially in view of current uncertainties"*. Acknowledging possible risks due to social unrest, geopolitical uncertainties or tensions in international trade, the UNWTO Secretary-General Zurab Pololikashvili reaffirmed confidently that *"in these times of uncertainty and volatility, tourism remains a reliable economic sector"*. One month later, the global COVID-19 pandemic forced the world to a standstill and put the entire tourism system on hold for a long while. New reports from UNWTO in 2021, at 18 months into the pandemic, announce a dramatic reduction of 85% in international tourist arrivals, calling this halt *"the biggest crisis in the history of tourism"*.

The period of inactivity imposed by the COVID-19 pandemic created a severe economic deficit that shocked the global tourism system to its core, forcing it to reboot. And although many are trying, it is unlikely that it will be possible to continue the same practices as before. Tourism businesses, destinations and local governments worldwide are struggling to make sense of the new conditions under which they need to operate: shortage of resources, high uncertainties and new perceptions about safety and closeness. With patterns of demand shifted in favour of domestic travels, destinations built for large volumes become ineffective investments and vulnerable models of development. Studies of system dynamics show that in complex systems such as tourism, getting out of critical points, such as the one following the COVID-19 crisis, is truly possible through dramatic reconfigurations of the system itself. Radical as it may sound, a reconfiguration is also an opportunity to rebuild and simultaneously to correct undesirable effects associated to paradigms of dominance, greed and control: over-tourism, the commodification of nature, the marginalisation or acculturalisation of indigenous population, or unethical management and governance.

As seen many times in practice, crucial elements that support communities or destinations overcome severe crisis are long traditions of collaboration and participation, while structures of power and dominance are likely to accentuate fragmentation and inequalities. Collaboration and participation are cornerstones of sustainable tourism initiatives, frequently associated to multi-stakeholder or hybrid partnerships of private and public actors. They are also core elements in building resilience in tourism destinations, enabling restoration and renewal after crisis. According to research, meaningful participation takes place when all social groups involved, regardless of economic or political status, have an active say in decision-making processes. However, the implementation of pluralistic initiatives is reduced to the mere formalities of involving stakeholders, and little effort is put into ensuring that multiple voices are being heard and their input is included in the decision-making process. Identifying and understanding the factors and conditions that consolidate stakeholders' participation in sustainable tourism and strengthen resilience in destinations remain desirable goals for policy, research and practice of tourism. So, what can be done to encourage tourism communities to dedicate efforts and resources to building meaningful participation with stakeholders in the aftermath of the COVID-19 pandemic?

One of the most important lessons that can be drawn from recent events is that singular perspectives and linear modes of thinking are not sufficient for handling complex challenges such as systems recovery or transformation to a sustainable society. Pluralistic forms of decision-making need new forms of learning from, and in spite of, differences between individual forms of knowledge. Tourism businesses have valuable experiences to share, as they make sense of the challenges to restart business operations after the COVID-19 restrictions. Skilled at evaluating changes in demand, businesses are well equipped for sensing and responding to new perceptions about travel risks. Furthermore, companies that already implement sustainable practices can share knowledge about saving precious resources with local communities that source their workforce. Stewards of land, nature and traditions, local communities often hold treasures of indigenous wisdom that celebrates plural views of life and knowledge, challenging dominant views of economic and political elites. Used to designing policies and action plans that encourage behaviours of businesses and individuals, policymakers are able to create conditions for equitable participation of different forms of knowledge and experiences. Mending tourism vulnerabilities exposed by the recent crisis, as well as creating sustainable systems for tourism production and consumption, requires that we reframe our thinking to appreciate differences as strengths and we learn to view insufficiencies as opportunities to unite in creating new understandings of the future.

Important sources of ancient wisdom, Asian and African cultures have valuable lessons to share about how solidarity and collaboration create solid ties without limiting individual freedom. Contributions presented in this book aim to question, explain and expand our current understandings of collaborative action while encouraging critical thinking about the validity of such frameworks in the context of sustainable tourism. Anticipating and maybe fostering a cultural shift, tourism welcomes such alternative cultural framework that can counter the dominant modernity-driven paradigms of growth, making a leap towards desirable sustainable futures.

Associate Professor, Department of Management,   Adriana Budeanu
Politics and Philosophy
Copenhagen Business School
Copenhagen, Denmark

Acknowledgements

This book is a collection of expertise of each chapter's contributors. Authors who have written within their area of specialised research fields have spent time and effort to improve and re-draft their chapters. We would like to acknowledge our team of authors' contributions. They all worked tirelessly throughout the pandemic to get this project completed.

We would also like to acknowledge our chapter reviewers for their voluntary contribution to offer expert peer-review which helped to refine each chapter to a quality completion. We acknowledge our chapter reviewers:

Associate Professor Harng Luh Sin, Sun Yat-Sen University and Singapore Management University
Fei Long, National University of Malaysia
Professor Amran Hamzah, University Technology Malaysia
Dr Loita Velita, Cebu Technological University
Associate Professor Adriana Budeanu, Copenhagen Business School
Dr Xueke Yang, Sun Yat-sen University
Yesaya Sandang, Faculty of Interdisciplinary Studies, Satya Wacana Christian University
Associate Professor Dr Mohd Hafiz Mohd Hanafiah, University Technology MARA
Professor Can Seng Ooi, University of Tasmania
Professor Heidi Dhales, University of Tasmania, Griffith University and Cambodia Development Resources Institute
Dr Velan Kunjuram, University Malaysia Kelantan
Professor Tazim Jamal, Texas A&M University
Professor Johan Edelheim, Hokkaido University
Dr Elaine Yang, Griffith University

Contents

1   **The Evolution of Sustainable Tourism in Asia** 1
Yue Ma and Ann Selvaranee Balasingam

Part I   Stakeholders Perspectives and Sustainability

2   **Partnerships Towards Sustainability: The Revival of Boracay's Wetlands** 19
Giovanni Francis A. Legaspi and Edieser D. L. Dela Santa

3   **Local Community Participation Towards Malaysian Homestay Sustainability** 39
Ann Selvaranee Balasingam

4   **Nurturing Sense of Place: Host Community Perspectives for Social Sustainability** 65
Paulin Poh Lin Wong and Balvinder Kaur Kler

5   **Sustainability and the Tourist Wall: The Case of Hindered Interaction Between Chinese Visitors with Malaysian Society** 81
Fei Long and Can-Seng Ooi

6   **Sustainable Tourism in Emerging Regional Destinations in China: Stakeholder Participation in Genhe** 101
Yue Ma and Lin Yang

Part II   COVID-19 and Its Impact on Tourism Sustainability

7   **Re-negotiating the Future for Indonesian Tourism After COVID-19: Sustainability as the New Normal?** 121
Mohamad Robbith Subandi, Karolina Doughty, and Rene van der Duim

8	**Tourism Sustainability in Indonesia: Reflection and Reformulation** 139
	Fandy Tjiptono, Lin Yang, Andhy Setyawan, Ida Bagus Gede Adi Permana, and I. Putu Esa Widaharthana

Part III Issues of Sustainable Tourism in Asia

9	**Scenarios of Sustainable Tourism Development in Cambodia** 163
	Heidi Dahles
10	**Sustainable Tourism and the Moral Limits of the Market: Can Asia Offer Better Alternatives** 177
	Can-Seng Ooi

Index... 199

Contributors

Heidi Dahles University of Tasmania, Sandy Bay, Australia
Griffith University, Gold Coast, Australia

Karolina Doughty Department of Environmental Sciences, Wageningen University & Research, Wageningen, The Netherlands

Rene van der Duim Department of Environmental Sciences, Wageningen University & Research, Wageningen, The Netherlands

Balvinder Kaur Kler Universiti Malaysia Sabah, Kota Kinabalu, Malaysia

Giovanni Francis A. Legaspi University of the Philippines Diliman, Quezon City, Philippines

Fei Long UKM-Graduate School of Business, National University of Malaysia (UKM), Bandar Baru Bangi, Malaysia

Yue Ma School of Social Sciences, University of Tasmania, Sandy Bay, Australia

Can-Seng Ooi School of Social Sciences, University of Tasmania (UTAS), Hobart, Australia

Ida Bagus Gede Adi Permana Faculty of Economics and Business, Universitas Airlangga, Surabaya, Indonesia

Edieser D. L. Dela Santa University of the Philippines Diliman, Quezon City, Philippines

Andhy Setyawan Faculty of Business and Economics, Universitas Surabaya, Surabaya, Indonesia

Ann Selvaranee Balasingam Nilai University, Nilai, Malaysia

Mohamad Robbith Subandi Department of Environmental Sciences, Wageningen University & Research, Wageningen, The Netherlands

Fandy Tjiptono School of Marketing and International Business, Wellington School of Business and Government, Victoria University of Wellington, Wellington, New Zealand

I. Putu Esa Widaharthana Hospitality Business Program, Politeknik Pariwisata Bali, Bali, Indonesia

Paulin Poh Lin Wong Quest International University, Ipoh, Malaysia

Lin Yang Tasmanian School of Business and Economics, University of Tasmania, Sandy Bay, Australia

Chapter 1
The Evolution of Sustainable Tourism in Asia

Yue Ma and Ann Selvaranee Balasingam

Abstract Prior to the COVID-19 pandemic, tourism in Asia had experienced a dramatic boom for the past three decades. Rich in cultural and natural heritage, Asia has attracted numerous tourists to both traditional touristic hotspots and emerging regional destinations. One question that researchers and practitioners should ask is whether the fast-growing tourism sector in Asia is sustainable. Are there localised examples of pursuing balanced tourism development? And what challenges and issues does Asian sustainable tourism face? Recognising the importance of sustainability, this edited volume brings together a collection of chapters that investigate sustainable tourism development in different Asian contexts; from stakeholders' perspectives, existing issues in the market, as well as the impacts of COVID-19 on tourism.

This introductory chapter describes the sustainable development concept and provides an overview of the history behind the conceptualization of sustainable tourism. It also briefly introduces the Asian sustainable tourism landscape and research in this field, followed by the key contributions of the collective works in this book.

Keywords Asia · Sustainability · Sustainable tourism · Research · Asian tourism

---

Y. Ma (✉)
School of Social Sciences, University of Tasmania, Sandy Bay, Australia
e-mail: yuem@utas.edu.au

A. Selvaranee Balasingam (✉)
Nilai University, Nilai, Malaysia
e-mail: annb@nilai.edu.my

© The Author(s), under exclusive license to Springer Nature Singapore Pte Ltd. 2022
A. Selvaranee Balasingam, Y. Ma (eds.), *Asian Tourism Sustainability*, Perspectives on Asian Tourism, https://doi.org/10.1007/978-981-16-5264-6_1

1.1 Introduction

The rapid economic growth in Asia with over half of the world's population, together with rising accessibility through air travel, facilitation of transport and large infrastructure projects, have boosted tourism in the region. According to UNWTO (2020a, b), the economic impact on Asia and the Pacific destinations' tourism earnings steadily increased from 17% of the world total in 2000 to 30% in 2019. This is equivalent to USD 443 billion in tourism receipts. This was on the incline until the COVID-19 pandemic hit the world in the beginning of 2020.

In the past decade, the booming Asian tourism industry may have neglected to achieve sustainable development. For example, Maya Bay, on the island of Phi Phi Leh, Thailand, has been closed since 2018 after realising the sharp rise in visitors had severely damaged the environment (BBC, 2019). Mass tourism poses challenges to local nature, biodiversity, wildlife, as well as local communities. In the midst of COVID-19, mass tourism is no longer an issue, however, sustainable tourism practices need to be prioritised and implemented to achieve the UNWTO 2030 Sustainable Development Goals to ensure the industry recuperates responsibly. Additionally, international hotel chains, investment and expatriates involved in many Asian tourism destinations cause financial leakage and only a small proportion of actual revenue from tourism remains in the host country benefiting the local communities. On the other hand, arguably, international tourism contributes to climate change (Kaiwa, 2017). Most tourism destinations of Asia, especially in developing countries suffer from water pollution and mismanagement of water resources which mean many local people suffer from water scarcity (Cole, 2014). It is imperative for tourism researchers, policy-makers and the society to address these unsustainable circumstances.

This book attempts to provide a further step in the comprehension of the nature of Asian sustainable tourism, including a basic understanding of Covid-19's early-stage impact on Asian tourism. This book, Asian tourism *Sustainability* which is part of the series of *Perspectives on* Asian Tourism, adds to this stream of literature with a strong focus on sustainable tourism and the sustainability of the industry in Asia.

This introductory chapter aims to provide the important contextual backgrounds of sustainable tourism and Asian tourism sustainability. We will first introduce the sustainable development concept, and then discuss the definition of sustainable tourism, its principles and historic steps. In the next section, we will present the current landscape of Asian tourism, discuss its sustainability, and briefly review Asian sustainable tourism research in comparison to Western research. We will highlight the existing gaps in knowledge concerning sustainable tourism in Asia. What follows after are the contributions of the collective works in this book and the highlights of the authors' key findings.

1 The Evolution of Sustainable Tourism in Asia

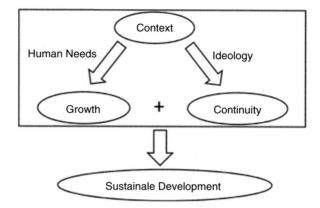

Fig. 1.1 The concept of sustainable development. (Zhang & Chan, 2020)

1.2 Sustainable Development

Sustainable Development is the parent paradigm of sustainable tourism. The concept was first introduced in the Brundtland Commission report, *Our Common Future*. Sustainable development is defined as "development that meets the needs of the present without compromising the ability of the future generation to meet their own needs" (WCED, 1987). This concept was developed due to the growing awareness of the possibility of an ecological crisis (Du Pisani, 2006). This ecological crisis was due to the environmental impact of tourism in mature destinations and increasing political support for environmental protection (Butler, 1999). The concept of sustainable development has a two-pronged view; nature and development view that concerns the resources or environmental continuity and human growth (Zhang & Chan, 2020). Part 2 of the Bruntland Report in 1987 addressed the population growth and resource limits, food security, species and ecosystems, energy, industry, and urban areas (Bruntland Report as cited in Zhang & Chan, 2020).

Figure 1.1 is a depiction of the concept of sustainable development by Zhang and Chan (2020) to emphasise that sustainable development concerns growth and continuity.

1.3 Sustainable Tourism

The concept of sustainable tourism has been evolving for the last 150 years and stems from multiple theories and concepts of development, resource conservation and management with the aim of achieving desired change in society. George Perkins Marsh, the originator of this concept authored the book Man and Nature Or, Physical Geography as Modified by Human Action in 1864 (Gossling et al., 2009). The foundation of his debate centered on ways to utilize natural resources for economic benefits. Later the United Nations [UN] adopted these concepts and published them widely for raising public awareness of world conservation. In 1980, the publication of the World Conservation Strategy was developed to protect and conserve the earth's biological resources in the face of international environmental problems such as deforestation, desertification, ecosystem degradation and destruction, species extinction and loss of genetic diversity, loss of cropland, pollution and soil erosion (Gossling et al., 2009). However, tourism was marginally mentioned in this strategy.

Sustainable tourism was introduced in the 1990s after the popularisation of sustainable development. The concept of sustainable tourism is defined as "'tourism which is in a form which can maintain its viability in an area for an indefinite period of time" (Butler 1993 as cited in Butler, 1999). Since the inception of the sustainable tourism concept, numerous definitions have emerged on sustainable tourism. Past academic authorities in the 1990s of sustainable tourism are Bramwell & Lane, Murphy, Archer, Cooper, Harries and Lieper (Berry & Ladkin, 1997) and Butler. The development of this definition has been critiqued over time with regards to their vagueness and broad coverage. In 2019, Zhang and Chan attempted to reduce the vagueness of this concept and they suggested that maintaining resource continuity and human growth or maintaining sustainable development within the context of tourism should be considered. Figure 1.2 depicts the concept of sustainable tourism that concerns the human growth of multiple stakeholders and the resource continuity from multiple perspectives.

Cottrell et al. (2004) propose that conceptual frameworks for sustainable tourism to incorporate three dimensions; ecological, socio-cultural and economic framework. However, the definitions and literature by Godfrey (1998); Churugsa (2007), Bramwell & Lane (2011); Hall (2011); Holladay and Powell (2013); Moyle et al. (2014) suggest the institutional dimension; while Zhang and Chan (2020) suggests

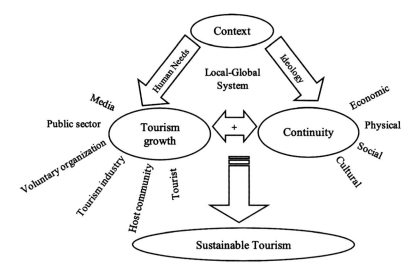

Fig. 1.2 Skeletons of sustainable tourism. (Zhang & Chan, 2020)

the cultural dimension. This indicates that tourism sustainability is multidimensional consisting of the economic, environmental, sociocultural, institutional and cultural impacts of tourism to the community today and for the future generations.

The economic dimension is defined as the stability of economic growth and the maintenance of benefits generated in terms of creating prosperity at different levels of society. This dimension also addresses the cost effectiveness of all economic activities, as well as the viability and activities of enterprises for long-term sustainability (Jitpakdee & Thapa, 2012; UNEP & WTO, 2005 as referenced in Hall, 2011). The institutional dimension addresses the governance or the management aspect, which is defined as a system and rules that govern the allocation of resources and exercising control and coordination (Bramwell & Lane, 2011). The institutional impact is the governing policies at all levels of governance to protect the industry. The levels of governance are categorized into the international, national, and local level of governance (Bramwell & Lane, 2011; Hall, 2011). The environmental dimension concerns the conservation and management of resources, especially those that are not renewable, but are nevertheless pertinent to human beings. It requires action to minimize pollution of air, land, energy, water, and waste and to conserve biological diversity and natural heritage and cultural systems (Hall, 2011; UNEP, 2011). The sociocultural dimension is defined as a means of respecting human rights and equal opportunities for all stakeholders, fair distribution of benefits with a particular focus on poverty alleviation. These efforts also emphasize on local communities, maintaining and strengthening their support systems, recognizing and respecting different cultures, avoiding any form of exploitation, preserving the local culture and norms, and maintaining community structures (Jitpakdee & Thapa, 2012; Phuakka et al., 2009; UNEP & WTO, 2005).

1.3.1 Historic Steps of Sustainable Tourism

There are some important historic steps in the world's development of sustainable tourism. In 1992's Rio Earth Summit, the concept of Sustainable Tourism Development (STD) was developed as a principle and objective of tourism organizations, businesses and academics. The ultimate recognition of this concept was when the UNWTO established a sustainable development entity alongside the World Travel and Tourism Council [WTTC] Blueprint for the New Tourism document in 2003 that created institutional level interest and recognition of the importance of this concept within the tourism system (Cooper et al., 2008).

In 2012, the 20th Conference in Rio: Conference on Sustainable Development marked full recognition of the concept of Sustainable Development (Jovicic, 2014). The conference focused on the two themes of finding ways to build a green economy to achieve sustainable development and lift people out of poverty; and ways to improve international coordination for sustainable development. Globally, $513 billion was pledged by UNWTO to build a sustainable future, which signalled a major step forward (UNWTO, 2013). As this industry is mutually reliant on the natural and cultural environment that needs to be preserved for the future generations, tourism then became an industry under the spotlight.

In 2015, the United Nations General Assembly introduced its updated set of 17 Sustainable Development Goals to be achieved from 2016 to 2030, emphasizing more on the continuity of human growth (Lane, 2018 as cited in Zhang & Chan, 2020). In 2015, the United Nation General Assembly also declared 2017 as the International Year of Sustainable Tourism for Development, recognizing the potential of tourism sector to lead 'economic growth, social inclusion and cultural and environmental preservation' (Khayrulloevna, 2020, as cited in Annual Report 2016, World Tourism Organisation, UNWTO). In 2017, the 17 Sustainable Development Goals (SDGs) were developed as an outcome of the 2012 RioC20 UN conference on Sustainable Development, and succeeded the Millennium Development Goals (MDGs).

1.3.2 Principles and Aims of Sustainable Tourism

The general principles and aims of sustainable tourism since 1987 to 2020 have evolved with the expanding definition of sustainable tourism and the policy goals that have been outlined by international organisation and scholars. Early in 1987, the World Commission on Environment and Development [WCED] outlined the four basic principles of sustainability concepts: (a) holistic planning and strategy-making, (b) the importance of preserving essential ecological processes (c) the need to protect both human heritage and biodiversity, and (d) development based on the idea that productivity can be sustained in the future (Lu & Nepal, 2009). Later in 1996, the Bellagio Principles were designed to implement sustainable development strategies. Nine principles were developed with the first principle as having a clear vision and definition of sustainable development, followed by the approach, practicality and participation by all stakeholders and ending with ongoing monitoring procedures and evaluation. Further, Tosun (2001) discussed three principles of sustainable development which are (a) its long-term perspective, (b) concern for the welfare of current and future generations and (c) applicable to any nation and industry irrespective of its social and economic standing. UNEP & UNWTO also outlines several aims (2005) that include economic viability, local prosperity, employment quality, social equity, visitor fulfilment, local control, community wellbeing, cultural richness, physical integrity and biological diversity.

The common thread amongst all authors is the principle of sustainable tourism involving future planning and thinking, current concerns from multiple perspectives, and incorporating stakeholders' involvement. In essence, these principles and aims inform strategic planning to be based on a clear vision; highlight the preservation of the environment, culture and human heritage; concern economic and social welfare; and most importantly focus on tourism players and stakeholders involved in a particular tourism effort; and finally it also incorporate monitoring and evaluation of the entire process. These aims and principles support the definition of sustainable tourism.

1.4 Asian Sustainable Tourism

1.4.1 Tourism Landscape in Asia

The international tourism landscape has changed tremendously in the past decades. Asia has emerged both as a prominent source market for international tourists, and a compelling destination for inbound travellers. The emergence of the Asia tourism market is contributed by the economic growth, the rise of the middle class and disposable incomes. Low-cost carriers and smartphone usage in travel planning and review sharing have also boosted the expansion of the market (Yang & Ong, 2020). The previous books from the same series *Perspectives on* Asian Tourism have highlighted that the Asian market is dynamic and evolving, and one should never generalise 'Asia' due to its unique history, background, cultural complexity and diversity, as well as political and social systems (Park et al., 2019; Yang et al., 2018). The editors of this book support this view. Nevertheless, the focus of tourism development in many Asian countries, especially in those developing countries has been commonly and explicitly led by the government, although the level and the extent of involvement of the governments in specific countries varies depending on political, cultural and economic backgrounds (Cochrane, 2007; Richter & Richter, 1985), The role of the government in most Asian countries have been played through various forms of funding allocation, tourism legislation, policy-making and promotion, such as the facilitation of ethnic tourism in China (Yang et al., 2008), the promotion of sustainable homestay program in Malaysia (Balasingam et al., 2017) and the welcome of the foreign investment in Cambodia (Po & Heng, 2019).

On the other hand, the unsustainability of tourism affects Asia in various aspects. Many regions in Asia, especially coastal destinations face considerable problems of water availability and quality, affecting their tourism sector and increasing competition with local residents and other industries (Cole et al., 2020). Southeast Asia, in particular, which heavily relies on tourism is also vulnerable to natural disasters, including cyclones, floods, earthquakes, tsunami, bushfires, droughts and volcanoes. In 2020, the COVID-19 hit the tourism sector hard, as governments worldwide implemented stay-at-home or lockdown measures to face the health crisis. The number of inbound visitors in Asia Pacific, among all the continents, was forecasted to drop the most by 83% (Americas −73%, Europe −69%, Africa −73% and Middle East −76%) (Statista, 2021).

1.4.2 Research into Asian Sustainable Tourism

Twenty-five years after the Brundtland Report was released, over 5000 publications on sustainable tourism were produced with most of the studies being concentrated in the regions of North-West Europe (16%), followed by Oceania (16%), North America (11%), South and Eastern Europe (11%), sub-Saharan Africa (6%), and North-East Asia (5%) (Ruhanen et al., 2015). Central Asia, West Asia, South Asia and South East Asia were areas that were under-researched (Yang & Ong, 2020). A bibliometric study of sustainable tourism showed a similar result that Europe was the primary area of research, with Asia and Australia having limited presence (Sánchez-Cañizares et al., 2018). Nonetheless, according to Mura and Khoo-Lattimore (2018), the West has played a pivotal role in constructing knowledge including Asian tourism knowledge. Consequently, there is a need to encourage 'Asianisation of tourism scholarship' including indigenous knowledge production, indigenous methodologies, and epistemologies (Ooi, 2019). Therefore, the aim of this book is to paint a more holistic picture of sustainable tourism and contribute to the decolonisation of tourism sustainability knowledge.

1.5 Contributions of Chapters in the Book

When proposing this book at the end of 2019, the world was at the peak of experiencing mass tourism. Many Asian tourism destinations and their practices were seen as unsustainable, including issues of over-tourism, overcrowding, over-commercialisation, environmental degradation and imbalanced socio-economic growth. When the book proposal was approved and at the time of calling for chapters in mid-2020, WHO had already declared the spread of coronavirus a global pandemic. The world has ever since experiencing regional lockdowns, and dramatic changes were happening in Asia, including the closure of borders, shift to work from home, social distancing; and numerous tourism and hospitality workers have had their employment affected. Many businesses have been struggling to survive. All stakeholders in the industry have fought for ways to recover.

The compilation of this book experienced the fast-changing tourism landscape of the Asian tourism market; and therefore, it consists of both sustainability discussions pre-COVID and the documentation of tourism in this pandemic era. The collection works in this book are therefore a timely contribution to extend and renew the existing understanding of Asian tourism sustainability.

For this book, we only received chapter proposals covering the tourism destinations from the South-east Asian countries and China, rather than from Western and Central Asia, even though when calling for chapters, we did not specify any particular geographical regions of Asia. This could be explained by Yang et al. (2018) that 'the identity of Asia is an evolving social imagination' (p. 6). This book addresses the above mentioned research gap by providing insights within the under-research areas of South East Asia, as well as on themes that include Asian stakeholder perspectives and impact studies.

The following chapters have been divided into three main parts, as an attempt to get closer to sustainable tourism in Asia, although the division of the boundaries is blurred:

Part 1. Stakeholders' perspectives and sustainability
Part 2. Covid-19 and its impact on Asian tourism sustainability
Part 3. Issues of sustainable tourism in Asia

Part 1 includes five chapters, which mainly discusses different stakeholders' perspectives in sustainable tourism development in order to achieve a balanced growth; yet Chaps. 2, 4 and 6 also mention more or less the influence of the pandemic on the destinations' tourism sustainability. Chapters constituting Part 2 mainly focus on the changes, challenges and opportunities that Covid-19 has brought to the destination, but also take stakeholders' perspectives into account. For instance, Chap. 7 indicates that the central government of Indonesia retained a dominant role in sustainable tourism agendas, but there was little evidence of including voices from the communities. Likewise, Part 3 scrutinizes multiple issues seen in the industry, but none of the chapters could avoid discussing stakeholders' roles and their participation; also, the pandemic has worsened some of the issues or shed light on certain problems.

The first part delves into the stakeholders' perspectives of sustainable tourism, while discussing a variety of contexts. Chapter 2 examines the partnerships towards sustainability, focusing on a Philippine tourism destination - Boracay Wetlands where the whole island was closed for 6 months in 2018 to be rehabilitated after years of environmental destruction. Legaspi and Santa in this chapter look into the implementation of Corporate Social Responsibility (CSR) initiatives. Carrying out from the lens of social learning, the case study analyzes public and private partnership in the revival of a wetland, with no cash outlay from the government, in the journey towards sustainable tourism development in the island. It identifies antecedents that lead to the involvement of particular organizations and stakeholders. It shows that the degraded nature of the ecosystem itself, and a clear cognition that a lack of resources or capacity would constrain actors from acting independently, galvanizes the action of stakeholders and influences the way rehabilitation and CSR is implemented. Driven by an internal desire to improve the general condition, private companies engage in CSR. Sustaining their participation are deeply-held family values to give back to communities, a goal which matches the state's aspirations. Besides calling attention to the role of the family and the state, the study points to the importance of collaboration among stakeholders, bound together by the common purpose of addressing serious environmental degradation, as a mechanism for CSR delivery. The chapter provides insights into how CSR for the environment is conceived and executed in the Philippines, and broadly, an understanding of how distinct CSR traditions in the Asian region are compared to the West, in ways that highlight the distinctness of Asian tourism sustainability.

Tracing back to 1992, the Agenda 21 perspective on sustainable development has already advocated community involvement in decisions on tourism planning and development (UN, 2021). A host community is a key stakeholder within the tourism system, but their participation in tourism is variable. Both Chaps. 3 and 4 discuss the significance of community participation and engagement in achieving tourism sustainability. In Chap. 3, Balasingam acknowledges that the local community provides important perspectives towards creating sustainable Malaysian homestays. Quantitative data was collected from four stakeholder groups, namely the homestay owner, government officials, tourists, and local residents and tested using the homestay sustainability conceptual framework to ascertain the extent that Malaysian homestays are sustainable for the future generations. The literature focuses on sustainable tourism and community-based tourism (CBT). Miso Walai Homestay is benchmarked as a successful case study. The chapter found that the four sustainability dimensions of economic, institutional, environmental and socio-cultural dimensions have significant relationships with homestay sustainability. The most profound impact is the environmental dimension as all stakeholders agree that homestays are a competitive destination, create jobs and create a multiplier effect for the local community. Within the context of Asian tourism sustainability, homestay sustainability considers the participation and input of multiple stakeholders.

Chapter 4 written by Wong and Kler provides a contextual understanding of the host community perspectives on destination sustainability, applying the concept - sense of place. This chapter focuses on social sustainability, specifically on one of the 15 areas, 'access to recreation'. It argues that tourism planning should consider these needs as a form of destination sustainability. In this chapter, the host community and their participation in tourism was defined as local residents who live in the vicinity of and participate in recreational activities at the Tunku Abdul Rahman marine park (TARP), Sabah, in the island of Borneo, Malaysia. Findings of this qualitative study produced both positive and negative themes which were used to refine the Pearce (2005) Sustainability Embedded Place Model. Themes were plotted into the components of activities, resources and conceptions. The chapter found that access to recreation is an essential element for the host community, and therefore future tourism development on TARP should consider these indicators to preserve social sustainability. By preserving these place-based indicators, the marine park authorities would have taken steps to enhance the Agenda 2030 Sustainable Development Goals (SDG), SDG 14 Life Below Water and SDG 15 Life on Land. This chapter suggests nurturing the host community's sense of place contributes to destination sustainability.

Following that, Long and Ooi in Chap. 5 assert that tourism is often considered a benign force to social sustainability and bring positive changes to host societies, but they argue that the assumption is inconclusive. The authors proposed a concept - the tourist wall, and used the lens of hindered interaction between Chinese visitors with Malaysian society to evaluate the social sustainability. By analyzing how Chinese tourists publicly review Malaysia on two top Chinese travel-sharing websites (i.e. Mafengwo.com and Qyer.com), it is found that there is a conspicuous silence on the discriminatory policy against Malaysian Chinese in those reviews even though the manifestations of that policy is omnipresent. Then, the chapter discusses how a Chinese tourist wall is constructed, how tourist businesses are inadvertently strengthening that wall, and how the wall limits the fulfillment of tourism's social sustainability goals. Arguably, the wall imposes a serious challenge for tourism to deliver considerable social benefits to the local community and eventually achieve social sustainability of tourism development. The newly-introduced concept of tourist wall facilitates us gaining a deeper understanding of the complexity of host-guest relations and the role of tourism that can play in social sustainability. Furthermore, the authors are suggesting the importance of interpreting tourists' silence when they describe their experiences. Tourists' ostensible silence may carry much hidden information that is neglected by previous tourism studies, which may help overseas destinations truly understand Chinese tourists.

Chapter 6 contributed by Ma and Yang explores the participation of different stakeholders in sustainable tourism in China, using Genhe, Inner Mongolia Autonomous Region as a case study. The case to some extent represents emerging regional destinations in China, where tourism has been advocated as a way to diversify the economy in the underdeveloped areas. Based on a desk-based research, this chapter reviews existing activities undertaken by the Destination management organization (DMO) and describes how the different stakeholders participate in achieving the region's development goals – environmental, social and economic sustainability. This chapter found that although the key decisions including the industrial transition from forestry to tourism are largely made based on the input from the different levels of the government bodies, other non-government stakeholders are also involved in the development process through various forms and levels of participation. All stakeholders follow the government policy, and voluntarily or involuntarily participate in the initiative from the government body. It is a government-centric view regardless of the benefits of their own entities. This is different from Western context where each stakeholder tends to look after their own institutes. The community's involvement is implicit in the tourism activities implemented by the DMO, though their role in the development of the destination is demonstrated through participation rather than planning and decision-making. This chapter also highlights the need that future research should investigate the motivations and relationships of the stakeholders in Chinese sustainable tourism development.

The two chapters in Part 2 examine the impact of COVID-19 on tourism sustainability from different angles and both focus on Indonesia, the largest economy in the Southeast Asian region, which is often under-represented in the literature. Chapter 7 entitled *Re-negotiating the future for* Indonesian tourism *after* COVID-19: Sustainability *as the* New Normal written by Subandi, Doughty and Duim analysed the emerging discourses – from March to September 2020 – as voiced by Indonesian tourism stakeholders and examined to what extent these discourses included the notion of sustainability. Their analysis clearly identified 'New Normal' as an overarching discourse which was consistently repeated and reproduced across the platforms the authors examined, where three issues prevailed: social distancing, health and hygiene protocols and Quality Tourism. It argues that social distancing could lead to an increase in the desire for nature-based tourism. In addition, although the link between the health and hygiene protocols and the New Normal in the context of the pandemic was obvious, it is less clear how these protocols relate to furthering sustainability agenda, except that the increased 'cleanliness' can contribute to overall environmental sustainability by reducing waste problem which is a major tourism issue in Indonesia. To capitalize on the suspension of activity caused by the pandemic and to push the Indonesian tourism sector toward a more sustainable direction, some stakeholders proposed a shift from quantity to quality as a 'solution' for the Indonesian tourism sector's poor performance.

Tjiptono, Yang, Setyawan, Permana and Widaharthana in Chap. 8 focus on the emergence, development, and challenges of sustainable tourism thought and practices in Indonesia. The chapter investigates how COVID-19 pandemic has severely disrupted the sustainability initiatives and efforts made by the government. This chapter offers important insights into how tourism and hospitality businesses in Bali, the largest and most popular tourism destination in Indonesia, respond and adapt during the COVID-19 pandemic and new normal. Although the specific responses varied across companies reflecting specific contexts, adaptability and flexibility of each player, the patterns of survival and recovery strategies are classified by the authors into the 4Rs strategies. Companies have navigated and survived the crisis by *restructuring* the business to improve their efficiency, *re-aligning* business processes in compliance to COVID-19 health protocols, *researching* and responding to new business opportunities, and/or *retargeting* the market. Interestingly, the strategies show that during the COVID-19 pandemic, which has been perceived as a 'death sentence' for many businesses, companies in the Indonesian tourism and hospitality industry have explored many innovative breakthroughs beyond survival. Such insights are relevant for other companies in the same and different industries as well as in different countries (e.g., Southeast Asian region) facing the COVID-19 crisis.

Part 3 addresses a few issues that exist in the Asian tourism developments' endeavour in pursuing sustainability. The growth of the Asian tourism market has not only posted opportunities but also challenges. This part covers the government level, the market level and the community level. The examples illustrated and the lessons learnt from the chapters are usually not alone within its own context. Dahles in Chap. 9 brings to readers a comparison of two scenarios that feature in Cambodia's tourism development: the government-driven growth scenario and the diversification scenario led by local initiatives that evolve under the banner of sustainable tourism. The discussion contributes to a critical assessment of major tourism trends in Cambodia from the perspective of the 'sustainable tourism development' narrative, which has risen to great prominence in current tourism research across academic fields. This chapter firstly shows that the government-driven growth scenario successfully employs tourism as an instrument for GDP growth but fails to provide economic benefits to local communities and create sustainable livelihoods. Then, the chapter raises critical questions about the diversification scenario designed to promote local participation in tourism development as initiatives rarely include the voice of the intended beneficiaries. Whilst social enterprises have the potential to channel a greater share of tourism benefits to communities and reduce revenue leakage, more investments in infrastructure, training and education, including basic business management, are called for to establish a meaningful local participation. In addition to that, it is advised that there is an increasing mismatch between the tourism product developed by Cambodia's social enterprises and the market which is shaped by increasing numbers of arrivals from East Asia. Finally, not alone in Cambodia, in view of the complete shutdown of the tourism industry as a consequence of the pandemic, local people should be encouraged by the government to diversify their business or trade with opportunities outside the narrow contours of the tourism industry to avoid the risks implied by a downturn in tourist arrivals.

The emergence of sustainable tourism arises within the context of a wider economic agenda that has dominated the development of modern societies, at the detriment to the environment and of local communities. After observing this major issue of the industry, in Chap. 10, Ooi critically assesses the two moral limits of the market. The first moral limit points to how economic exchange transforms products, services and/or experiences in ways that denigrate and even destroy the intrinsic value of what is being sold. Revered sites lose their sacred values when economically transacted, for instance. The second moral limit of the market points to how the market fails to distribute benefits of market exchange equitably. Accessibility to goods and services are based on people's ability to pay rather than on their needs, and that the benefits do not necessarily go to deserving parties. For example, slum tourism has enriched tour operators and provided interesting experiences to tourists but does little to lift the slum communities. Ooi in this chapter also comprehensively evaluates some methods and models that are used in Asia to promote their versions of sustainable tourism and mitigate the consequences arising from the inherent moral limits of the market. It includes the application of the triple bottom lines in diverse tourism businesses, public authorities being responsible for the welfare of society, the Public-Private Partnership (PPP) model, redesign and regulation of the visitor market, and the community-led tourism model. Interestingly, Ooi's answer to his ultimate question - Can Asia offer alternatives to doing better sustainable tourism? His answer is: yes, but with caveats.

1.6 Concluding Remarks

This edited book draws together empirical research from across a range of Asia-Pacific destinations and conceptual discussions on the sustainability of Asian tourism. We hope this book can provide a consolidated and updated reference to researchers, industry practitioners, decision-makers and students for understanding Asian tourism sustainability, although this brief volume is only a partial representation of the vast Asia landscape. It is also noteworthy that the tourism landscapes in Asia have been undergoing unprecedented rapid and structural change on a global scale in the current pandemic era.

References

Balasingam, A. S., Bojei, J., Awang, K. W., & Radzi, S. M. (2017). Institutional sustainability of Malaysian homestays: Government perspective. *Journal of Tourism, Hospitality & Culinary Arts, 9*(3), 85–103.

BBC. (2019). Thailand: Tropical bay from 'The Beach' to close until 2021. *BBC News, Asia*. https://www.bbc.com/news/world-asia-48222627

Berry, S., & Ladkin, A. (1997). Sustainable tourism: A regional perspective. *Tourism Management, 18*(7), 433–440.

Bramwell, B., & Lane, B. (2011). Critical research on the governance of tourism and sustainability. *Journal of Sustainable Tourism, 19*(4–5), 411–421.

Butler, R. W. (1999). Sustainable tourism: A state-of-the-art review. *Tourism Geographies, 1*(1), 7–25.

Cochrane, J. (Ed.). (2007). *Asian tourism: Growth and change*. Elsevier.

Cole, S. (2014). Tourism and water: from stakeholders to rights holders, and what tourism businesses need to do. *Journal of Sustainable Tourism, 22*(1), 89–106.

Cole, S. K., Mullor, E. C., Ma, Y., & Sandang, Y. (2020). "Tourism, water, and gender"—An international review of an unexplored nexus. *Wiley Interdisciplinary Reviews: Water, 7*(4), e1442.

Cooper, C., Fletcher, J., Fyall, A., Gilbert, D., & Wanhill, S. (2008). *Tourism: Principles and practise*. Pearson Education.

Cottrell, S., Van Der Duim, R., Ankersmid, P., & Kelder, L. (2004). Measuring the sustainability of tourism in Manuel Antonio and Texel: A tourist perspective. *Journal of Sustainable Tourism., 12*(5), 409–431.

Churugsa, W., McIntosh, A. J., & Simmons, D. (2007). Sustainable tourism planning and development: Understanding the capacity of local government. *Leisure/ Loisir, 31*(3), 453–473.

Du Pisani, J. A. (2006). Sustainable development – Historical roots of the concept. *Environmental Sciences, 3*, 83–96.

Godfrey, K. B. (1998). Attitudes toward 'sustainable tourism' in the UK: A view from local government. *Tourism Management, 19*(3), 213–224.

Gossling, S., Hall, M., & Weaver, D. B. (2009). *Sustainable tourism futures: Perspectives on systems, restructuring and innovations*. Routledge.

Hall, C. M. (2011). Policy learning and policy failures in sustainable tourism governance: From first- and second- order to third-order change? *Journal of Sustainable Tourism, 19*(4–5), 649–671.

Holladay, P. J., & Powell, R. B. (2013). Resident perceptions of social–ecological resilience and the sustainability of community-based tourism development in the Commonwealth of Dominica. *Journal of Sustainable Tourism, 21*(8), 1188–1211.

Jitpakdee, R., & Thapa, G. B. (2012). Sustainability analysis of ecotourism on Yao Noi Island, Thailand. *Asia Pacific Journal of Tourism Research, 17*(3), 301–325.

Jovicic, D. Z. (2014). Key issues in the implementation of sustainable tourism. *Current Issues in Tourism, 17*(4), 297–302.

Khayrulloevna, A. M. (2020). The substantial economic benefits of tourism. *Academy, 3*(54).

Kaiwa, E. (2017). *Sustainable tourism in Asia – Current situations, trends, and existing practices*. World Scientific Publishing Company.

Lu, J., & Nepal, S. K. (2009). Sustainable tourism research: An analysis of papers published in the Journal of Sustainable Tourism. *Journal of Sustainable Tourism, 17*(1), 5–16.

Moyle, B. D., Mclennan, C. J., Ruhanen, L., & Weiler, B. (2014). Tracking the concept of sustainability in Australian tourism policy and planning documents. *Journal of Sustainable Tourism, 22*(7), 1037–1051.

Mura, P., & Khoo-Lattimore, C. (2018). *Locating Asian research and selves in qualitative tourism research. Asian qualitative research in tourism, perspectives on Asian tourism*. Springer Nature.

Ooi, C. S. (2019). Asian tourists and cultural complexity: Implications for practice and the Asianisation of tourism scholarship. *Tourism Management Perspectives, 31*, 14–23.

Park, E., Kim, S., & Yeoman, I. (2019). *Eating in Asia: Understanding food tourism and its perspectives in Asia* (Food tourism in Asia, perspectives on Asian tourism). Springer Nature.

Pearce PL (2005) Tourist behaviour: Themes and conceptual schemes. Channel View Publications, Clevedon.

Phuakka, R., Sarkki, S., Cottrell, S. P., & Siikamaki, P. (2009). Local discourses and international initiatives: Sociocultural sustainability of tourism in Oulanka National Park Finland. *Journal of Sustainable Tourism, 17*(5), 529–549.

Po, S., & Heng, K. (2019). Assessing the impacts of Chinese investments in Cambodia: The case of Preah Sihanoukville province. *Pacific Forum (Issues & Insights), 19*, 1–19.

Richter, L. K., & Richter, W. L. (1985). Policy choices in South Asian tourism development. *Annals of Tourism Research, 12*(2), 201–217.

Ruhanen, L., Weiler, B., Moyle, B. D., & McLennan, C. L. J. (2015). Trends and patterns in sustainable tourism research: A 25-year bibliometric analysis. *Journal of Sustainable Tourism, 23*(4), 517–535.

Sánchez-Cañizares, S. M., Castillo-Canalejo, A. M., & Cabeza-Ramírez, L. J. (2018). Sustainable tourism in sensitive areas: Bibliometric characterisation and content analysis of specialised literature. *Sustainability, 10*(5), 1525.

Statista. (2021). *Inbound tourism visitor growth worldwide in 2019, with a forecast to 2023, by region. Travel, Tourism & Hospitality.* https://www.statista.com/statistics/274010/inbound-visitor-growth-forecast-worldwide-by-region/

Tosun, C. (2001). Challenges of sustainable tourism development in the developing world: The case of Turkey. *Tourism Management, 22*, 289–302.

United Nations. (2021). *Agenda 21, UNCED 1992. Sustainable development goals knowledge platform.* Retrieved from https://sustainabledevelopment.un.org/outcomedocuments/agenda21

United Nations World Tourism Organisation. (2013). *UNWTO world tourism highlights 2013 edition.* Retrieved from http://mkt.unwto.org/en/barometer

United Nations Environmental Program and the United Nations World Tourism Organization. (2005). *Making tourism more sustainable: A guide for policy makers.* United Nations Environmental Programme.

United Nations Environment Programme. (2011). *The global partnership.* Retrieved from http://www.unep.org/resourceefficiency/Business/SectoralActivities/Tourism/Activities/TheGlobalPartnershipforSustainableTourism/tabid/78818/Default.aasp

UNWTO. (2020a). *UNGA sustainable tourism resolutions.* Retrieved from https://www.unwto.org/sustainable-development/unga

UNWTO. (2020b). *International tourism highlights – 2020 edition.* UNWTO.

United Nations Environmental Programme & World Tourism Organisation. (2005). *Making tourism more sustainable, guideline for policy makers.* Retrieved from http://www.unep.fr/shared/publications/pdf/DTIx0592xPA-TourismPolicyEN.pdf

World Commission on Economic Development. (1987). *UN Documents: Gathering a body of global agreements, our common future: Report on the World Commission on Environment and Development.* Retrieved from: http://www.un-documents.net/wced-ocf.htm

Yang, E. C. L., & Ong, F. (2020). Redefining Asian tourism. *Tourism Management Perspectives, 34* https://doi.org/10.1016/j.tmp.2020.100667.

Yang, E. C. L., Lee, J. S. H., & Khoo-Lattimore, C. (2018). Asian cultures and contemporary tourism: Locating Asia, cultural differences and trends. *Asian cultures and contemporary tourism, perspectives on Asian tourism* (pp. 1–17). Springer, Singapore.

Yang, L., Wall, G., & Smith, S. L. (2008). Ethnic tourism development: Chinese Government Perspectives. *Annals of Tourism Research, 35*(3), 751–771.

Zhang, S., & Chan, E. S. (2020). A modernism-based interpretation of sustainable tourism. *International Journal of Tourism Research, 22*(2), 223–237.

Yue Ma is currently a lecturer in tourism and society, and a member of the Tourism Research and Education Network (TRENd) at the University of Tasmania. She received her PhD in December 2019 from University of Tasmania. Her research has included: water-gender-tourism nexus; sustainable development of Chinese national parks; tourism education during pandemic, Chinese outbound tourism, Chinese culture and social media in research.

Ann Selvaranee Balasingam is a Head for the School of Hospitality and Tourism in Nilai University in Malaysia. She has been working in the hospitality industry since her teenage years and in academia since 2008. She has been teaching business and hospitality courses at the undergraduate and post-graduate level. Her area of research is in sustainable tourism with a focus on Malaysian homestays.

Part I
Stakeholders Perspectives and Sustainability

Chapter 2
Partnerships Towards Sustainability: The Revival of Boracay's Wetlands

Giovanni Francis A. Legaspi and Edieser D. L. Dela Santa

Abstract The past decade has seen significant growth in the tourism and hospitality literature on corporate social responsibility (CSR). However, limited literature exists on public and private partnerships in the revival of tourist destinations, with no cash outlay from the government, towards sustainable tourism development. This case study addresses this gap by looking into how government agencies and private organizations, through their CSR, worked together to rehabilitate Boracay wetlands. The focus is on the rehabilitation of the nine wetlands, and in particular wetland number 2 into a conservation park that features endemic tree and animal species rescued from extinction.

In the process, the chapter identifies antecedents that lead to the involvement of particular organizations and stakeholders. It highlights traditional values and the primacy of the family, in pushing CSR onto the agenda. It accentuates the enabling function of the state and the importance of partnerships as mechanisms for CSR delivery. It is argued that considering all these factors, underpinned by social learning, lead to a good understanding of CSR for the environment in the Philippines and assist in ascertaining the place and trajectory of corporate social responsibility for sustainability among businesses in the Asian region.

Keywords Corporate social responsibility · Public and private partnerships · Boracay wetlands · Social learning · Sustainable tourism

2.1 Introduction

The past decade has seen significant growth in the tourism and hospitality literature on corporate social responsibility (Font & Lynes, 2018). This growth in scholarship has emerged notwithstanding debates on the nature of corporate social

---

G. F. A. Legaspi (✉) · E. D. L. Dela Santa
University of the Philippines Diliman, Quezon City, Philippines
e-mail: galegaspi@up.edu.ph; eddelasanta1@up.edu.ph

© The Author(s), under exclusive license to Springer Nature Singapore Pte Ltd. 2022
A. Selvaranee Balasingam, Y. Ma (eds.), *Asian Tourism Sustainability*, Perspectives on Asian Tourism, https://doi.org/10.1007/978-981-16-5264-6_2

responsibility (CSR), its overlap with other concepts such as business ethics and difficulties in its measurement (Cherapanukorn & Focken, 2014; King et al., 2019; Mitnick et al., 2020). The broad interest in this field of study has led to a robust characterization of Western models of CSR. Among the early frameworks, including Carroll's in 1991, CSR was seen as forming a pyramid that covers the economic, legal, ethical and philanthropic dimensions of business operations. There were explicit and implicit aspects (Matten & Moon, 2020). As corporations tried to meet the "triple bottom line", they sought opportunities to adhere to global standards of transparency and accountability (Cherapanukorn & Focken, 2014).

Certainly, these ideas have found their way into Asia via institutions such as foundations that tended to replicate their experience (Sciortino, 2017), to the extent that CSR initiatives of local companies has been dubbed as "Western mimicry" (Srisuphaolarn, 2013). Nonetheless, questions have been raised regarding this hegemonic interpretation. It is emphasized that Asian values and ideals impact distinctly on CSR, and hence, should be the focus of studies (Pang et al., 2018).

This chapter contributes to the discussion by looking into the implementation of CSR initiatives in a Philippine tourism destination, Boracay Island. The whole island was closed for 6 months in 2018 to be rehabilitated after years of environmental destruction. The specific objective of the case study is to analyze public and private partnership in the revival of a wetland, with no cash outlay from the government, in the journey towards sustainable tourism development in the island. The analysis is carried out from the analytical lens of social learning.

In the process, the case study identifies antecedents that lead to the involvement of particular organizations and stakeholders. The analysis shows that the degraded nature of the ecosystem itself, and a clear cognition that a lack of resources or capacity would constrain actors from acting independently, galvanizes the action of stakeholders and influences the way rehabilitation and CSR is implemented. Driven by an internal desire to improve the general condition, private companies engage in CSR. Sustaining their participation are deeply-held family values to give back to communities, a goal which matches the state's aspirations. Besides calling attention to the role of the family and the state, the study points to the importance of collaboration among stakeholders, bound together by the common purpose of addressing serious environmental degradation, as a mechanism for CSR delivery.

It is argued that considering these factors, all underpinned by social learning, lead to a good understanding of CSR for the environment in the Philippines. Moreover, the paper provides insights into how distinct CRS traditions in the Asian region are compared to the West, as well as assist in ascertaining the place and trajectory of corporate social responsibility for sustainability among businesses in the Asian region.

2.2 Corporate Social Responsibility in Tourism

Scholars have been noting the significant growth in the CSR literature in tourism and hospitality. Font and Lynes (2018), in a recent review of the extant literature, tracked close to 370 published articles in the Web of Science database, 70% of which were published in the preceding 5 years. Working on a different database, Wong et al. (2019) also note a prolific period of research for tourism and hospitality academics between 1995 and 2018, with the hotel industry topping the list in terms of industrial field.

This healthy growth in research has emerged notwithstanding debates on the nature of CSR. Like some discourses in tourism, the space occupied by CSR is contested (Mitnick et al., 2020) and the scope of firms' socially responsible behavior is difficult to define and measure (Cherapanukorn & Focken, 2014; King et al., 2019). Yet, some scholars suggest that CSR has achieved its conceptual development and could be replaced by corporate sustainability (Abad-Segura et al., 2019).

One dimension of this debate pertains to regional and cultural differences in the way CSR is conceived and practiced. That is, researchers find that the orthodoxies of CSR in the West are not similar with those of Asian countries. In the first place, it has been observed that there has been an overwhelming focus on European and US cultures (Kang et al., 2015). From the Western tradition, Carroll (1991) framed it as forming a pyramid of corporate social responsibility that covers the economic, legal, ethical and philanthropic dimensions. Under this approach, the main concern is about "how companies make their money, not only how they spend it once they have made it" (Sharma, 2013, p.14). Matten and Moon (2008) conceptualized CSR as comprising the explicit and implicit. As explained, explicit CSR "describes corporate activities that assume responsibility for the interests of society [and] consists of voluntary corporate policies, programs and strategies" (p. 410); implicit CSR "describes corporations' role within the wider formal and informal institutions for society's interests and concern [and] consists of values, norms, and rules that result in (often codified and mandatory) requirements for corporations" (p. 410). Corporations seek incentives and opportunities to adhere higher standards of governance, accountability and transparency (Cherapanukorn & Focken, 2014), as they try to live up to the triple bottom line imposed by tripartism, neocorporatism and law (Matten & Moon, 2020).

The robust growth in the Western literature can be contrasted to the sparse literature on CSR in Asia (Pang et al., 2018). This is not to say that CSR has not spread in the region or has remained as largely a Western hegemonic phenomenon (Srisuphaolarn, 2013). It is rather prominent and is reflected in a spectrum of activities. In a 10-country study of CSR in Asia, Sharma (2013) describes these activities as ranging from philanthropy, legal compliance, self-regulation and business models that respond to social needs including the private provision of public goods, social enterprises, green technology and others. Of late, many business leaders have been looking into sustainability and social responsibility, going so far as to adopting ISO standards on social responsibility, energy management and environmental management (Cherapanukorn & Focken, 2014). Sciortino (2017) observes that through philanthropic forms, many Asian companies concentrate generally on education via the provision of scholarships and construction of buildings, and to a lesser extent, medical care. Sciortino adds that there is minimal support for arts and culture, human rights, gender equity and mitigating environmental impacts. To Sharma

(2013), all these suggest that Asian CSR is focused on giving back to communities, and not geared towards structural change.

Within the Asian context, this variation has been attributed to many factors, not least of which is the national political and socio-cultural milieux. Recent studies in the tourism and hospitality sector confirm this claim. For example, Horng et al. (2017) extol Confucianism as the basis of Chinese tradition and culture, and the foundation for ethics in business organizations. They emphasize the connection of tourism-related issues on stakeholders, philanthropic practices, financial performance, and others with Confucianism as "the axis of Chinese social operation" (p. 1276). They argue that ethics as influenced by Confucianism is the fundamental element of CSR, rather than a tertiary-level element of Carroll's CSR pyramid. In Indonesia, Rahmawati et al. (2019) raise the importance of spirituality in CSR in Balinese tourism industry, arguing that it facilitates the creation of a favorable external environment, provides inspiration for business leaders and complements the governance of stakeholders and issues. Nonetheless, it must be said that individual stakeholder perception might play a role. The study by Latif et al. (2020) cautions that the "way tourists understand CSR is quite homogenous across different geographical contexts," (p. 11), thereby suggesting that researchers rethink the national differences argument.

Another major factor cited is family connection. As emphasized by researchers, the family remains as the locus of business and philanthropic activities among Asian countries (dela Rama, 2012), and in East Asia, not only are family units the more popular ownership form, they also are able to exercise excess control over other shareholders, such as in *chaebols* in Korea (Choi et al., 2019). El Ghoul et al. (2016) hypothesize that the power of controlling families to expropriate minority shareholders reduces CSR activities, while their concern to enhance the family's reputation through CSR would have the opposite effect. Another mechanism by which families influence CSR is through the formation of foundations connected to family corporations. Sciortino (2017) observes that these entities are generally supported by members of a single, oftentimes multi-generational family who maintain ties with the family enterprises. Huge Southeast Asian family foundations such as the Tahir Foundation in Indonesia and Ayala Foundation in the Philippines, all strongly connected with conglomerates, are prime examples.

The family brings to the fore the identity of stakeholders who have been the subject of CSR investigations. In their review of CSR research in tourism and hospitality, Font and Lynes (2018) note the "fundamental role that stakeholders play within a firm's CSR practices" (p. 1028). The prominence of stakeholders is a nod to Freeman's stakeholder theory, commonly used in CSR papers, which emphasizes the responsibility of businesses to stakeholders rather than shareholders (Khatter et al., 2019). Thus, investigations have been carried out regarding the relationship of CSR with host communities (Bohdanowicz et al., 2011), employees (Holcomb et al., 2007; Tsai et al., 2012; Cherapanukorn & Focken, 2014), customers (Latif et al., 2020) suppliers (Sanfiel-Fumero et al., 2017) or a combination of these stakeholders (Truong & Hall, 2017; Kang et al., 2015).

Within the above context, there is a noticeable strand that deals with sustainable tourism and CSR. Scholars have noted the involvement through CSR of the tourism industry, particularly hotels, with sustainability issues although this engagement is observed to sometimes fall short of requirements with regard to fragile destinations (Sanfiel-Fumero et al., 2017). According to Khatter et al. (2019), there is momentum in the adoption of environmentally sustainable policies and practices (ESPPs) but the degree to which hotel establishments implement these measures remain uneven due to internal factors such as firm size and variation in the intensity of external pressures received. Their own analysis of ESPPs among hotels in Melbourne, Australia show that most hotels in the study did not effectively report their activities. Moreover, they found a link between the size and affiliation of the hotel and website-based environmental disclosures, observing that larger hotels tend to display environmental information more than lower star rated properties. This is supported by research on Asian luxury hotels by Cherapanukorn and Focken (2014) who assert that while the properties are keen "to be seen as caring for the world" (p. 206), they are motivated in their CSR activities by the need to sustain the basis of their operations.

Compared to accommodation establishments, NGOs and governments are noticeably absent from CSR assessments. This is unfortunate, since in the Asian context, governments have been observed to play a role in encouraging CSR (Sharma, 2013), even if the extant tourism literature ignores their contribution (Font & Lynes, 2018). This is due not only to the heavy presence of government in the corporate sector via ownership, control or links to the market, but because of policies and regulations that provide an enabling environment for CSR to thrive. In China, for example, state-owned enterprises comprise the bulk of the economy. Thus, the relatively youthful CSR in China has been labelled as "top-down", that is, national government through meta-governance, steers its implementation through local governments and state enterprises (Tang et al., 2018).

In the Philippines, CSR has had a much longer history. Some scholars trace its beginnings to the 1960s, describing that period as the decade of donations whereby companies ameliorated social problems by giving donations to charitable institutions (Rafael, 2015). The ensuing years saw the growth and development of CSR in response to societal forces, which gave birth to a diverse set of organizational channels. According to Anonuevo (2013), the usual means is for companies to form their own foundations, incorporate themselves into a network of companies such as the Philippine Business for Social Progress or Philippine Business for Education, work within a network of foundations such as the League of Corporate Foundations, or engage themselves in the activities of a consortia. A frequent object of investigation are conglomerates (e.g. Azanza, 2009; Buera 2012; Anonuevo, 2013) which have been observed to engage mainly in philanthropic activities.

Research and publication on CSR activities of the local tourism industry is largely confined to non-academic medium, but some players in the industry are known to engage with communities. These include Philippine Airlines Foundation which capitalizes on its air assets to assist in social development, for example, by airlifting aid to victims of calamities or flying indigent patients for medical treatments. Another is El Nido Foundation, attached to El Nido Resorts in Palawan, which undertakes environmental conservation and social amelioration programs such as reef restoration, malaria control, skills training and market linkaging with members of the local community in El Nido. While CSR is argued as a myth in the country, from "a lack of ethics" and being focused on the "front stage" (Lorenzo-Molo, 2009), it is noteworthy that efforts by such organizations as El Nido Foundation have been recognized with awards for sustainability.

No doubt, such honors were facilitated by active partnerships with other organizations. As previously explained, collaboration by like-minded corporations, foundations, donors, universities, and other actors is a feature of Philippine CSR. This by no means suggests that working together for CSR is the norm across the international tourism industry, as a cursory review of the academic literature shows little evidence thereof. The closest is the work by Buijtendijk et al. (2018) who developed a framework, inspired by Actor Network Theory, to investigate the development of a web-based carbon management application in the Dutch travel industry. The paper showed how the collaboration involved many tour operators and research centers over many years and described the unfolding of the eco-innovation over four overlapping moments beginning with the emergence of collaboration on uniform carbon measurement through to rising disputes among representative spokespersons.

Collaboration among stakeholders to address intractable problems such as environmental degradation, and the open-ness of the government for such coordination mechanism has been argued as evidence of social learning (Islam et al., 2018). As an analytical framework, it is usually categorized into first- or second-order learning, or single- and double-loop learning (Schäpke et al., 2017). Dwyer (2018) notes its importance in changing mindsets of tourism stakeholders from engaging in extractive activities to one of rejuvenating destinations. With a focus on the interaction among actors, social learning has been applied within the tourism context to study the dynamics of stakeholders (Dela Santa, 2015; Wray, 2011; Koutsouris, 2009) and to examine conservation management in wild animal populations in response to anthropogenic stimuli (Higham, 2012). Other applications include analysis of social learning as a contributor to tourism destination governance, where Islam et al. (2018) found that social learning was instrumental in building consensus following communicative actions such as debates among stakeholders of a protected area in Bangladesh. The collaborative processes associated with social learning, they argue, have led to a better understanding of structural and ecological challenges facing the protected area, and via single-loop through to triple-loop learning, have resulted in behavioral as well as policy changes towards sustainability. Hoppstadius and Möller (2018) acknowledge that the social aspects involved in learning and sustainability are complex and intricate processes, particularly when conceptualized with spatial considerations in mind and related to everyday life. The outcome, they suggest, are sustainability views that connects the professional with the personal backgrounds of individuals. These concepts find resonance in the rehabilitation of Boracay's wetland described below; hence, applied as the analytical lens through which the restoration is analyzed.

2.3 Methodology

To meet the objectives of the study, a variety of methods were used. Interviews were conducted with key informants, tourism officers in the locale, representatives from the local government unit and other tourism related organizations in Boracay and select members of the Boracay Inter-Agency Task Force (BIATF). The interviews were assisted by and coordinated through the Philippine Department of Tourism Region VI Office and its satellite office in Boracay Island. On-site visit in the different wetlands that allowed access were done with the assistance of the tourism officer in Boracay Island. Interviews with select representatives from the visited wetlands were done to get information relevant to this study. All these were carried out in 2019 as part of wider research program to study overtourism and rehabilitation in the island. In addition, interviews with the head of Watershed and CSR Department of Energy Development Corporation and the project head of its rehabilitation project in Boracay wetland 2 were conducted in September 2020. This was to further explain and better understand the unique characteristics of its CSR, anchored on strong family values, beyond economic and social gains.

Moreover, information from published articles, books, website of the private and government institutions involved in the rehabilitation of Boracay wetlands, were used as secondary sources of data in this study. Particular attention was focused on policy documents produced by the BIATF. The idea was to strengthen, describe, and analyze the information gathered during the actual site visit in the research situ and personal interviews conducted.

Data from the fieldwork were subsequently transcribed and analyzed. Analytical codes used in the study followed social learning theories. These included key concepts such as collaboration, technical and conceptual learning, learning in everyday life, and lesson-drawing. The researchers also considered important categories associated with social learning such as the search for integrated strategies, the utilization of scientific information, and the priority placed on environmental and social issues. All these were used to interpret the ideas and alternative views of CSR and social learning as argued in the distinct Asian context and discussed in this study.

2.4 Findings

In April 2018, Philippine President Rodrigo Duterte ordered the closure of the island to tourists for 6 months saying pollution had turned the waters of Boracay into a cesspool. To facilitate the rehabilitation of the island and ensure its ecological sustainability, Executive Order 53 (EO53) created the Boracay Inter-Agency Task Force (BIATF). The Task Force was composed of various government agencies with the Department of Environment and Natural Resources (DENR) as the lead agency in coordinating and implementing the Medium-Term Boracay Action Plan (BAP). The plan sought to address areas requiring attention such as: strict enforcement of laws and regulations, pollution control and prevention, sustainability of island activities, and rehabilitation and recovery of the ecosystem. "It primarily provides the strategic interventions to ensure the island's rehabilitation over the medium term and sustainable management over the long term" according to the National Economic Development Authority Undersecretary Adoracion M. Navarro (Interagency task force adopts Boracay Action Plan, 2019).

The Department of Environment and Natural Resources (DENR), as the lead government agency in the rehabilitation of Boracay Island, partnered with private enterprises to undertake environmental projects to achieve the government's goal of saving Boracay environment and ecosystem. One of the projects was the restoration of the nine wetlands in the 1032-hectare Boracay Island. DENR Secretary Roy Cimatu noted how wetlands had been among the most neglected and impaired ecosystems in Boracay. This is despite their importance in regulating natural water flow in the island. Following this, DENR initiated activities, together with other stakeholders, including the relocation and demolition of all establishments and structures encroaching on forestlands, wetlands and other water bodies in Boracay (Moaje, 2020).

Wetlands are areas where the environment and the associated plant and animal life are mainly controlled by water. They are among the most valuable ecosystems on the planet (Mitsch et al., 2015). Wetlands are described as *kidneys of the landscape* because they function as the downstream receivers of water and waste from both natural and human sources (Mitsch & Gosselink, 2015). They are also important environment resource as they act as catch basins and avert flooding during heavy rains and thunderstorms. When wetlands are destroyed, the local population loses the benefits wetlands once provided, including protecting shores from wave action and preventing flooding (De Guzman, 2018).

Boracay's nine wetlands constitute a total of 37.81 hectares. Eight are located in forest lands, and one is in an area classified as alienable and disposable, as identified in the Boracay Inter-Agency Task Force (BIATF)-drafted Boracay Action Plan. However, an older map of Boracay revealed that there are actually a dozen wetlands on the island, but the unbridled development had caused these important water bodies to vanish over the years (Mayuga, 2018). Construction involved draining the wetlands and changing their hydrology (Cruz & Legaspi, 2019). Thus, of the remaining nine original wetlands in Boracay, five have disappeared. The remaining four wetlands are occupied by business establishments (shops, resorts and boarding houses) and illegal settlers (De Guzman, 2018).

Social learning relies on cognitive gains derived from the assimilation of evidence about the world (Dela Santa, 2015). This was seen in the wetlands. After evaluating their condition, which in some cases employed experts from the academe, it was found that some of the wetland ecosystems were still intact and might actually be saved from further destruction.

However, DENR Secretary Roy Cimatu mentioned that they needed partners with resources and long-term vision to collaborate with the government. "The government, on its own, cannot guarantee our natural ecosystems' sustainability". This is in keeping with social learning, which emphasizes partnership and collaboration to overcome challenges (Islam et al., 2018). Thus, a partnership with owners of private business establishments for the rehabilitation and co-management of the island's wetland ecosystem was born: The Adopt-a-Wetland Program, where the private sector committed to rehabilitate and restore wetlands at no cost to the government. The adopt-a-wetland was patterned after the successful "Adopt-an-Estero/River" program implemented by the DENR's Environmental Management Bureau (EMB). The latter is an example of lesson-drawing in social learning, where successful models across time and space are emulated (Wolfram et al., 2019).

CSR was seen to play a big role. As DENR Undersecretary Jonas Leones explained: "we want to maximize the support coming from the private sector. Business establishments should help the government in its rehabilitation effort by making the assistance a part of their corporate social responsibility to protect and conserve Boracay's wetlands." He even stressed the idea that the private company's responsibility is not just limited to cleaning the wetlands. They encouraged private businesses to invest in structures to enhance the wetland as ecotourism areas even as the development was primarily focused on ensuring the ecological balance and environmental sustainability of the wetlands.

While private businesses took on a lot of responsibilities, the government was expected to lay the foundations. For its part, the DENR provided assistance in the processing or issuance of documentary requirements, including environmental compliance certificate, certificate of non-coverage, other necessary permits and clearances. The DENR was likewise responsible in identifying the areas where the rehabilitation plan and restoration would be implemented; clearing the area; profiling of the wetland; creating information campaign materials; preparing sustainability plan for the continuity and completion of the project.

The rehabilitation project was to last for 3 years covering three phases. The first phase involves studies on the wetlands' existing state that includes bathymetric surveys, profiling, and biodiversity assessment. The second phase is the formulation and drafting of the rehabilitation plan centered on enhancing the touristic values of the wetland while preserving the ecosystem. The third phase covers the full implementation and completion of the rehabilitation plan.

Of the nine Boracay wetlands identified for rehabilitation, five were adopted by private companies that were funding and undertaking Boracay wetlands' rehabilitation and development as part of their CSR activities. These are the Lopez-led Energy Development Corp. (Wetland No. 2), San Miguel Corp. (Wetland No. 3), Aboitiz Equity Ventures (Wetland No. 4), the Lucio Tan-controlled Boracay Tubi System Inc. (Wetland No. 6) and the Gokongwei-led JG Summit Petrochemical Corp. (Wetland No. 8).

San Miguel Corporation (SMC), partnered with DENR to adopt and restore Wetland 3 in the district of Balabag in Boracay. The rehabilitation and development of wetland 3 highlights the commitment of SMC to invest in social projects beyond its business interests. They believe that the private sector needs to do its part for communities to prosper. As most of its operations rely on natural resources, they share the responsibility for environmental preservation, protection, and sustainable development. The development in wetland 3 consists of a floating deck boardwalk, an observation deck, an amphitheater, and a footbridge to access the viewing deck. These structures will complement and highlight the natural features and attraction of the environment that is perceived to be the most attractive among the wetlands that still exist in Boracay. In addition, they also engage in community development initiatives through resource management training programs as means to improve and develop the local's full potential, keystone of strong community life.

The Aboitiz Group, through its social development arm, Aboitiz Foundation, has adopted and rehabilitated Boracay Wetland 4. They readily agreed to be the DENR's partner as preservation of the environment is one of the long-standing advocacies of the company. Wetland 4 will be fitted with structures that will enhance the greening of the environment through its ecological footprint, water plants, fishing areas, and water aerators to increase oxygen levels in the wetland and improve the natural systems beneath the water surface. The wetland was converted into a linear urban park to enhance its touristic potential. The development features three thematic areas: recreational, highlighting low-impact eco-tourism design; educational, defining the purpose and the importance of wetlands; and experiential, enjoining tourists and locals to be active partners in the cleanup, conservation and preservation, and protection efforts of the wetland.

Lucio Tan owned and controlled Boracay Tubi System, Inc., (BTSI) a water concessionaire in the island, commits to restore Wetland 6 in accordance with the action plan of the Boracay Inter-Agency Rehabilitation Management Group (BIARMG). BTSI has been operating in Boracay for about 20 years providing potable water in the island and operates treatment facilities for wastewater discharged from homes and other establishments in Boracay. Wetland 6 with an area of 8.5 hectare is the biggest wetland in Boracay. The rehabilitation of wetland 6, also known as the Dead Forest, will incorporate vegetative enhancement through planting mangrove seedlings. Through this initiative, 2500 seedlings were planted in the wetland, reviving its original ecosystem that provide source of food for animal and plant species in the area. A boardwalk is also constructed that will serve as an eco-park and a bridgeway allowing visitors to see the wetland and its surrounding ecosystem.

The leading supplier of innovative world-class petrochemical products and solutions in the Philippines, JG Summit Petrochemicals Group (JGSPG), adopts Wetland 8. The company recognizes the importance of the rehabilitation of Boracay wetlands as they provide ecosystem services, protection of the riverbanks and coastlines in the island, and promote ecological sustainability of the island. JGSPG President and CEO Patrick Henry Go emphasized the importance of government and the private sector "to work together in efforts that aim to protect and preserve our planet and the environment." The rehabilitation of wetland 8, a 1.8-hectare swamp and marshland in the district of Manoc-manoc in Boracay, is anchored on environmental stewardship and community partnership, contributes to achieving UNSDG Goal 15 on the protection, restoration, and promotion of "sustainable use of terrestrial ecosystems and sustainably manage forests." One of the critical components of the project is the rehabilitation of vegetation in the area. To achieve this, 483 seedlings were planted on top of the 550 seedlings distributed to residents in the district in order to sustain tree-planting activities in the wetland.

Energy Development Corporation (EDC), a leader in geothermal energy, partnered with DENR to adopt wetland 2. A brackish water swamp turned into construction dump over the years, the project seeks to rescue remaining endemic trees and animal species in Boracay by putting up a tree park with a bird-watching platform. Under the agreement, EDC spent P10 million over the three-year term in support of the government's efforts to rehabilitate Boracay Wetland No. 2 and restore its natural resources as part of its partnership with DENR. In addition, ecological path walks were constructed to manage tourist access and movement within the area that will minimize ecological disturbance. These consist of more than a thousand leaf step pads ideally positioned to manage tourist access to areas within the BWCP. A bird watch platform is also constructed to allow visitors to view the birds and bats that have been sighted in the area. EDC also built an information center for visitors that will serve as reception and exhibit areas for visitors. These will provide opportunities to orient and educate visitors on the rehabilitation efforts of the area and serve as information in promoting native plants of Boracay wetlands.

2.4.1 CSR and Social Learning in Wetland 2

The partnerships between the private organizations and DENR continue as they have common interests, shared values, and commitment for the protection and rehabilitation of the environment, aligned with their CSR programs. The DENR identified support for the rehabilitation of Boracay wetlands from these institutions who had previous and existing projects with them. The successful outcome of previous projects that stood strongly on their CSR programs, capabilities, and resources, allowed these organizations to consider wider opportunities to help DENR carry out the rehabilitation program of Boracay Wetlands. These antecedents directed these organizations to remain as valuable partners in the Adopt a Wetland project, achieving the DENR's goal of rehabilitating the wetlands and abatement of cost to the government (Fig. 2.1).

However, the particular interest of EDC in adopting wetland 2 goes beyond the economic and social gains, often descriptive of CSR initiatives. EDC's perspective on CSR is strongly anchored on the Lopez credo and values. This is consistent with assertions in the literature that social and spatial processes of learning for sustainability connect both the private and public spheres of one's everyday life (Hoppstadius & Möller, 2018). The Lopez family believes that the company should grow with the community. Atty. Allan Barcena, head of Watershed and CSR Department of EDC, explained that the "community gives us the social license to operate, hence we are active in helping them". "We have to build them, develop their abilities and connect them with other stakeholders to be more sustainable. Through education and environmental programs, we grow the company and the community as well." Barcena further explained. Due to the owner's espoused values, all members of the Lopez Group of Companies are expected to conduct business in a

Fig. 2.1 Actual site condition of Boracay Wetland 2 prior to its rehabilitation. (Photo by courtesy of EDC)

manner that creates mutual benefits to all stakeholders, become responsible stewards of all resources, and be cognizant of their obligation to generations, present and future.

Since 1928, the distinctive Lopez values has remained unchanged. These values are guided by the ABUNSIE philosophy, an acronym that stands for: A pioneering entrepreneurial spirit, Business excellence, Unity, Nationalism, Social Justice, Integrity, Employee welfare and wellness. These values, known from generations of experience, serve as cornerstone in managing their businesses and building their framework for CSR (Figs. 2.2, 2.3 and 2.4).

Consistent with these values, EDC through BINHI, its flagship environmental program committed to adopt wetland number 2, where part of the development and rehabilitation plan is to create an awareness campaign on the critical flora and fauna of the area and the importance of their coexistence in the island. These recommendations were based on the result of a rapid biological assessment of the area conducted by experts from the academe, highlighting a learning approach towards conservation management and sustainability (Higham, 2012). Foresters of the BINHI program had successfully located samples of these species and had them planted within the development site in wetland 2, also known as Boracay Wetland Conservation Park (BWCP). "The trees planted are clustered into families and there will be 29 species of trees that can be seen here, 21 of which are part of the 96 threatened species that EDC BINHI rescued from extinction and is propagating in their state-of-the-art automated nurseries" according to Atty. Allan Barcena, head of Watershed and CSR Department of EDC. "By planting these tree seedlings now, we hope in a few years' time, Boracay will not only boast of its clean waters and crystal white sands but will also show off their native tree arboretum which can become an added source of pride by the community," Barcena added.

Social learning centers on interactions and communications with various stakeholders (Wray, 2011). In the case of wetland 2, EDC continues to serve as an active partner of DENR and Boracay Inter-Agency Rehabilitation and Management Group

Fig. 2.2 Boracay Wetland Conservation Park marker. (Photo by courtesy of EDC)

Fig. 2.3 Bird watching platform. (Photo by courtesy of EDC)

Fig. 2.4 Endemic trees planted as part of the rehabilitation of BWCP. (Photo by courtesy of EDC)

(BIARMG) through the Boracay Wetland Bayanihan Program: We Clean and Heal as One. The program provides community volunteers 5 kilograms of rice per household in exchange for weekly cleanup of Boracay Wetlands. "We aim to raise greater awareness on the need to protect and maintain the wetlands and also help residents who are experiencing economic hardships," according to Natividad Bernardino, BIARMG general manager. In a move that shows learning in everyday life (Hoppstadius & Möller, 2018), a similar program was also afforded to volunteers who joined the first food-for-work cleanup activity during April–October in 2018 when Boracay was temporarily closed to tourists for the rehabilitation of the island. The program supported by the local government of Malay and the private organizations, including EDC, provided food in exchange for work to around 120 volunteers, most of whom live within or near the wetlands. Through these initiatives, EDC takes its mission as a renewable energy provider and goes beyond sustainability by investing in programs and partnering with the government that enhance the environment and empower its partner communities in Boracay.

2.5 Discussion

This chapter has been concerned with analyzing the implementation of CSR initiatives involving public and private partnership. The geographic context was Boracay Island, whose wetlands were rehabilitated along with the general restoration of the island's physical environmental. The analysis showed that the degraded nature of the ecosystem itself galvanized the action of stakeholders and influenced the way rehabilitation and CSR would be conducted. These stakeholders, from academic experts, private companies to government agencies, were bound together by the common purpose of addressing serious environmental degradation of the island's beaches and wetlands. It was also observed how CSR was based on deeply-held values by family owners. The government, admitting to a lack of resources to carry out restoration of state resources, was found to play an enabling role in CSR implementation.

These findings provide insights into how CSR for the environment is conceived and executed in the country, in ways that highlight the distinctness of Asian sustainability. The first is social learning among stakeholders for the ecosystem. The restoration of the wetlands in Boracay was a gargantuan task for the Department of Environment and Natural Resources alone to complete. Thus, partners were brought in from the private sector, who in turn mobilized their own networks, for the task. This resulted in the commitment of several stakeholders to rehabilitate the wetlands. All these reinforce previous analyses of social learning in Philippine tourism and the environment (Dela Santa, 2015), where government was observed to accept capacity constraints, to engage in horizontal communication with non-state actors, and to enhance the role of civil society in environmental policy implementation. Amidst the persistence of certain practices that impinge on governance processes and lead to the destruction of the environment (Maguigad et al., 2015; Dela Santa, 2018), highlighted by the closure of Boracay island, it is noteworthy that certain stakeholders have been determined to achieve sustainable outcomes.

Among the stakeholders involved in CSR, two stand out in the analysis. The first is the family-controlled enterprise represented by the Energy Development Corporation, which rehabilitated wetland 2. More specifically, it is the values of the Lopez family, captured by the acronym ABUNSIE, that are found to be more important in sustaining the CSR programs of the company than regulatory compliance or adherence to global standards. Besides social learning, this is unmistakably connected to a family's concern for enhanced reputation (El Ghoul et al., 2016) as the CSR program itself is dubbed as the greening legacy not just of the company but the rest of the Lopez businesses as well. As one of the most influential families in the country whose significance dates back to Spanish Philippines (McCoy, 2015), keeping a favorable family name for the long-term is a strong concern.

The second is the government and how it has played an enabling role in CSR. It is clear from the findings that it was the Department of Environment and Natural Resources which invited private companies it had known before to partner with it in rehabilitating the wetlands of Boracay, thus, opening the gates through which CSR programs can pass. Despite general criticisms of the weakness of the state (Abinales & Amoroso, 2017), as perfectly shown by analysis of events leading to the closure of Boracay Island (Cruz & Legaspi, 2019), the government remains as the fulcrum of governance processes. In the restoration of the wetlands and the island as a whole, it was the government that provided active leadership, underscoring its centrality in resolving sustainability issues.

That the government relied on partners it had worked with before, such as in the national greening program, to rehabilitate the wetland shows not just the importance of social learning but also the interconnectedness of networks. It also highlights the significance of network ties in forging CSR initiatives, as clearly the Boracay wetlands would not have been on the radar of EDC had it not been for DENR. These modern concepts, which have been investigated in connection with CSR by scholars from China and Japan (e.g., Akiyama, 2010; Zou et al. 2019), find resonance in the traditional Filipino values of bayanihan, a concept associated with kinship, mutual assistance, and cooperative spirit. Many philanthropic activities and initiatives have been launched with bayanihan in mind, including the government's official policy responses to the Covid-19 pandemic: Bayanihan to Heal as One Act (Republic Act No. 11469) and the Bayanihan to Recover as One Act (Republic Act No. 11494). Indeed, bayanihan is culturally ingrained as to drive collaboration for CSR.

The above discussion goes to show that the local socio-cultural context provides a fertile ground for the identification of antecedents of Asian CSR for the environment. In the case of wetland restoration in Boracay, the underlying basis appears to be the overall degradation of the physical environment and a clear cognition that a lack of resources or capacity would constrain actors from acting independently. Driven by an internal desire to improve the general condition, moved in no small part by traditional values such as bayanihan, private companies engage in CSR. Sustaining the participation of business enterprises are deeply-held family values to give back to communities, a goal which matches the state's aspirations.

Some of these factors and mechanisms of cooperation have similarities with the Western tradition. The facilitating role of government is one. Researchers have noted how governments in the West have ensured that CSR would be possible through the provision of legal protection for investors, enhancing the competitiveness of capital markets, strengthening the role of outside shareholders, setting up standards and policy frameworks, offering fiscal incentives for CSR. Matten and Moon (2020) explain that it was government that led the way towards the emergence of European explicit and implicit CSR policies and practices. They likewise point out the changing governance status of CSR, "with closer entailment of governments in CSR regulation… and with corporations and other private regulators in the cocreation of new governance systems" (p. 10).

The new governance system referred to above speaks of collaborative structures between government and non-state actors on a range of issues including CSR. Researchers have long noted the benefits of collaboration including shared costs and benefits. A hallmark of social learning, such an approach is advocated when dealing with difficult problems such as environmental degradation and other societal concerns. CSR is no less an exception, with work on pressing environmental issues having been carried out based on collaboration (e.g., Buijtendijk et al., 2018). It has been observed that such arrangements continue to grow in the West and are being observed as well in Asia and other regions (Matten & Moon, 2020).

Yet, distinctions can be made between the Western and Asian traditions of CSR. From the paper, the Filipino traditional values of bayanihan was strongly identified as a main driver of CSR. This is not unique to the Philippines, since it has been observed that in Singapore, Brunei, and Malaysia, the traditional values of *gotong royong* is argued to drive mutual aid (Sciortino, 2017), while it is Tri Hita Karana for the Balinese of Indonesia (Rahmawati et al., 2019), and Confucianism for many countries in East Asia (Horng et al. 2017). Furthermore, the family connection cannot be missed. Family values definitely account for far more in the region, not just in economic relations, but in philanthropic activities too. In other words, traditional Asian values associated with devotion to the family and to others set it apart from Western models of CSR for the environment.

Unfortunately, while the findings of the study emphasized the generally known philosophical similarities and differences between the East and West, it also exposed the glaring lack of engagement of the tourism industry to major environmental rehabilitation efforts. Not one of the major resorts operating in Boracay was involved in wetlands restoration, even if the wetlands were literally in their backyards; most were focused on complying with directives to correct environmental violations. This is a cheerless reinforcement to observations that the tourism industry in the Asian region is not sufficiently engaged in sustainable practices (Tolkach et al., 2016).

2.6 Conclusion

Moving forward, efforts must be made by stakeholders for greater engagement towards sustainability through CSR. In particular, the experience of Boracay shows the need to strengthen compliance with environmental laws, adhere to standards of compliance, disclosure and transparency. A chief concern is how to get the tourism industry engaged more deeply with sustainability issues, that is, how industry players could be encouraged to go beyond the basis of their operations. Forming social learning networks, glued by traditional Asian values of mutual assistance and togetherness, where members could assimilate new knowledge and co-construct new visions and plans could be a good step. Working closely with the government in broadening these governance mechanisms is necessary, given its centrality in the sustainability process.

The government itself is encouraged to continue with its horizontal coordination and to rope in other stakeholders in its processes. It is noted that NGOs have not been involved in the rehabilitation of wetlands, but they too can be strong partners and channels of transformative learning for sustainability. All of this is actually easier said than done. As Schäpke et al. (2017) noted, sustainability transitions even with social learning are fraught with challenges. For the Philippines, Dela Santa (2015) found that these obstacles include the persistence of traditional institutional practices, financial and human resource constraints and most of all, the resilience of features of a patrimonial state, all of which were observed in Boracay prior to its closure and rehabilitation. Perhaps, in thinking about how to shift mindsets towards a "sustainable futures" perspective (Dwyer, 2018) via CSR and related endeavors, researchers could begin reflecting on Asian values and how they might be integrated with restorative and regenerative activities.

References

Abad-Segura, E., Cortés-García, F. J., & Belmonte-Ureña, L. J. (2019). The sustainable approach to corporate social responsibility: A global analysis and future trends. *Sustainability, 11*(19), 5382.

Abinales, P. N., & Amoroso, D. J. (2017). *State and Society in the Philippines*. Rowman & Littlefield.

Akiyama, T. (2010). CSR and inter-organizational network management of corporate groups: Case study on environmental management of Sekisui House Corporation Group. *Asian Business & Management, 9*(2), 223–243.

Anonuevo, A. T. (2013). Characterizing Corporate Social Responsibility (CSR) Practices in the Philippines. *UP Los Banos Journal, XI*, 44–57.

Azanza, R. T. (2009). Corporate social responsibility (CSR) as an effective and sustainable approach to workplace and community relations. *Philippine Journal of Labor and Industrial Relations, 29*(1&2), 80–87.

Bohdanowicz, P., Zientara, P., & Novotna, E. (2011). International hotel chains and environmental protection: An analysis of Hilton's we care! Programme (Europe, 2006–2008). *Journal of Sustainable Tourism, 19*(7), 797–816.

Buera, J. A. T. (2012). Comparative analysis of corporate social responsibility practices of selected Philippine conglomerates. *UP Los Banos Journal, 10*, 28–42.

Buijtendijk, H., Blom, J., Vermeer, J., & van der Duim, R. (2018). Eco-innovation for sustainable tourism transitions as a process of collaborative co-production: The case of a carbon management calculator for the Dutch travel industry. *Journal of Sustainable Tourism, 26*(7), 1222–1240.

Carroll, A. B. (1991). The pyramid of corporate social responsibility: Toward the moral management of organizational stakeholders. *Business Horizons, 34*(4), 39–48.

Cherapanukorn, V., & Focken, K. (2014). Corporate social responsibility (CSR) and sustainability in Asian luxury hotels: Policies, practices and standards. *Asian Social Science, 10*(8), 198.

Choi, D., Chung, C. Y., & Young, J. (2019). An economic analysis of corporate social responsibility in Korea. *Sustainability, 11*(9), 2676.

Cruz, R. G., & Legaspi, G. F. A. (2019). Boracay beach closure: the role of the government and the private sector. In R. Dodds & R. W. Butler (Eds.), *Overtourism: Issues, realities and solutions* (pp. 95–110). De Gruyter.

De Guzman, C. (2018). DENR: 5 of 9 Boracay wetlands damaged; 4 to be reclaimed. *CNN Philippines*, 4 March. http://cnnphilippines.com/new/2018/03/03/DENR-5-of-9-Boracay-wetlands-damaged-4-to-be-reclaimed.html. Accessed 10 Sep 2020.

dela Rama, M. (2012). Family-owned Asian business groups and corporate governance. In T. Clarke & D. Branson (Eds.), *The SAGE handbook of corporate governance* (pp. 406–427). Sage.

Dela Santa, E. (2015). The evolution of Philippine tourism policy implementation from 1973 to 2009. *Tourism Planning & Development, 12*(2), 155–175.

Dela Santa, E. (2018). Power and politics in tourism policy and planning in the Philippines. In *Managing Asian destinations* (pp. 23–34). Springer.

Dwyer, L. (2018). Saluting while the ship sinks: The necessity for tourism paradigm change. *Journal of Sustainable Tourism, 26*(1), 29–48.

El Ghoul, S., Guedhami, O., Wang, H., & Kwok, C. C. (2016). Family control and corporate social responsibility. *Journal of Banking & Finance, 73*, 131–146.

Font, X., & Lynes, J. (2018). Corporate social responsibility for sustainable tourism. *Journal of Sustainable Tourism, 26*(7), 1027–1289.

Higham, J. E. (2012). Wildlife social learning should inform sustainable tourism management. *Animal Conservation, 15*(5), 438–439.

Holcomb, J. L., Upchurch, R. S., & Okumus, F. (2007). Corporate social responsibility: What are top hotel companies reporting? *International Journal of Contemporary Hospitality Management, 19*(6), 461–475.

Hoppstadius, F., & Möller, C. (2018). 'You have to try being a role model' – Learning for sustainability among tourism entrepreneurs in a Swedish biosphere reserve. *European Journal of Tourism Research, 20*, 28–45.

Horng, J. S., Hsu, H., & Tsai, C. Y. (2017). The conceptual framework for ethics and corporate social responsibility in Taiwanese tourism industry. *Asia Pacific Journal of Tourism Research, 22*(12), 1274–1294.

Inter-agency task force adopts Boracay Action Plan. (2019, January 7). *Republic of the Philippines National Economic and Development Authority*. https://www.neda.gov.ph/inter-agency-task-force-adopts-boracay-action-plan/. Accessed 30 Oct 2020.

Islam, M. W., Ruhanen, L., & Ritchie, B. W. (2018). Exploring social learning as a contributor to tourism destination governance. *Tourism Recreation Research, 43*(3), 335–345.

Kang, J. S., Chiang, C. F., Huangthanapan, K., & Downing, S. (2015). Corporate social responsibility and sustainability balanced scorecard: The case study of family-owned hotels. *International Journal of Hospitality Management, 48*, 124–134.

Khatter, A., McGrath, M., Pyke, J., White, L., & Lockstone-Binney, L. (2019). Analysis of hotels' environmentally sustainable policies and practices. *International Journal of Contemporary Hospitality Management, 31*(6), 2394–2410.

King, A. K. F., Wong, F., Kim, S., & Lee, S. (2019). The evolution, progress, and the future of corporate social responsibility: Comprehensive review of hospitality and tourism articles. *International Journal of Hospitality & Tourism Administration*, 1–33.

Koutsouris, A. (2009). Social learning and sustainable tourism development; local quality conventions in tourism: A Greek case study. *Journal of Sustainable Tourism, 17*(5), 567–581.

Latif, K. F., Pérez, A., & Sahibzada, U. F. (2020). Corporate social responsibility (CSR) and customer loyalty in the hotel industry: A cross-country study. *International Journal of Hospitality Management, 89*, 102565.

Lorenzo-Molo, M. C. F. (2009). Why CSR remains a myth: The case of the Philippines. *Asian Business & Management, 8*(2).

Maguigad, V., King, D., & Cottrell, A. (2015). Political ecology, island tourism planning, and climate change adaptation on Boracay Island. *Urban Island Studies, 1*, 152–179.

Matten, D., & Moon, J. (2008). "Implicit" and "explicit" CSR: A conceptual framework for a comparative understanding of corporate social responsibility. *Academy of Management Review, 33*(2), 404–424.

Matten, D., & Moon, J. (2020). Reflections on the 2018 decade award: The meaning and dynamics of \ corporate social responsibility. *Academy of Management Review, 45*(1), 7–28.

Mayuga, J. (2018). Adopt-a-wetland seen for Boracay. *Business Mirror*. https://businessmirror.com.ph/2018/06/14/adopt-a-wetland-seen-for-boracay/. Accessed 25 Oct 2020.

McCoy, A. W. (2015). A tale of two families: Generational succession in Filipino and American family firms. *TRaNS: Trans-Regional and-National Studies of Southeast Asia, 3*(2), 159–190.

Mitsch, W. J., Bernal, B., & Hernandez, M. E. (2015). Ecosystem services of wetlands. *International Journal of Biodiversity Science, Ecosystem Services & Management, 11*(1), 1–4. https://doi.org/10.1080/21513732.2015.1006250

Mitsch, W. J., & Gosselink, J. G. (2015). *Wetlands* (5th ed.). Wiley.

Mitnick, B. M., Windsor, D., & Wood, D. (2020). CSR: Undertheorized or essentially contested? *Academy of Management Review*. https://doi.org/10.5465/amr.2020.0239. Accessed 10 Aug 2020.

Moaje, M. (2020, July 28). *DENR to start restoration of another recovered wetland*. Republic of the Philippines, Philippine News Agency. https://www.pna.gov.ph/articles/1110409. Accessed 2 Nov 2020.

Pang, A., Lwin, M. O., Ng, C. S. M., Ong, Y. K., Chau, S. R. W. C., & Yeow, K. P. S. (2018). Utilization of CSR to build organizations' corporate image in Asia: Need for an integrative approach. *Asian Journal of Communication, 28*(4), 335–359.

Rahmawati, P. I., Jiang, M., Law, A., Wiranatha, A. S., & DeLacy, T. (2019). Spirituality and corporate social responsibility: An empirical narrative from the Balinese tourism industry. *Journal of Sustainable Tourism, 27*(1), 156–172.

Rafael, E. (2015). Building the case for CSR: Philippine corporate discourse on the role of business in social development from the 1970s to the present. In *Filipino generations in a changing landscape* (pp. 171–190). Philippine Social Science Council.

Sanfiel-Fumero, M. A., Armas-Cruz, Y., & González-Morales, O. (2017). Sustainability of the tourist supply chain and governance in an insular biosphere reserve destination: The perspective of tourist accommodation. *European Planning Studies, 25*(7), 1256–1274.

Schäpke, N., Omann, I., Wittmayer, J. M., Van Steenbergen, F., & Mock, M. (2017). Linking transitions to sustainability: A study of the societal effects of transition management. *Sustainability, 9*(5), 737.

Sciortino, R. (2017). Philanthropy in Southeast Asia: Between charitable values, corporate interests, and development aspirations. *ASEAS-Austrian Journal of South-East Asian Studies, 10*(2), 139–163.

Sharma, B. (2013). *Contextualising CSR in Asia: Corporate social responsibility in Asian economies*. Lien Centre for Social Innovation.

Srisuphaolarn, P. (2013). From altruistic to strategic CSR: How social value affected CSR development – A case study of Thailand. *Social Responsibility Journal, 9*(1), 56–77.

Tang, Y., Ma, Y., Wong, C. W., & Miao, X. (2018). Evolution of government policies on guiding corporate social responsibility in China. *Sustainability, 10*(3), 741.

Tolkach, D., Chon, K. K., & Xiao, H. (2016). Asia Pacific tourism trends: Is the future ours to see? *Asia Pacific Journal of Tourism Research, 21*(10), 1071–1084.

Tsai, H., Tsang, N. K., & Cheng, S. K. (2012). Hotel employees' perceptions on corporate social responsibility: The case of Hong Kong. *International Journal of Hospitality Management, 31*(4), 1143–1154.

Truong, V. D., & Hall, C. M. (2017). Corporate social marketing in tourism: To sleep or not to sleep with the enemy? *Journal of Sustainable Tourism, 25*(7), 884–902.

Wolfram, M., Van der Heijden, J., Juhola, S., & Patterson, J. (2019). Learning in urban climate governance: Concepts, key issues and challenges. *Journal of Environmental Policy & Planning, 21*(1), 1–15.

Wong, A. K. F., Kim, S., & Lee, S. (2019). The evolution, progress, and the future of corporate social responsibility: Comprehensive review of hospitality and tourism articles. *International Journal of Hospitality & Tourism Administration*, 1–33.

Wray, M. (2011). Adopting and implementing a transactive approach to sustainable tourism planning: Translating theory into practice. *Journal of Sustainable Tourism, 19*(4–5), 605–627.

Zou, H., Xie, X., Meng, X., & Yang, M. (2019). The diffusion of corporate social responsibility through social network ties: From the perspective of strategic imitation. *Corporate Social Responsibility and Environmental Management, 26*(1), 186–198.

Giovanni Francis A. Legaspi is an Assistant Professor at the University of the Philippines, Asian Institute of Tourism. He has been in the academe since 2007 and has been teaching core and elective courses in tourism – Integrated Resort Management, Organization and Behavior in Tourism Enterprise, and Human Resource Management in Travel and Tourism. His research interests focus on human resource management, rural and island communities, organizational development, flexible work and work life balance, and corporate social responsibility, in tourism.

Edieser D. L. Dela Santa, Ph.D., is a Professor at, and former Dean of, the University of the Philippines Asian Institute of Tourism. His recent works and publications have examined the politics of tourism policy, the representation of culture and heritage, and tourism and hospitality curriculum development. He is currently involved in research projects that look into the governance aspects of protected area tourism, small islands tourism, and tourism education.

Chapter 3
Local Community Participation Towards Malaysian Homestay Sustainability

Ann Selvaranee Balasingam

Abstract Sustainable tourism has been part of the Malaysian tourism agenda for more than a decade and is evident in several of its tourism product since the first National Ecotourism Plan 1996. Sustainable tourism efforts are evident through green hotels, marine protected areas, forest reserves, homestays, and heritage preservation efforts. The purpose of this chapter is to provide evidence that sustainable tourism has been successfully implemented into the Malaysian tourism industry through Malaysian homestays. The underpinning theory is the concept of community-based tourism and sustainable tourism. The article will describe the success of The Miso Walai Homestay that has adopted the principles of community-based tourism. To justify Malaysian homestay sustainability, a homestay sustainability conceptual framework was tested using quantitative research methods. Surveys were collected from four main stakeholders directly involved namely, the homestay owner, government officials, tourists, and local residents. These stakeholders agree that the four dimensions of sustainable tourism have significant relationship with Malaysian homestay sustainability. Thus, Malaysian homestays are a successful community-based sustainable tourism product based on the successful adoption of the key features of community-based tourism and sustainable tourism.

Keywords Homestay · Sustainable tourism · Community-based tourism · Malaysia

---

A. Selvaranee Balasingam (✉)
Nilai University, Nilai, Malaysia
e-mail: annb@nilai.edu.my

© The Author(s), under exclusive license to Springer Nature Singapore Pte Ltd. 2022
A. Selvaranee Balasingam, Y. Ma (eds.), *Asian Tourism Sustainability*, Perspectives on Asian Tourism, https://doi.org/10.1007/978-981-16-5264-6_3

3.1 Introduction

Malaysia is a developing nation located in the centre of the South East Asian region that makes it a popular centre for international tourists to stopover. The natural and cultural resources that attract tourists to Malaysia include sandy beaches and islands, rainforest, mountains, caves, and the multi-cultural diversity of its people, cities, and cuisine. Since 1980, the Malaysian Tourism, Arts, and Culture Ministry has developed tourism products into various tourism components that include shopping, accommodation and passenger transport, automotive fuels, and food and beverage (Department of Statistics Malaysia, 2020). The Malaysian tourism industry is the second highest foreign exchange earner in the country, next to the manufacturing sector. According to the 2019 Travel and Tourism Competitiveness Index (World Economic Forum [WEF], 2019), Malaysia is ranked twenty nine due to its rich natural and cultural resources, strong price competitiveness, and policy environment that promotes tourism development and encourages foreign investment.

Table 3.1 displays the significance of the Malaysian tourism industry in terms of its economic contribution from the years 2008 to 2019. Table 3.1 shows positive and promising performance of the industry with a steady performance in contribution to GDP, the number of tourist arrivals, and share of tourism-related employment to total employment and tourism receipts within the years of 2008 to 2019. Malaysia's international tourist arrivals in 2019 were 26.1 million arrivals and receipts totalling MYR 86.1billion (Tourism Malaysia, 2020). The top five key tourists markets for Malaysia is Singapore, Indonesia, China, Thailand, and Brunei. The industry's overall performance was at an incline but during the period of this research, the global tourism industry has faced the onset of the COVID-19 pandemic since March 2020. Prior to the COVID-19 pandemic, the federal government envisioned the nation to become a high income and globally competitive nation by the year 2030

Table 3.1 Key performance indicators of the Malaysian tourism industry, 2008–2019

Key statistics	2008	2009	2010	2011	2012	2013	2;014	2015	2016	2017	2018	2019
Contribution to GDP (%)	11.2	12.7	12.6	12.4	12.5	13.1	14.9	14.4	13.7	14.6	15.2	15.9
Tourist arrivals (million)	22.5	23.65	24.58	24.71	25.03	25.72	27.44	25.7	26.75	25.9	25.83	26.1
% of Tourism employment to total employment	15.7	16.1	15.6	16.4	16.4	13.6	13.0	20.6	22.5	22.9	23.5	23.6
Tourism receipts (RM billion)	49.6	53.4	56.5	58.3	60.6	65.4	72	69.1	82.1	82.1	84.1	86.1

Adapted from Department of Statistic Malaysia (2014, 2015a, b, c, d, 2020), Economic Planning Unit [EPU] (2020), The Sun Daily (2015), WTTC (2015, 2017) and MOTAC (2015) as part of the nations' Shared Prosperity Vision 2030 (Ministry of Economic Affairs, 2019). This vision was meant to be translated into action within the Malaysian Tourism industry.

Malaysia's strategic planning has incorporated sustainable tourism development as a government agenda since 1996 when a National Ecotourism Master Plan was drafted. This plan was further enhanced in the 9th Malaysian plan developed from 2011–2015 that integrated global action for sustainability to preserve and enhance natural cultural assets (EPU, 2020; Siti Nabiha et al., 2008). The latest plan is the National Ecotourism Plan 2016 to 2025 with an emphasis on local communities and environmental conservation (MOTAC, 2020a, b). Malaysia's effort to integrated sustainable tourism into its tourism agenda is currently evident through its green hotels, gazetted tourism destinations like marine protected areas, forest reserves, and heritage preservation efforts (Nair & Thomas, 2013). The purpose of this chapter is to provide evidence that sustainable tourism has been successfully implemented into the Malaysian tourism industry through Malaysian homestays. The chapter will firstly describe the key underpinning concepts of sustainable tourism and community-based tourism (CBT). Next, the chapter will review one of Malaysia's most successful sustainable community-based tourism products, the Miso Walai Village Homestay. Next, a homestay sustainability framework is introduced and supported with the results of a quantitative survey. This tested conceptual framework is evidence that Malaysian homestays are sustainable tourism products. In addition, the conceptual framework will justify the way the Malaysian homestays have achieved the objectives of the concept of community-based tourism and tourism sustainability. Finally, implications and areas for further research will be identified.

3.2 Literature Review

3.2.1 Sustainable Tourism

The two underpinning concepts for this chapter is sustainable tourism and community-based tourism. Sustainable tourism is defined as "tourism that takes full account of its current and future economic, social and environmental impacts, addressing the needs of visitors, the industry, the environment, and host communities" (UNWTO, n.d.). The overarching theory of this concept is the theory of sustainable development. The concept of sustainable tourism is concerned with development and conservation and considers a multi-dimensional perspective of all types of destinations that range from mass to niche tourism destinations. Cottrell et al. (2004); Bramwell and Lane (2011); Churugsa et al. (2007), Godfrey (1998); Hall (2011); Holladay and Powell (2013) and Moyle et al. (2014) suggests conceptual frameworks for sustainable tourism incorporates four dimensions; ecological, sociocultural, economic and institutional dimensions. To attain sustainable tourism, there needs to be a balance between each dimension (UNWTO, n.d.) The aim and objective of this concept is decent employment, economic viability and growth, social equity, visitor satisfaction, local community concerns, cultural richness, physical integrity, and biological diversity (UNEP & WTO, 2005). United Nations has also developed the Sustainable Development Goals as an opportunity to advance the tourism industry. In light of the COVID-19 pandemic, researchers highlight the pressing need for tourism organisations to implement sustainable tourism policies but the capitalist, short-term economic pressures faced by many tourism enterprises may cause sustainable tourism to be placed on hold until the industry recovers (Jones & Comfort, 2020). Sustainable tourism differs from CBT as sustainable tourism is concerned with macro-level dimensions of sustainability of large tourism enterprises in comparison to CBT that concerns the grassroots level, local community, and local enterprises. CBT is mainly implemented in developing regions like Asia, Africa, and Latin America (Dangi & Jamal, 2016).

3.2.2 *Community-Based Tourism (CBT)*

The concept of CBT began in 1980s as a form of alternative tourism as an option to combat mass tourism and aid in the development of the rural local community (Dangi & Jamal, 2016). CBT is defined as tourism that considers the economic, environmental, social, and cultural sustainability that is managed by the community to create tourist awareness of the local community (Hamzah, 2014). In developing countries, community-based rural tourism is used as a catalyst for socio-economic development (Hall & Jenkins as cited in Harun et al., 2012). In essence, CBT is intended as a tourism development effort with local participation for the benefit of the community. The objective of CBT is community development, capacity building, local control and local enterprise, development, sustainable livelihoods, and poverty alleviation (Dangi & Jamal, 2016). There are three characteristics that a CBT initiative should meet that includes *"(1) located within a community (e.g. on communal land or within community area of influence such as physical borders, land used by the community for subsistence and economic activities) (2) owned, managed or co-managed by one or more community members (i.e. for the benefit of one or more community members) (3) be one initiative with central leadership structure (managing organization) that may include more sub-initiative"* (Zielinski et al. 2020). The benefit of CBT is mainly economic and social well-being that includes economic gain, leadership, empowerment, and employment with the community (Dangi & Jamal, 2016). The model CBTs in the Asian region do not vary much from other regions as it is dependent on the influence of the leader or initiator. CBTs could be initiated by NGOs, government, or local communities but is commonly developed by an NGO (Sustainability Leaders Project, 2020). Research indicates that less than 10% of CBTs worldwide are successful in empowering the local community due to lack of local capacity and skills, leadership, organisation, poor understanding of the market, and dependency (Sustainability Leaders Project, 2020;

Zielinski et al., 2020). However, key success factors for CBT include (1) the development from a local champion to a broader-based community development, (2) strong financial and organisational capacity, (3) sustaining commercial viability and developing career paths, and (4) establishing partnership with tour operators (Hamzah, 2014).

3.3 Malaysian Community Based Tourism Efforts: Malaysian Homestay

Homestays are a subset of CBT that is built on the pillars of sustainable tourism and incorporate the characteristics of CBT (Pakshir & Nair, 2011). Malaysia boasts of one of its most successful community-based sustainable tourism efforts which is the Malaysian homestay. The objective of this effort was to benefit the local community and the tourists. The local community was to benefit through involvement in the tourism sector to increase living standards in the rural community and create local tourism entrepreneurs. For the tourist, homestays were to offer a unique rural and cultural experience. The first Malaysian homestay was officially launched in 1995, but this concept can be traced back to the early 1970s, where a local woman welcomed long-staying drifters or hippies and provided meals and accommodation within her home (Amran as cited in Pusiran & Xiao, 2013, pg. 1). Small rural villages followed suit this arrangement to gain the benefits of the influx of domestic and international tourists who are looking for a different travel experience to learn and experience culture through homestays.

The Malaysian homestays require tourists to stay with the host's family to experience the local Malaysian lifestyle (MOTAC as cited in Ibrahim & Razzaq, 2009, pg. 10). A homestay experience in Malaysia usually begins with a festive welcome greeting by the local school children playing traditional musical instruments and the local youth club exhibiting local cultural performance or a traditional game. Throughout the guest stay, the homestay programs include village tours, souvenirs and handicrafts making, and communal eating with the hosts to truly immerse in the village lifestyle (Pusiran & Xiao, 2013).

To develop homestay programs, government support, and funding was essential. The Malaysian Government allocated substantial funds to grow and expand the Homestay program (Liu, 2006). The Malaysian homestay entrepreneurs have received high government funding and support through grants from several government agencies to promote homestay tourism. As a result of this investment by the government, the number of operators grew steadily in the years 2006 to 2019 as displayed in Fig. 3.1.

The increase in tourist arrivals and receipts to Malaysian homestays over the years of 2006 to 2019 indicates growth as displayed in Table 3.2. Table 3.3 displays the proportion of international to domestic tourists' arrivals to Malaysian registered homestays. The proportions of domestic tourists outweigh the international tourist.

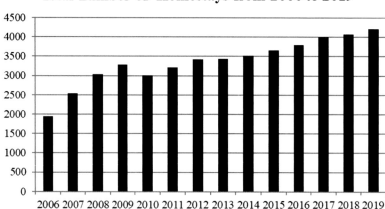

Fig. 3.1 Number of Homestay Operators in Malaysia from 2006 to 2019. (Ahmad et al., 2014; Che Leh, & Hamzah, 2012; Kayat, 2008; MOTAC, 2015, 2016, 2020a, b; The Star Online, 2013)

Table 3.2 Tourist arrival and receipts to Malaysian homestays

Year	International	Domestic	Total arrivals	Total receipts (RM)
2006	14,458	24,507	38,965	2.065 m
2007	21,368	51,055	75,562	4.92 m
2008	23,117	68,416	91,533	6.25 m
2009	31,523	130,038	161,558	10.9 m
2010	49,126	147,346	196,472	12.4 m
2011	59,657	195,324	254,999	15.7 m
2012	65,835	259,423	325,258	18.55 m
2013	62,847	288,107	350,954	21.5 m
2014	71,034	296,439	339,360	21.7 m
2015	71,034	319,395	319,225	28.4 m
2016	57,178	353,344	410,522	27.7 m
2017	61,846	321,115	382,961	30.12 m
2018	82,332	290,153	372,475	27.6 m
2019	85,341	373,558	458,899	29.6 m

Adapted from Bhuiyan et al. (2012), Jamal et al. (2011), MOTAC (2012, 2015, 2016, 2020a, b) and Performance Management and Delivery Unit [PEMANDU] (2013)

To launch the Malaysian homestay program and create awareness, local and foreign secondary schools and local universities student were attracted to the homestay (Ministry of Tourism Malaysia, 2006). The Ministry of Tourism and Culture (MOTAC) also initiated collaborations with the Singaporean and Japanese Education ministry in 2006 to attract the foreign student market (Ministry of Tourism Malaysia, 2006). Domestic tourists mainly include students, local government agencies, and local tourists visiting friends and families in the village to attend weddings. Local tourist also includes familiarization trips by homestay owners as organized by

3 Local Community Participation Towards Malaysian Homestay Sustainability

Table 3.3 Proportion of foreign to local tourist to Malaysian homestays

Year	International	%	Domestic	%	Total arrivals
2006	14,458	37	24,507	63	38,965
2007	21,368	32	51,055	68	75,562
2008	23,117	25	68,416	75	91,533
2009	31,523	19	130,038	80	161, 558
2010	49,126	25	147,346	75	196,472
2011	59,657	23	195,324	77	254,999
2012	65,835	20	259,423	87	325,258
2013	62,847	18	288,107	82	350,954
2014	71,034	21	296,439	87	339,360
2015	71,034	18	280,538	82	319,225
2016	57,178	14	353,344	86	410,522
2017	61,846	16	321,115	84	382,961
2018	82,332	22	290,153	78	372,475
2019	85,341	19	373,558	81	458,899

Adapted from Bhuiyan et al. (2012), Jamal et al. (2011) and MOTAC (2015, 2020a, b)

MOTAC. International tourists are foreign tourists' groups as organized by MOTAC. International tourists originate from South Korea, Japan, China, Singapore, Europe, Indonesia, Australia, the USA, Korea, and Taiwan (Bhuiyan et al., 2013; MOTAC, 2015, 2020a, b).

Tourist that are attracted to homestays is categorised as allocentric type tourists who are motivated to discover new experiences and are from the upper-income band (Cooper et al., 2008). International tourists visit homestays for the experiential and emotional value of homestay living, fun, excitement, culture, lifestyle, and uniqueness (Jamal et al., 2011; Wang, 2007). The most important value perceived by the homestay tourists include the experiential value through the activities, knowledge, culture, and host-guest interaction) and functional value through the establishment and price (Jamal et al., 2011).

To mark the success of the Malaysian homestay, in 2012, the Malaysian homestays received recognition from UNWTO (Malaysian Observer, 2012). The award was labelled the UNWTO Ulysses Award for Innovation in Public Policy and Governance. Malaysia was chosen by the ASEAN Ministry of Tourism to lead the homestay program within the ASEAN nations. This marks the success of this program at the international level (Malaysian Observer, 2012).

3.3.1 Successful Homestay – Miso Walai Village Homestay

Miso Walai Homestay is a Malaysian homestay that has successfully adopted the principles of community-based tourism and recognised as one of the 10 successful CBT projects in the Asia Pacific Economic Corporation Economies (APEC) (Hamzah, 2014). Miso Walai Homestay is located in Lower Kinabatangan, Sabah,

East Malaysia. The homestay was established in 1996 by the WWF Norway who viewed tourism as a source of income and an opportunity to create jobs for the local youth due to the timber and agricultural works that were diminishing (Harun et al., 2012). The initial funding was from local and international NGOs followed by support from the state tourism ministry. Several factors contribute towards a successful Malaysian homestay program that is developed by the community and for the benefit of the community. These factors include the location of the homestay, the awareness, knowledge, and skill of the local community, the management structure, the central leadership, and local commitment and vision.

3.3.1.1 Homestay Community Locations

The first essential characteristic of a community-based tourism product is the product needs to be located within a community (Zielinski et al., 2020). The tourism ministry guideline for the establishment of Malaysian homestay states that homestays must be in rural Malaysian family homes surrounded by natural resources or agricultural efforts. Besides, the homestays must be within a village or community. The minimum number of homes that are required to participate is 10 or more homes within the same community (MOTAC, 2019). Miso Walai Homestay consists of 19 homes within two neighbouring villages (MOTAC, 2020a, b). The natural resources that the Miso Walai Homestay has to offer include farming and wildlife encounters like encounters with several species of hornbill, orang-utan, macaques, and a host of other rainforest birds unique to the locality (CREST Sustainable Tourism Planning, n.d.). Thus, the locality of a homestay within a community with natural resources and agricultural efforts is essential in the success of the Malaysian homestay programme.

3.3.1.2 Awareness, Knowledge and Skill of Local Community

Secondly, awareness, knowledge, and skill of the local community are important for homestays to succeed. The lack of awareness, knowledge, and skill causes the limited involvement of the local community. In the context of the Miso Walai Homestay, the core group that first initiated the homestay effort, took 3 years to build awareness knowledge, and skill amongst the local community through dialogues, research, exposure trips, brainstorming, planning, and convincing the older locals (Harun et al., 2012). Skills training was provided to the locals based on the needs that included courses like English language courses, computers, catering, tour guiding, receptionist, marketing, handicrafts, agriculture, and others. It was only after these efforts that the local community was aware, knowledgeable, and equipped with the needed skills to support this effort collectively. Today, for all successfully registered homestay providers, there is a structured training program by two government ministries that include MOTAC and INFRA once the homestay has passed the inspection stage.

3.3.1.3 Management Structure

Another essential characteristic of a CBT is owned and managed by one or more community members (Zielinski et al., 2020). The management structure adopted by the Miso Walai homestay and other top performing homestays in Malaysia adopts the model of a tourism corporative. The leadership of the cooperative is by the homestays committee members. In its initial stage of conception, a simple association organisation structure was adopted. However, after facing resistance from funders for lack of financial transparency, Miso Walai was forced to form a transparent business model. The tourism corporative fit the business model and received the support of the local community. The structure allowed the local community to sit in the cooperative while the homestay committee members were the implementers. The Village Development and Security Committee (JKKK) was invited to sit on the board (Mohammad & Hamzah, 2012).

In contrast with most of the Malaysian homestays, the initial stage of conception, the Village Welfare and Security Committee (JKKK) would form a committee that constitutes of the village head, the homestay coordinator, homestay owners, and the local residents. The committee is responsible for registration, planning, organizing, and running the homestays. The committee would report to the state level homestay chairman or coordinator. The coordinator would be responsible to report to the state-level Ministry of Tourism. The state-level would finally report to eight federal level governing bodies. After a homestay cluster is successfully established, MOTAC encourages the JKKK to establish itself to register as a cooperative with the Malaysian Co-operatives Societies Commission. After 3 years of operation, a compliance inspection will be conducted by the MOTAC (Ahmad et al., 2014). The Miso Walai Homestay management structure allows the homestay committee that has been initiated by the local residents to take the lead as opposed to the village head taking the leadership. Despite the difference in the organisation between the Miso Walai Homestay and the majority of the Malaysian homestays, homestay management is a community effort.

3.3.1.4 Central Leadership

Central leadership is another essential characteristic of a successful CBT. The central leadership of successful Malaysian homestay programmes is the homestay coordinators or the local champions who are solely dedicated to developing the homestay programme. In the Miso Walai Homestay, an Australian tour guide was the local champion who then mentored a local graduate to coordinate between the homestay committee, head of the village, and the villagers (Harun et al., 2012; Hamzah 2014). Eventually, the central leadership developed into a committee that steered the village forward for the tourism effort of the community.

3.3.1.5 Local Commitment and Vision

The Miso Walai Homestay through local commitment and vision has now developed from a committee to a local business entity in the form of a corporative with 260 members with ownership through shares. Local communities have a choice of direct or indirect involvement. The local cooperative named KOPEL consist of member, chairman, and bureaus that include the bureau of boat service, bureau of homestay, bureau of culture, bureau of transport, bureau of communication, and bureau of tourists. KOPEL has further diversified its efforts and has received grants and tenders' bids nationally (Harun et al., 2012). KOPEL also establishes partnerships with tour operators to ensure a steady stream of tourist arrivals (Hamzah, 2014). The success of the Miso Walai Homestays is because it embraces the CBT concept.

3.3.1.6 Homestay Sustainability Conceptual Framework

This section introduces the Homestays sustainability conceptual framework that was developed in the year 2018 to prove that Malaysian homestay is sustainable. The framework is depicted in Fig. 3.2 below. The homestay sustainability conceptual framework was developed based on the four sustainability dimensions; economic, institutional, environmental, and socio-cultural dimensions, and is underpinned by the concept of sustainable tourism. Each dimension as depicted in the

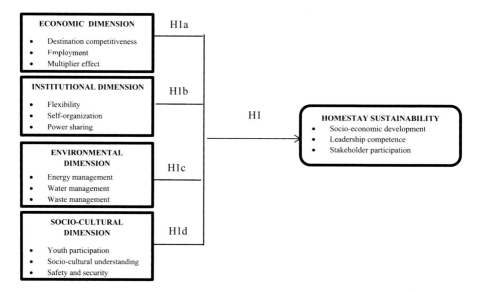

Fig. 3.2 The homestay sustainability conceptual framework. (Source: Dwyer & Kim, 2003; Holladay & Powell, 2013; McCool & Lime, 2001; UNEP& WTO, 2005; Weaver & Lawton, 2010, Balasingam, 2018)

conceptual framework below was tested to establish a relationship with homestay sustainability.

Economic Dimension

The economic dimension refers to economic impacts in terms of growth, cost-effectiveness, and the economic viability of enterprises for a long period. The economic impact of tourism can be categories as direct and indirect economic impacts. Direct tourism economic impact is usually measured in terms of tourist arrivals, receipts, taxation revenue, contribution to GDP, profit, rate of return and indirect measures includes multiplier effect, employment, revenue leakages (Dwyer & Kim, 2003; Roberts & Tribe, 2008; Weaver & Lawton, 2010). Malaysian homestay tourists' arrivals and receipts before 2020 were indicating growth. To determine if the Malaysian homestays were sustainable from the economic dimension, three economic indicators were chosen to ascertain the economic impact of Malaysian homestays. The chosen indicators include destination competitiveness, job opportunities, and multiplier effect.

Destination Competitiveness

The first indicator, destination competitiveness refers to a destination that is superior in its appeal and experience offered to tourists in comparison to other destinations (Dwyer & Kim, 2003). Often destination competitiveness is used to measure the attractiveness of a country as a tourism destination however this research measures the destination competitiveness of each Malaysian homestay. Each Malaysian homestay destination offers a different comparative and competitive advantage. These comparative advantages include access to resources like the climate, scenery, flora, and fauna surrounding the rural homestay location. The competitive advantage also refers to the capability to use the resources for the long term (Nadalipour et al., 2019). The competitive advantage refers to the availability of the supporting facilities namely the common hall or 'balai raya' and the display of the cultural heritage through cultural events and cultural games and sports, unique to each homestay village.

Employment

The second indicator used to determine homestay sustainability is the creation of job opportunities. Homestays were initiated by the government to create job opportunities for rural communities solely dependent on agriculture or farm-based industry. Direct employment is through the job of a homestay owner and operator. MOTAC reported a total of 4227 homestay owners alone in Malaysia in 2019 (MOTAC, 2019). Bhuiyan et al. (2012) stated that Malaysian homestays are mostly managed and operated by the homestay owner and family members. Most homestays surveyed had between one to two employees. Miso Walai Homestay alone created 206 tourism-related jobs and 34 homestay operator jobs for the local community in 2012 (Mohamad & Hamzah, 2012). Indirect employment is also evident as homestay owners hire locals to assist in the caretaking of the homestay, cooking, and cleaning, transporting guests, and acting as tour guides (Kannegieser, 2015; Kayat, 2010). Tourists would also create employment opportunities for small-scale local handicrafts, food, and traditional medication producers as the tourist would seek to purchase local souvenir items (Kayat, 2010). Total jobs created by the Malaysian homestay programme in 2018 totalled 10,000 jobs (Ab Malek, 2019).

Multiplier Effect

The third indicator of the economic sustainability of the Malaysian homestay is the multiplier effect. The multiplier effect of homestays is the amount of tourist dollars spent to consume the products at homestays and the monies retained within the homestays rather than leaving the homestays. The first round of indirect impact is when the payment is made by the tourist and items are purchased by the operator and wages are paid to employees. The second round of impact is when the operators purchase supplies for their use (Weaver & Lawton, 2010). A case study on the Kampung Pelegong Homestay program by Kayat (2010) resulted in low leakage as the income generated from tourists was paid to helpers within the community. In another study by Shahudin et al. (2017) the findings also revealed the homestay multiplier effect of homestays within the state of Selangor in Malaysia indicate little leakage of the economic benefits outside the Malaysian homestays in that state (Cooper et al., 2008; Shahudin et al., 2017). The multiplier effect ensures the economic impact within the local village is higher than leakage outside the local village or surrounding towns, which leads to homestay sustainability.

Institutional Dimension

The second dimension used to measure homestay sustainability is the institutional dimension. Three indicators were used to determined homestay sustainability that includes flexibility, self-organization, and power-sharing. These three measures helped to determine the adaptability, planning, legislation coordination, and cooperation by the homestay's decision-makers. These include the eight government bodies, the state level tourism ministry, the state-level homestay chairman, and the homestay hosts.

Flexibility

The first indicator, flexibility refers to governance structures that promote learning and adaptive management for change (Holladay & Powell, 2013). Within the Malaysian homestays, the governance structures promote learning and adaptive management for change at all levels of governance, considering all the stakeholders' involved. Sustainable tourism policies are likely to be improved if there is flexibility. Thus, flexibility was used as an indicator in determining the flexibility of the homestay committee and the federal and state-level governing bodies' ability to work together and adapt quickly to changing problems.

Self-Organization

The second indicator, self-organization is local organizing behaviour supported by legislation, funding, networks, and collaborative learning (Holladay & Powell, 2013). The self-organizing process is the tourism development process as summarized by Churugsa et al. (2007) as the planning, legislation and regulation and coordination, and cooperation by the government to achieve the tourism program's objective.

Power Sharing

The third indicator, power-sharing is the joint decision making between the local, national and community (Holladay & Powell, 2013). For example, within the Kampong Pelegong homestay, high power and authority belong to the government officials, program committee members, homestay operators, guest, organizers, and 52 operators (Kayat, 2008). Low power is assigned to the local residents based on their interest in the homestay program. Nonetheless, there is a need for power sharing or joint decision making between each stakeholder for homestays to succeed.

Environmental Dimension

From the environmental dimension, three indicators were used to determine Malaysian homestay sustainability which were energy management, water usage, and waste management. Energy management refers to the use of energy-saving techniques and renewable sources for the program like the use of energy-saving light and renewable power like solar power sources (Buckley & Araujo, 1996; UNEP & WTO, 2005). Water usage measures tourist water consumption and the use of water-saving devices like water saving showerheads, not washing linen daily and installing rainwater tanks (Buckley & Araujo, 1996; McNamara & Gibson, 2008). Drinking water quality was measured using the number of homestays with water treated to international standards and the frequency of water-borne illnesses UNEP and WTO (2005). Waste management was measured based on the waste volume produced by the destination per month and the volume recycled (UNEP & WTO, 2005).

Past research on the environmental dimension by McNamara and Gibson (2008) indicates a low adoption rate of environmental initiatives by small accommodation facilities along the Australian coastal zones because small facilities believe environmental initiatives were not applicable to them and small facilities cause lesser damage. Smaller accommodation businesses tend to spend less effort on environmental sustainability than larger companies due to size, the impact of smaller businesses that are less damaging to the environment, and limited resources like finance, time, and human resource to deal with environmental concerns. Chin et al. (2014) in testing the relationship between conservation efforts and destination competitiveness in Malaysian homestays resulted in insignificant relationships. Finally, a study on sustainability criteria of Malaysian homestays ranked conservation of community resources as the sixth most important sustainability criteria (Kasim et al., 2016). Khan et al. (2017) reported minimal environmental efforts by homestays in the state of Kelantan, Malaysia.

Socio-Cultural Dimension

The fourth and final dimension used to measure homestay sustainability is the socio-cultural perspective. Within the Malaysian homestay program, suitable indicators adapted and adopted from UNWTO (2013) and Holladay and Powell (2013) includes the inclusion of youth in tourism, promotion of socio-cultural understanding, and the level of safety and security (UNWTO, 2013).

Youth in Tourism

Firstly, the inclusion of youth in tourism is evident through youth participation. Youth participation is crucial to the success of the homestay program for ownership (Pusiran & Xiao, 2013). At Kampung Pelegong Homestay in Negeri Sembilan, the community was supportive of the homestay efforts as the presence of the visitors would have an impact on the young people curious to know the happenings in the village and the guests (Kayat, 2008). On the contrary, there is evidence of lack of interest and commitment by Generation Y or the youth to continue developing the program for the future as youth tend to migrate to cities for better employment opportunities (Pusiran & Xiao, 2013).

Promotion of Socio-Cultural Understanding

The second indicator of the socio-cultural dimension is the promotion of socio-cultural understanding to tourists or the lack thereof. This refers to the positive or negative perception that the tourist will have of the local community (UNWTO, 2013). Past Malaysian homestay research indicated there exists a communication barrier between host and guest. As most hosts are not fluent in English, the interaction between the hosts and the guests may be limited to facial gestures, sign languages, and the use of local Malaysian homestays tourists as translators (Pusiran & Xiao, 2013). This finding is supported by Shuib et al. (2010) that homestay operators have basic level English proficiency. This may reduce the interaction between the hosts and guests and lead to communication breakdown. This problem is important as it will affect the perception of tourists towards the host-guest interaction within the program.

Level of Safety and Security

The third indicator is the level of safety and security that refers to the evidence of the rise of crime and other social problems with the development of the homestay program (UNWTO, 2013). Tourist safety and security are vital in the tourist decision-making process to travel (Pearce as cited Kunjuraman & Hussin, 2017). The two issues raised within the Malaysian homestay relate to tourist safety and privacy breaches while staying in unregistered homestays and the invasion crisis in Lahad Datu that affected the Dagat Village homestay program foreign tourist arrivals (Kunjuraman & Hussin, 2017). These issues raise the need to measure the level of safety and security in Malaysian homestay.

3.4 Methodology

A quantitative study conducted has proven the sustainability of the Malaysian Homestay through surveys collected from four main stakeholders directly involved in West Malaysian homestays. The quantitative research collected was based on the homestays sustainability theoretical framework as depicted in Fig. 3.2. The four dimensions are adopted and adapted from the concept of sustainable tourism. Each variable with the dimension was developed from numerous sources on sustainable tourism and homestay. Data were collected using self- administered survey questionnaires and online surveys that employed a 5-point Likert scale. Survey questionnaires were distributed to four different stakeholders: 254 homestay owners, 115 government officials, 96 tourist, and 57 local residents. Convenience sampling strategy was used to collect the survey results. Table 3.4 provides an overview of the profile of the four stakeholders who responded to the survey. There are two quantitative methods used to analyse the survey results which include a descriptive assessment analysed using SPSS followed by a second more rigorous data analysis method which is the Partial Least Square (PLS) approach to Structural Equation Modelling (SEM).

3.5 Findings and Discussion

The homestay sustainability conceptual framework that comprises four dimension is further measured using indicators that are unique to Malaysia homestays based on the past literature on the concept of sustainable tourism as well as literature on Malaysian homestays. The indicators of each dimension are described and the results of the quantitative analysis using these indicators from the perspective of the four stakeholders in terms of their significance in relationship to homestay sustainability are described. Tables 3.5 and 3.6 provides a summary of the findings and discussion.

Table 3.4 Demographic profile of the respondents

Variable	Role Variable	Homestay owner Frequency	%	Government officials Frequency	%	Local resident Frequency	%	Tourists Frequency	%
Gender	Female	165	65	65	56	42	74	64	66
	Male	89	35	50	43	15	26	32	34
Age	Below 20	0	0	0	0	0	0	42	44
	20–29 years	6	2	22	19	9	16	8	8
	30-39 years	18	7	49	43	16	28	2	2
	40–49 years	50	20	28	24	17	30	5	5
	50–59 years	125	49	16	14	9	16	27	28
	60 and above	55	22	0	0	6	10	12	13
Race	Malay	251	99	97	84	57	100	45	47
	Chinese	3	1	1	1	0	0	22	23
	Indian	0	0	3	3	0	0	18	19
	Bumiputera (Sabah/Sarawakian)	0	0	14	12	0	0	3	3
	Others							8	8
Role	Government officials	0	0	115	100	0	0	0	0
	Homestay owner	232	91	0	0	57	100	0	0
	Local residents	0	0	0	0	0	0	0	0
	Homestay coordinator	22	9	0	0	0	0	0	0
	Tourists	0						96	100
Years of involvement	1–2 years	3	1	68	59	9	16		
	3–5 years	50	20	23	20	26	46		
	6–9 years	107	42	14	12	15	26		
	More than 9 years	94	37	10	9	7	12		
Education	No formal education	13	5	8	7	2	4	2	2
	Secondary or lower	219	86	11	10	40	70	74	77
	Diploma	13	5	43	37	10	18	2	2
	First degree	8	3	41	36	4	7	13	14
	Master's degree	1	1	12	10	1	2	5	5

3 Local Community Participation Towards Malaysian Homestay Sustainability

Table 3.5 Summary of the descriptive assessment

Hypothesis	Research findings			
	Homestay owners	Government officials	Local residents	Tourists
H1: There a significant relationship between the economic, institutional, environmental, and socio-cultural dimensions and homestay sustainability?	Yes	Yes	Yes	Yes
H1a: There a significant relationship between economic dimension and homestay sustainability?	Yes	Yes	Yes	Yes
H1b: Is there a significant relationship between the institutional dimension and homestay sustainability?	Yes	Yes	Yes	Yes
H1c: Is there a significant relationship between environmental sustainability and homestay sustainability?	Yes	Yes	Yes	Yes
H1d: Is there a significant relationship between socio-cultural dimension and homestay sustainability?	Yes	Yes	Yes	Yes

Table 3.6 Summary of research findings using SEM-PLS

Hypothesis	Homestay owners	Government officials	Local residents	Tourists
H1: There a significant relationship between the economic, institutional, environmental, and socio-cultural dimensions and homestay sustainability?	Yes	Yes	Yes	Yes
H1a: There a significant relationship between economic dimension and homestay sustainability?	Yes	Yes	Yes	Yes
H1b: Is there a significant relationship between the institutional dimension and homestay sustainability?	Yes	Yes	Yes	No
H1c: Is there a significant relationship between environmental sustainability and homestay sustainability?	Yes	No	No	No
H1d: Is there a significant relationship between socio-cultural dimension and homestay sustainability?	Yes	Yes	No	Yes

Table 3.5 is a summary descriptive assessment of the surveys collected from the four stakeholders. The survey questionnaires with an average mean that was above 3 on a five-point Likert scale indicated agreement to the statements in the survey questionnaire. The mean results of each questionnaire were derived using SPSS software. Further rigorous testing was conducted using SEM-PLS as reflected in Table 3.6. These results findings indicate the hypotheses developed have a

significant or insignificant relationship between each construct. Below is an in-depth discussion of the findings of Table 3.5 and Table 3.6 based on the four sustainability dimensions.

3.5.1 Economic Dimension

The results of the descriptive assessment and SEM PLS analysis from the perspective of the homestay owner, government official, tourists, and local residents resulted in all stakeholders' agreeing that homestays are a competitive destination that is superior in appeal and experiences compared to other destinations (Balasingam, 2018; Balasingam & Bojei, 2019). The results of the quantitative study conducted indicate that all stakeholder agreed that job opportunities has increased for all age groups within the homestay community (Balasingam, 2018; Balasingam & Bojei, 2019). The results of the quantitative study of the third indicator multiplier effect indicate that all stakeholders agree to the existence of the multiplier effect of Malaysian homestays (Balasingam, 2018).

Overall, the results of both the descriptive assessment and SEM-PLS shows a significant relationship from the perspective of all stakeholders (See Tables 3.5 and 3.6). The homestay owners, government officials, residents, and tourists agree that the higher the values of the economic dimension, the higher;the degree of homestay sustainability. These results indicate that the Malaysian homestay has achieved the sustainable tourism objective of decent employment and economic viability and growth.

3.5.2 Institutional Dimension

The descriptive assessment results indicate there is a significant relationship between the institutional dimension and homestay sustainability from each stakeholders' perspective (See Table 3.5). However, a more rigorous quantitative analysis using SEM-PLS indicates that the result from the perspective of only the homestay owners, government, and local residents the institutional dimension and homestay sustainability was able to show significant results (See Table 3.6). The results of the survey indicate that three stakeholders believe the homestay administration is flexible and adaptable to change and indicate in the descriptive assessment that the government plays a pivotal role in the success of this program. These results also indicate that the governance within the homestay is a collective effort between the homestay committee, homestay owners, and the multiple government bodies. Thus, leadership and governance as a collective rather than autocratic decision-making process by the government and the homestay committee and power-sharing are necessary (Balasingam, 2018). The governance is still collective governance between various stakeholders. From the perspective of local residents, the institutional dimension and homestay sustainability were also significant because local residents have witnessed village development (Kayat, 2008). From the perspective of tourists, the institutional dimension and homestay sustainability was unable to show significant results because tourists primarily have a recreational interest rather than a governance interest (Kayat, 2008). The key success factors for a successful homestay was for the management structure to adopt the tourism cooperatives business model that leads to a strong financial and organisational structure. However, the adoption rate of the Malaysian homestays to become cooperative is still low at the rate of 18% of the total homestays (Ahmad et al., 2020).

3.5.3 Environmental Dimension

The results from the descriptive assessment from the perspective of the homestay owner, local residents, and tourists indicate that there is a relationship between the environmental dimension and homestay sustainability (See Table 3.5). The SEM PLS results are contrary to the descriptive assessment as only one stakeholder which is the homestay owner agrees to the relationship of the environmental dimension and homestay sustainability. The other three stakeholders disagree (See Table 3.6). These results indicate a lack of exposure of the stakeholders on environmental concerns and behaviour within the homestay program (Balasingam, 2018). Thus, the environmental dimension is a concern for the homestay owner, but these efforts are not evident to the government officials, local residents and tourist.

3.5.4 Socio-Cultural Perspective

The results from the descriptive assessment from the perspective of the homestay owner, local residents, and tourists indicate that there is a relationship between the socio-cultural dimension and homestay sustainability (See Table 3.5). The result of the descriptive assessment regarding the first indicator which is youth involvement reflects that all stakeholders agree that youth are involved in the program. Youth involvement is essential for the succession planning of this effort. The quantitative study results indicate that the hosts' inability to communicate in English and the use of sign language and facial gestures as a form of communication is not an issue as indicated by stakeholders. Other sociocultural interaction issues include the negative impact of the tourists who visit the homestays' and disrespect the culture, the social norms, and values of the hosts. At the initial stage, some villagers experienced culture shock discovering the way of life of foreign tourists (Pusiran & Xiao, 2013). This issue causes sociocultural differences between the hosts and the guests and becomes a reason to deter community participation. The quantitative survey results indicate that all stakeholders agree that social norms and values are maintained and not altered. Past findings by Lo et al. (2013) has proven that the local residents in rural tourism areas believe that preservation of social norms and values are the main concern for rural tourism destinations to maintain the image of the destination. The social values and norms of tourists may differ from the local residents and lead to potential conflicts or disruptive behaviour in a destination (Deery et al., 2012). As local residents in past studies have expressed culture shock with the tourist way of life at the initial stage of the program (Pusiran & Xiao, 2013), findings of the descriptive assessment indicate this issue has resolved over time.

The assessment of the level of safety and security indicates that all stakeholders agree that the level of safety and security within the program is satisfying. Therefore, safety and security concerns are proven to be satisfying within the context of the Malaysian homestays in this study.

The PLS-SEM result shows that from the perspective of the homestay owner, government, and tourists, the three sociocultural dimension measures and homestay sustainability have shown a significant relationship. However, from the perspective of the local resident's socio-cultural dimension and homestay sustainability was unable to show a significant relationship (See Table 3.6). The local residents were unable to support this relationship (Balasingam, 2018). Past findings using PLS have confirmed that there is a significant relationship between the cultural aspect to homestay development in Malaysia from the perspective of homestay owners (Shukor et al., 2014). The sustainable tourism objectives of social equity and visitor's satisfaction are evident in Malaysia homestays.

The homestay sustainability conceptual framework proves that the Malaysian homestays are sustainable from the economic dimension. Malaysia homestays are sustainable from the institutional dimension from the perspective of the homestay owner, government official, and local resident and not from the tourist perspective. The Malaysia homestay is sustainable from the socio-cultural dimension from the perspective of the homestay owner, government official, and tourists but not the local resident. Finally, Malaysian homestays are sustainable from the environmental dimension from the perspective of the homestay owner only. Thus, the economic sustainability of the Malaysian homestay is assured from the perspective of all the stakeholders involved followed by institutional and socio-cultural sustainability. Environmental sustainability is lacking in Malaysian homestays.

3.6 Conclusion and Implications

Malaysia as a country strongly advocates sustainable tourism within its tourism agenda. The concept of sustainable tourism is evident through the Malaysian homestay. Successful homestays factors as exemplified through the Miso Walai Homestay includes the location of the homestay, the awareness, knowledge, and skill of the local community, the management structure, the central leadership, and local commitment and vision. In research conducted, to test the homestay sustainability framework, results have proven that the sustainability conceptual framework can be adopted in determining Malaysian homestay sustainability from four dimensions that include the economic, institutional, environmental, and socio-cultural dimensions. These four stakeholders collectively concur that the economic impact of the Malaysian homestays in terms of destination competitiveness, job opportunities, and the multiplier effect led to homestay sustainability. The other three sustainability dimensions- institutional, environmental, and socio-cultural have a significant relationship with homestay sustainability but not from the perspective of each of the four stakeholders, indicating areas for improvement for the local homestays industry.

Implications of the research are for the homestay owners is to persist in current economic efforts but further pursue partnerships with tour operators to manage the seasonality of demand (Hamzah, 2014). In terms of institutional sustainability, the homestay committee should benchmark its governance and management to the Miso Walai homestays and setup tourism cooperatives that empower the local community and ensures succession planning for the next generation. The slow adoption rate of the existing homestay operators to become tourism cooperatives requires urgent advocacy from the tourism authorities. The homestay owners also need to make more effort in energy, water, and waste management as this is an area that stakeholders' have not seen much effort. Finally, the socio-cultural dimension needs to be further enhanced by motivating the youth to participate by creating awareness of the benefits of the homestays. The promotion of socio-cultural exchange needs to be promoted using updated marketing tools. The limitations of the research were the inability to test the conceptual framework developed to the Miso Walai Homestay in East Malaysia and other homestays in East Malaysia due to the inability of the researcher to collect data from the East Malaysia homestay stakeholders. Areas for further research include the exact number of jobs created by each homestay, the multiplier effect by each Malaysian homestay, the reason for Malaysian homestay's slow adoption of the tourism corporative business models, and the current effort by the homestays to become more environmentally friendly.

References

Ab Malek, R. (2019, January 28). *Berita Harian. Inap desa wujud 10,000 peluang pekerjaan – Mohamaddin.* https://www.bharian.com.my/berita/nasional/2019/01/524910/inap-desa-wujud-10000-peluang-pekerjaan-mohamaddin. Accessed 6 Nov 2020.

Ahmad, H., Saifuddin, M. S. M., Jusoh, H., Choy, E. A., & Jali, M. F. M. (2020). Pendekatan Koperasi Dalam Membangunkan Inap Desa: Penerimaan Komuniti Inap Desa (Cooperative Approach in Developing Homestay: Acceptance from Homestay Community). *Akademika, 90*(1), 129–145.

Ahmad, S. Z., Jabeen, F., & Khan, M. (2014). Entrepreneurs choice in business venture: Motivations for choosing home-stay accommodation businesses in Peninsular Malaysia. *International Journal of Hospitality Management, 36*, 31–40.

Balasingam, A. S., & Bojei, J. (2019). Homestay owners' perspective of economic sustainability of the registered Malaysian homestay. *Pertanika Journal of Social Science & Humanities, 27*(2), 1367–1390.

Balasingam, A. S. (2018). *Multi-dimensional perspective of homestay sustainability in Malaysia moderated by carrying capacity* (Doctoral dissertation). University Putra Malaysia.

Bhuiyan, M. A. H., Siwar, C., Ismail, S. M., & Islam, R. (2012). Homestay accommodation for tourism development in east coast economic. *American Journal of Applied Science, 9*(7), 1085–1090.

Bhuiyan, M. A. H., Siwar, C., & Ismail, S. M. (2013). Socio-economic impacts of home stay accommodations in Malaysia: A study on home stay operators in Terengganu state. *Asian Social Science, 9*(3), 42–49.

Bramwell, B., & Lane, B. (2011). Critical research on the governance of tourism and sustainability. *Journal of Sustainable Tourism, 19*(4–5), 411–421.

Buckley, R., & Arajou. (1996). Environmental performance in tourism accommodation, research notes and reports. *Annals of Tourism Research, 24*(2), 465–469.

Che Leh, F., & Hamzah, M. D. (2012). Homestay Tourism and Pro-poor tourism strategy in banhguris, Selangor, Malaysia. *Elixir Geoscience, 45*, 7602–7610.

Churugsa, W., McIntosh, A. J., & Simmons, D. (2007). Sustainable tourism planning and development: Understanding the capacity of local government. *Leisure/ Loisir, 31*(3), 453–473.

Chin, C. H., Lo, M. C., Songan, P., & Nair, V. (2014). Rural tourism destination competitiveness: A study on Annah Rais Longhouse Homestay Sarawak. *Procedia-Social and Behavioural Sciences, 144*, 35–44.

CREST Sustainable Tourism Planning. (n.d.). *MESCOT Sustainable Tourism & Conservation Initiatives*. http://www.mescot.org/village_homestay_home.htm. Accessed 9 Nov 2020.

Cottrell, S., Van Der Duim, R., Ankersmid, P., & Kelder, L. (2004). Measuring the sustainability of tourism in Manuel Antonio and Texel: A tourist perspective. *Journal of Sustainable Tourism, 12*(5), 409–431.

Cooper, C., Fletcher, J., Fyall, A., Gilbert, D., & Wanhill, S. (2008). *Tourism: Principles and practise*. Pearson Education.

Dangi, T. B., & Jamal, T. (2016). An integrated approach to "sustainable community-based tourism". *Sustainability, 8*(5), 475.

Deery, M., Jago, L., & Fredline, L. (2012). Rethinking social impacts of tourism research: A new research agenda. *Tourism Management, 33*(1), 64–73.

Department of Statistics Malaysia. (2014). *Tourism satellite account Malaysia 2005–2014*. http://www.statistics.gov.my Accessed 19 Aug 2020. Accessed 30 Aug 2020.

Department of Statistics Malaysia. (2015a). *Characteristics of household 2010*. https://www.statistics.gov.my. Accessed 6 Sept 2020.

Department of Statistics Malaysia. (2015b). *Economic characteristics of the population 2010*. https://www.statistics.gov.my. Accessed 5 Nov 2020.

Department of Statistics Malaysia. (2015c). *Salaries and wages survey report 2014*. https://www.statistics.gov.my. Accessed 30 Aug 2020.

Department of Statistics Malaysia. (2015d). *Service statistics accommodation 2015*. http://www.dosm.gov.my/v1/index.php?r=column/cthemeByCat&cat=326&bul_id=UXM5VmxqYnBGU01tSSs1YkQzdDhEZz09&menu_id=b0pIV1E3RW40VWRTUkZocEhyZ1pLUT09. Accessed 5 Nov 2020.

Department of Statistics Malaysia. (2020). *Tourism satellite account 2019*. https://www.dosm.gov.my/v1/index.php?r=column/cthemeByCat&cat=111&bul_id=dEZ6N0dYUDJEWkVxMzdOalY3UUJSdz09&menu_id=TE5CRUZCblh4ZTZMODZIbmk2aWRRQT09. Accessed 16 Nov 2020.

Dwyer, L., & Kim, C. (2003). Destination competitiveness: Determinants and indicators. *Current Issues in Tourism, 6*(5), 369–414.

Economic Planning Unit, Prime Minister's Department Malaysia, *Key Policies: Tourism 2013*. http://www.epu.gov.my/en/pelancongan?p_p_id=56_INSTANCE_G8nA&p_p_lifecycle=0&p_p_state=normal&p_p_mode=view&p_p_col_id=column-4&p_p_col_count=1&page=1. Accessed 29 June 2020.

Godfrey, K. B. (1998). Attitudes toward 'sustainable tourism' in the UK: A view from local government. *Tourism Management, 19*(3), 213–224.

Hall, C. M. (2011). Policy learning and policy failures in sustianble tourism governance: From first- and second- order to third-order change? *Journal of Sustianble Tourism, 19*(4–5), 649–671.

Hamzah, A. (2014). Critical success factors for creating community-based tourism. In A. A. Lew, C. M. Hall, & A. M. Williams (Eds.), *The Wiley Blackwell companion to tourism* (pp. 589–599).

Harun, H., Hassan, R., Abdul Razzaq, A. R., & Mustafa, M. Z. (2012). *Building local capacities towards sustaining community-based tourism development (CBET): Experience from Miso Walai Homestay*. Kinabatangan Sabah.

Holladay, P. J., & Powell, R. B. (2013). Resident perceptions of social–ecological resilience and the sustainability of community-based tourism development in the Commonwealth of Dominica. *Journal of Sustainable Tourism, 21*(8), 1188–1211.

Ibrahim, Y. & Razzaq, A.R.A (2009). *Homestay programme and rural community development in Malaysia*. http://www.ritsumei.ac.jp/acd/re/k-rcs/hss/book/pdf/vol02_03.pdf

Jamal, S. A., Othman, N. N., & Muhammad, N. M. (2011). Tourist perceived value in a community-based homestay visit: An investigation into the functional and experiential aspect of value. *Journal of Vacation Marketing, 17*(1), 5–15.

Jones, P., & Comfort, D. (2020). The COVID-19 crisis, tourism and sustainable development. *Athens Journal of Tourism, 7*(2), 75–86.

Kannegieser, I. (2015). *A home in the hills: Examining the socioeconomic benefits of homestay tourism on rural women and their communities in the Darjeeling district*. http://digitalcollections.sit.edu/isp_collection/2205/

Kasim, M. M., Kayat, K., Ramli, R., & Ramli, R. (2016). Sustainability criteria for the Malaysia homestay programme. *International Review of Management and Marketing, 6*(7), 250–255.

Kayat, K. (2008). Stakeholders perspective toward a community based rural tourism development. *European Journal of Tourism Research, 1*(2), 94–111.

Kayat, K. (2010). The nature of cultural contribution of a community based homestay programme. *Tourismos: An International Multidisciplinary Journal of Tourism, 5*(2), 145–159.

Khan, N. F. A. H., Aziz, R. C., Munir, N. M. N. M., Shuaib, A. S. M., & Hamsani. (2017). Provision of green practises amongst homestay operators in Kelantan. *Journal of Tourism, 2*(4), 48–58.

Kunjuraman, V., & Hussin, R. (2017). Challenges of community-based homestay programme in Sabah, Malaysia : Hopeful or hopeless ? *Tourism Management Perspectives, 21*, 1–9.

Liu, A. (2006). Tourism in rural areas: Kedah, Malaysia. *Tourism Management, 27*, 878–889.

Lo, M. C., Songan, P., & Mohamad, A. A. (2013). Rural tourism and destination image: Community perception in tourism planning. *The Macro-theme review, 2*(1), 102–118.

Malaysian Observer. (2012, November 20). *Malaysia Homestay Experience Programme won an award in 2012 UNWTO Ulysses Awards [Video file]*. http://www.youtube.com/watch?v=tWzi_DWkv4E

McCool, S. F., & Lime, D. W. (2001). Tourism carrying capacity: Tempting fantasy or useful reality? *Journal of Sustainable Tourism, 9*(5), 372–388.

McNamara, K., & Gibson, C. (2008). Environmental sustainability in practice? A macro-scale profile of tourist accommodation facilities in Australia's coastal zone. *Journal of Sustainable Tourism, 16*(1), 85–100.

Ministry of Economic Affairs. (2019). *Prime Minister's Office of Malaysia Shared Prosperity Vision 2030*. https://www.pmo.gov.my/2019/10/shared-prosperity-vision-2030-2/. Accessed 25th Jan 2021.

Ministry of Tourism Malaysia. (2006). *Study on the demand, expectations and satisfaction levelled of Japanese youths at homestays in Malaysia*. MOTOUR.

Ministry of Tourism and Culture Malaysia. (2012). *Official Portal: Ministry of Tourism and Culture Malaysia*. http://www.motac.gov.my/. Accessed 20 Jan 2020.

Ministry of Tourism and Culture Malaysia [MOTAC]. (2015). *Official Portal: Ministry of Tourism And Culture Malaysia*. http://www.motac.gov.my/en/. Accessed 11 Oct 2020.

Ministry of Tourism and Culture Malaysia [MOTAC]. (2016). *Official Portal: Ministry of Tourism And Culture Malaysia*. http://www.motac.gov.my/en/. Accessed 29 Oct 2020.

Ministry of Tourism and Culture Malaysia [MOTAC]. (2019). *Official Portal: Ministry of Tourism And Culture Malaysia.* http://www.motac.gov.my/en/. Accessed 9 Nov 2020.

Ministry of Tourism and Culture Malaysia [MOTAC]. (2020a). *National ecotourism plan 2016-2025: Executive summary.* http://www.motac.gov.my/en/download/category/86-pelan-eko-pelancongan-kebangsaan-2016-2025. Accessed 20 Jan 2020.

Ministry of Tourism and Culture Malaysia [MOTAC]. (2020b). *Malaysian homestay experience statistics report August 2020.* http://www.motac.gov.my/muat-turun/category/11-homestay. Accessed 20 Jan 2020.

Moyle, B. D., Mclennan, C. J., Ruhanen, L., & Weiler, B. (2014). Tracking the concept of sustainability in Australian tourism policy and planning documents. *Journal of Sustainable Tourism, 22*(7), 1037–1051.

Mohamad, N. H., & Hamzah, A. (2012). Tourism cooperative for scaling up community-based tourism. *Worldwide Hospitality and Tourism Theme, 5*(4), 315–328.

Nair, P. K., & Thomas, T. K. (2013). Sustainable tourism in Malaysia. Policies and practices. *Mondes du Tourisme, 8*, 60–69.

Nadalipour, Z., Khoshkhoo, M. H. I., & Eftekhari, A. R. (2019). An integrated model of destination sustainable competitiveness. *Competitiveness Review: An International Business Journal, 29*, 314–335.

Pakshir, L., & Nair, V. (2011). Sustainability of homestay as a form of Community-based tourism (CBT): A case study of the rural community in Bavanat-Iran. *TEAM Journal of Hospitality and Tourism, 8*(1), 5–18.

Performance Management and Delivery Unit. (2013). *Economic transformation programme.* http://etp.pemandu.gov.my. Accessed 9 Jan 2020.

Pusiran, A. K., & Xiao, H. (2013). Challenges and community development: A case study of homestay in Malaysia. *Asian Social Science, 9*(5), 1–17.

Roberts, S., & Tribe, J. (2008). Sustainability indicators for small tourism enterprises – An exploratory perspective. *Journal of Sustainable Tourism, 16*(5), 575–594.

Siti-Nabiha, A. K., Abdul Wahid, N., Amran, A., Haat, H. C., & Abustan, I. (2008). Towards a sustainable tourism management in Malaysian. *LESIJ-ET Scientia International Journal, 15*(2), 301–312.

Shahudin, F., Abdullah, A. M., Radam, A., Latif, I., & Yacob, M. R. (2017). Estimating output multiplier of homestay programme of Selangor, Malaysia. *South East Asia Journal of Contemporary Business, Economics and Law, 12*(2), 9–15.

Shuib, M., Kamil, S. R. A., Abdullah, S., & Mapjabil, J. (2010). A study of homestay operators and international guest English language oral interaction. In B. Mohamed (Ed.), *Proceedings of regional conference on tourism research: The state of the Art and its Sustainability, Penang, Malaysia.* http:eprints.usm.my/26626/1/PROCEEDINGS_RCTR_2010.pdf

Shukor, M. S., Salleh, N. H. M., Othman, R., & Idris, S. H. M. (2014). Perception of homestay operators towards homestay development in Malaysia. *Jurnal Pengurusan, 42*, 3–17.

Sustainability Leaders Project. (2020). *Amran Hamzah on community-based tourism in Malaysia and building resilience in the aftermath of COVID-19.* Available via: https://sustainability-leaders.com/amran-hamzah-interview/. Accessed 3 Oct 2020.

The Star Online. (2013, October 9) *Nazri Aziz: Malaysia to reap RM168bil from tourism by 2020.* http://www.thestar.com.my/News/Nation/2013/10/09/nazri-aziz-tourism/. Accessed 5 Jan 2020.

The Sun Daily. (2015, October 19). *Tourism industry now 6th largest GDP contributor, says Najib.* http://www.thesundaily.my/news/1586311

Tourism Malaysia. (2020). *Official website of tourism Malaysia.* Available via: http://www.tourism.gov.my/en/my

United Nations Environmental Programme [UNEP] & World Tourism Organisation [WTO]. (2005). *Making tourism more sustainable, guideline for policy makers.* http://www.unep.fr/shared/publications/pdf/DTIx0592xPA-TourismPolicyEN.pdf. Accessed 5 Jan 2020.

United Nations World Tourism Organisation. (2013). *UNWTO world tourism highlights 2013 edition*. http://mkt.unwto.org/en/barometer. Accessed 17 Feb 2020.

United Nations World Tourism Organisation. (n.d.). *Sustainable development*. http://mkt.unwto.org/en/barometer. Accessed 1 Oct 2020.

Wang, Y. (2007). Customized authenticity begins at home. *Annals of Tourism Research, 34*(3), 789–804.

World Travel and Tourism Commission. (2015) *Travel and tourism economic impact 2015, Malaysia*. http://www.wttc.org/media/files/reports/economic%20impact%20research/countries%202015/malaysia2015.pdf. Accessed 17 Oct 2020.

World Travel and Tourism Council. (2017). *Travel and tourism economic impact 2017, Malaysia*. https://www.google.com/search?=wttc+%2B+malaysia+2016&oq=wttc+%2B+malaysia+2016&aqs=chrome..69i57j0l3j69i64.6257j0j8&sourceid=chrome&ie=UTF-8

World Economic Forum. (2019). *The Travel and Tourism Competitiveness Report 2019: Travel and Tourism at a tipping point*. http://www3.weforum.org/docs/WEF_TTCR_2019.pdf

Weaver, D., & Lawton, L. (2010). *Tourism management* (4th ed.). Wiley.

Zielinski, S., Kim, S. I., Botero, C., & Yanes, A. (2020). Factors that facilitate and inhibit community-based tourism initiatives in developing countries. *Current Issues in Tourism, 23*(6), 723–739.

Ann Selvaranee Balasingam is a Head for the School of Hospitality and Tourism in Nilai University in Malaysia. She has been working in the hospitality industry since her teenage years and in academia since 2008. She has been teaching business and hospitality courses at the undergraduate and post-graduate level. Her area of research is in sustainable tourism with a focus on Malaysian homestays.

Chapter 4
Nurturing Sense of Place: Host Community Perspectives for Social Sustainability

Paulin Poh Lin Wong and Balvinder Kaur Kler

Abstract Sense of Place is a useful indicator for social sustainability. Host community sense of place towards an urban marine park in Malaysian Borneo was explored using a qualitative research design. Twenty participants described what experiences made Tunku Abdul Rahman Marine Park a meaningful place. A TARP Host Meanings model identified positive and negative place meanings: hedonia-seeking, companionship, aesthetics appreciation, ephemeral escapade, being host, crowdedness, observing island changes, and underwater devastation. The model could be translated into place-based indicators for social sustainability in the context of access to recreation. Essentially, a more community-centred tourism business model is needed which encourages domestic tourism. Suggestions are made to incorporate SoP to ensure future tourism development protects and preserves experiences that are meaningful for host community visitors.

Keywords Sense of place · Host community · Marine park · Meanings · Social sustainability

4.1 Introduction

Tourism literature is replete with ideals that tourism benefits the host community (Zaei & Zaei, 2013; Nair & Thomas, 2013). Tourism destination sustainability emphasises a successful balance between three pillars: people, planet, and profits.

P. P. L. Wong (✉)
Quest International University, Ipoh, Malaysia
e-mail: paulin.wong@qiu.edu.my

B. K. Kler
Universiti Malaysia Sabah, Kota Kinabalu, Malaysia
e-mail: balvinder@ums.edu.my

© The Author(s), under exclusive license to Springer Nature Singapore Pte Ltd. 2022
A. Selvaranee Balasingam, Y. Ma (eds.), *Asian Tourism Sustainability*, Perspectives on Asian Tourism, https://doi.org/10.1007/978-981-16-5264-6_4

Higgins-Desbiolles (2018) urged these pathways to sustainable tourism be redefined and managed in the wider context of sustainability asserting the need to reclaim tourism for its higher purposes: social cohesion, inclusivity, and well-being. The 'people' pillar focuses on care and social justice for all stakeholders involved in tourism. Gaps remain in our understanding of some facets of social sustainability, for example residents' experiences of sharing public space with tourists and how it impacts their quality of life (Helgadóttir et al., 2019). One neglected indicator of social sustainability is Sense of Place (SoP), the emotional attachments of residents to 'place' (Stedman, 1999). SoP has a strong influence on community well-being and place sustainability (Stedman, 1999; Kyle & Chick, 2007; Sullivan et al., 2009; Halpenny, 2010). We form attachments to meaningful places in our lives. National parks are one example of public space shared between hosts and guests as a site for outdoor recreation. Access to recreation is also one form of social sustainability (McClinchey, 2017) with direct links to well-being. The application of SoP for sustainability is growing (Chapin & Knapp, 2015; Masterson et al., 2017; McClinchey, 2017; Jarratt et al., 2018; Ferrari & Gilli, 2018; Christou et al., 2019). This chapter focuses on understanding host community SoP towards a marine park to clarify the impact of sharing public space with tourists and its influence on social sustainability in the context of access to recreation.

We approach host community perspectives of tourism development through the lens of Place theory (Pearce, 2005). In the context of tourism, place is an amalgam of destination qualities and relationships between residents and visitors (Christou, 2020). Place may generate strong positive emotions over time; attachments provide a sense of belonging and meaning. Alteration of places could result in the loss of its SoP, its uniqueness and authenticity leading to placelessness (Christou, 2020). The research setting, Tunku Abdul Rahman Marine Park (TARP) transformed from a public picnic ground into an international tourist destination in Sabah, Malaysia. The research questions asked what experiences make TARP meaningful for the host community? How have they experienced tourism development and how has it impacted them? Data from an exploratory qualitative study employed a triangulated method of focus group interviews, visitor-employed photography, and an adapted Q-methodology. Analysis produced the TARP Host Meanings model which delineates meaningful experiences. Themes were translated into indicators for social sustainability which contribute to Agenda 2030 Sustainable Development Goals (SDG), SDG 11 Sustainable Cities and Communities. Indicators could be applied in ensuring universal access to safe, inclusive, and accessible green and public spaces for the residents of Kota Kinabalu (KK), a thriving tourism city. TARP is a mere 3 kilometres offshore from KK, a twenty-minute boat ride and is in fact an urban national park.

4.2 Literature Review

Three key concepts contribute to the theoretical foundations of this study: host community, SoP and destination sustainability. Brief overviews of each are presented next.

4.2.1 Host Community

Residents of a tourist destination are the 'host community' and key stakeholders within the tourism system whose views should be incorporated in tourism planning (Goeldner & Ritchie, 2012; Ferrari & Gilli, 2018). Often, this stakeholder has no influence on the development of the industry (Ashworth, 2003; Mowforth & Munt, 2009). When a host community has positive perceptions of tourism impacts, they will reap the benefits that come with place development (Ferrari & Pratesi, 2012). Residents evaluate their support for tourism depending on what they value (Sharpley, 2014). Both positive and negative perceptions of tourism impacts have significant influences on the residents' attitudes (Eusebio et al., 2018).

Here, two inherent points arise: the contested notion of what constitutes a "host community" and also their "participation in tourism". Contextual literature on Sabah utilises host community mainly through studies on community-based tourism (CBT) as a tool for development (home-stay programmes), nature conservation, and poverty alleviation through tourism cooperatives and entrepreneurship (Hamzah & Mohammad, 2012; Goh, 2015; Kunjuraman & Hussin, 2017). However, in this study, the host community are defined as residents in and around the vicinity of high amenity areas, who are directly or indirectly involved with, and/or affected by tourism development (Stedman et al., 2006). We define residents of KK as the 'host community' because they visit this urban national park to participate in leisure and recreation. Essentially, a heterogenous group of residents with shared experiences of TARP who have witnessed changes due to tourism development. In line with SDG 11, their access to green and public spaces contributes to the sustainability agenda.

4.2.2 Sense of Place

Space itself is lifeless. Awakened through human experiences, relationships, emotions and thoughts, space converts into Place (Stedman et al., 2004). Tourism developers should assess how residents feel about their 'place' because "quality tourism experiences depend on maintaining the SoP held by residents of a tourism destination" (Bricker & Kerstetter, 2006, p.109). This need to preserve host community SoP arises to protect the unique character of a destination (Sullivan et al., 2009).

Scannell and Gifford (2010) emphasized that the thoughts and emotional relationship people have with places will influence how they will behave. Understandably, it takes time to explore and understand place; it is conceivable that residents are more likely to have deeply embedded values towards place, over a transient visitor (Budruk et al., 2011). Intangible place meanings, or SoP are vital to understanding the experiences of place users (Budruk et al., 2011). SoP is akin to the characteristics that some places have, and others do not, but it is also people's perceptions of these characteristics (Christou, 2020). What makes place meaningful to a host community is worth protecting and could contribute to the tourist experience. Christou (2020) highlights the significance of emotional connections between people and place, generating 'topophilia' – deep affection for specific qualities of place that foster attachment and encourage investment in protecting how the destination was prior to tourism.

4.2.3 Social Sustainability

Sustainability is widely discussed as an important element for tourism development (Kuhlman & Farrington, 2010). The United Nations World Tourism Organization (UNWTO) (2005:12) defined sustainable tourism as "tourism that takes full account of its current and future economic, social and environmental impacts, addressing the needs of visitors, the industry, the environment and host communities". Management strategies for tourism development should protect the natural and man-made resources of a destination for future growth. Masterson et al. (2017) stressed to develop and apply strategic development goals for destination sustainability, we must first consider what people care about. Yet, 'people', or social sustainability remains under-researched (Mowforth & Munt, 2009; McClinchey, 2017). Although policy-makers seek to incorporate social sustainability in urban community planning, its application lacks clarity. Social sustainability relates to "identity creation, social, political and cultural capital, and even happiness and sense of place" (McClinchey, 2017, p.5). Host community SoP for a recreation site as a currency of social sustainability has not been conceptualised. For their well-being, the social or 'people' pillar should ensure equity for residents of tourist destinations (Higgins-Desbiolles, 2018). Helgadóttir et al. (2019) suggest social sustainability is conceived in both substantive (ends) and procedural (means) terms. Substantive referring to the needs, rights, and well-being of people, and, procedural to the means of achieving those ends (access to information, empowerment, and democratic governance) (Helgadóttir et al., 2019). They suggest a need for greater scrutiny between the link between quality of life and tourism development specifically when residents share public space with tourists. How can we understand such experiences?

A Tripartite Sustainability Embedded Place model for tourist sites is available (Pearce, 2005) as depicted in Fig. 4.1. According to Pearce (2005), this model be used for understanding and promoting sustainable on-site tourist behaviours and to

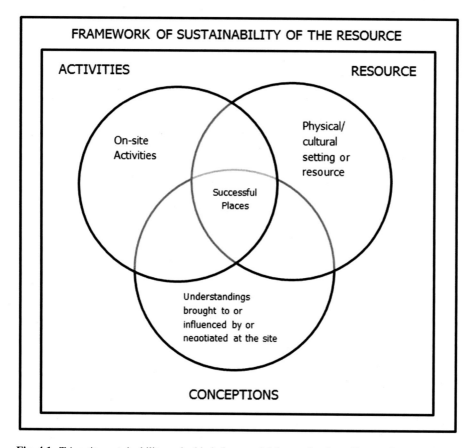

Fig. 4.1 Tripartite sustainability embedded place model for tourist sites. (Source: Pearce (2005))

discuss tourists' on-site experiences with the sites and settings visited, or Place(s). This model could be used to understand what a host community care about, then preserve it to ensure quality tourism experiences for all visitors. 'Activities' denotes both active and passive activities for participation; 'Resource' represents tangible facilities and physical resources and 'Conceptions' signifies meanings influenced by or negotiated at the site. Pearce (2005) suggests a successful tourist site would intersect all three dimensions to achieve destination sustainability. He suggested a good and sustainable tourist site was likely to promote positive visitor experiences, provide a clear understanding of the site for the public, offers activities that are understood and accessible, and that the physical environment of the site was unique and aesthetically pleasing.

We applied the Pearce (2005) model to understand sustainability at a tourist destination in Borneo.

4.3 Research Setting

TARP is the first marine national park in Sabah, Malaysian Borneo consisting of five tropical islands gazetted in 1974, covering an area of 50 square kilometers (Spait, 2001). The islands are named Gaya, Manukan, Mamutik, Sapi and Sulug. Hutton (2010) referred to TARP as one of Kota Kinabalu's greatest treasures with its lowland forests, sandy beaches, forest trails, shallow waters, coral reefs, mangrove forests, birds, and wildlife. TARP is perceived as one of the most desirable marine destinations in Sabah where visitors may participate in a vast range of activities, accommodation, and services. Activities include SCUBA diving, snorkeling, paddle-boarding, island-to-island zipline, windsurfing, sea-walking, picnicking, parasailing, kayaking, and trekking. Accommodation caters to different markets, from camping sites to luxurious resorts. The marine park is under the management of the Board of Trustees of Sabah Parks, an agency of the Ministry of Tourism, Culture and Environment (Sabah). The second Tourism Master Plan 2011–2025 emphasizes sustainable development for TARP. 'Sabah Parks' objectives for marine parks includes to protect the environment; safeguard livelihoods; promote sustainable use of natural resources; encourage environmentally sensitive development; and, build public awareness on the importance of parks (IDS, 2007: p.185).

As the marine park is only three kilometers offshore in Gaya Bay, visitors hop on a twenty-minute boat ride from the city to arrive in TARP for leisure and recreation. TARP is mainly a destination for day trips to the islands, its beaches, and as a hub for recreational activities. TARP transformed into the most popular urban national park for international tourists to KK. Prior to the COVID-19 pandemic, visitor arrivals averaged about half a millions per year, mainly international tourists (Tourism Malaysia, 2018). The international to Malaysian visitor arrivals showed a 70:30 ratio. No attention was given to the low number of domestic visitors. The focus was on the high numbers of international visitors who paid higher fees for park entrance, recreational activities, and avail tour packages.

In March 2020, Malaysia implemented a Movement Control Order (MCO) which closed international travel borders and all national tourism destinations. Between June 2020 and May 2021, TARP has re-opened as the pandemic situation improved in Sabah. Since international borders remained shut, the state travel industry shifted its focus to domestic tourism incorporating health and safety protocols (Miwil, 2020). With this shift of focus, it is timely and sensible to focus on social sustainability or 'people' as the way forward to support the 'planet' and 'profit' pillars. After all, the vision, mission, and goals of Sabah Parks projects a symbiotic relationship with the "people of Sabah" (Sabah Parks, 2021). Post-pandemic, accessibility to TARP should be balanced with clearer policies that support the needs of both park management and all visitors.

4.4 Research Design

This exploratory study employed an interpretive inquiry paradigm to explore meaningful experiences of TARP for the host community. This focus on lived experiences seeks understanding of the multi-faceted reality of participants' experiences displayed through the researcher's interpretations (Henn et al., 2006). The research design applied method triangulation combining focus group interviews, Visitor Employed Photography (VEP) and an adapted Q-methodology for data collection. A purposive sample of twenty participants met the recruitment criteria of (i) KK resident; (ii) regular visitors to TARP; (iii) deep affiliation to TARP as a recreation site. Four groups of five homogenous participants were categorised as Generation-X, Generation-Y, tourism industry employees, and expatriates living in KK for a minimum of 5 years. These groupings mirrored the heterogenous nature of the host community.

The two-part study commenced with focus group interviews about their past and present experiences with TARP to gain an in-depth understanding (Braun & Clarke, 2013). Part two combined the VEP method and a Q-sort process (Exel & Graaf, 2005) which guided the second focus group interview. For both VEP, and the Q-sort, elements of photo-elicitation guided choice of photos taken or chosen for discussion. The purpose of this combination was to gain an understanding on collective meanings and reasonings based on the pattern and ranking-results of the photographs. After the first focus group interview, participants proceeded to visit islands in TARP and took as many photos as they liked to depict examples of meaningful places, experiences and activities. In total, 761 photos were taken by participants. This initiated the process of an adapted Q-method where the researcher as the instrument picked the concourse set of photos known as the 'Q-set' (250 photos). Participants then sorted the Q-set into categories of positive, neutral, and negative photos, the act known as a 'Q-sort'. From the three piles, a further sorting of less positive, more positive, less negative, and more negative was conducted from each pile. Part Two concluded with another round of focus group interviews to discuss results from the Q-sort process. This combination of methods was systematic and illuminated an in-depth understanding of participants' SoP towards TARP over conventional individual or focus group interviews. A thematic analysis proceeded to identify attributes that contribute to host community SoP based on eight sets of interview transcriptions, 250 photographs and the Q-sort. ATLAS.ti 7 qualitative data analysis software assisted data interpretation. A total of 113 codes were created from 1407 quotations coded in the software programme. Codes were analysed thematically resulting in five positive (two sub-themes each) and three negative themes contextual to this study.

4.5 Findings

Themes provide an insightful understanding of experiences at TARP. Table 4.1 depicts 'TARP Host Community Place Meanings', essentially identifies the intangible SoP. TARP is experienced as a site of recreation, leisure, and escapism. Participants value the opportunity to act as protectors for the environment and as informal guides for tourists. Sharing public space uplifts sense of pride. These intangible place meanings are akin to destination wealth which contributes to participants' well-being and quality of life. However, negative place meanings have seeped into this perfect picture and informs their SoP. We suggest these recreation-based place meanings be translated into social sustainability indicators. Access to positive meaningful recreational experiences should remain available and negative experiences be reduced as these are detrimental to overall SoP.

Drawing upon the Tripartite Sustainability Embedded Place Model for Tourist Sites (Pearce, 2005), place meanings were plotted within three place dimensions of Activities, Resource, and Conceptions. Figure 4.2 depicts the TARP Host Meanings model.

Pearce suggested all three components are necessary for destination sustainability. Our model incorporating place meanings identifies the need to preserve social sustainability as 'Conceptions' of TARP result from recreation-based SoP within TARP. We elucidate these suggestions using extracts from our data next.

4.5.1 Positive Sense of Place

Hedonia-seeking 'Active Adventure' represents a significant purpose of participants' visits, to seek challenging activities and experience thrills. Different types of adventurous experiences are described based on both the physical setting of TARP and activities on offer.

Table 4.1 TARP host community place meanings

Type	Themes	Sub-themes
Positive	Hedonia-seeking	Active adventure
		Passive pursuit
	Companionship	Reconnection
		Creating shared memories
	Aesthetics appreciation	Beauty
		Experiences
	Ephemeral escapade	Being away
		Seclusion
	Being host	To visitors
		For environment
Negative	Crowdedness	
	Observing island changes	
	Underwater devastation	

4 Nurturing Sense of Place: Host Community Perspectives for Social Sustainability

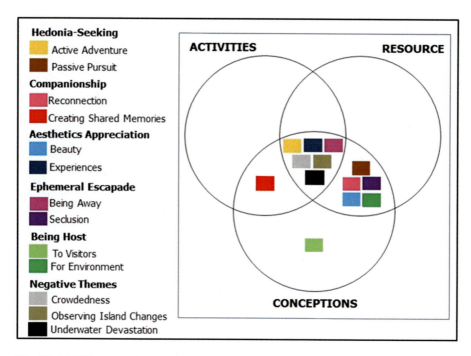

Fig. 4.2 TARP host meanings model

> "Zip line is above all. It is because I feel it is more adventurous and challenging. I like a challenge." (Zal, 35)

'Passive Pursuit' describes the nature of achievement through simple activities and sometimes simple pleasure of being on the island(s). Participants expressed feeling 'satisfied', 'relaxed', 'calm', 'peace', 'quiet' and 'refreshed' when they are in TARP.

> "Satisfaction. More relaxed. It's like a weekend getaway from all the hectic environment. We can see the blue, blue sky and greeneries everywhere because you don't see it every day at your work or around your house." (Abelle, 25)

Companionship 'Reconnection' highlights pre-existing relationships with friends and family where visits are platforms to strengthen bonds. SoP in this context falls under the resource dimension where the focus is on passive participation requiring physical space on the islands for reconnection.

> "If you go there with your friends and family, then you can spend some quality time. At home, you can be together as well but it will be, do this, do that. There you can just talk and be together." (Reka, 31)

'Creating Shared Memories' advances on new memories and experiences created in a social environment when one spends time completing activities with significant others or new acquaintances in TARP. New memories are created even as activities are repeated with the same person.

Fig. 4.3 Picture 38 – Photograph taken by a participant (part of the Q-set)

"Special memories. That time when my girlfriend brought me here on my birthday. That's the first time we go to an island together. She blind-folded me so it's kind of sweet and she taught me how to swim." (Adial, 25)

Aesthetics Appreciation 'Beauty' is an explicit reference to physical qualities exuding pleasure to the senses. Participants referred to the attractiveness and splendour of TARP, the natural physical attributes (sun, sea, sand, forests). Participants smiled thinking about their favourite spots on the islands alluding to a connection between beauty and joy. Beauty in nature is the competitive advantage which attracts visitors (see Fig. 4.3).

"Picture 38. This is what I look for. When I go to the islands… this is exactly what I look for and every time I see blue water, I take pictures of it. Even though I have got 1000 pictures of blue water already…, every time I go and see this, I am like wow, this is beautiful. Sabah is beautiful. No matter how many times I see blue water I am still super excited about it and amazed. Yeah, this is so beautiful." (Maggie, 33).

'Experiences' that are intangible were vivid in the thoughts of participants when asked about their involvements in TARP. Participants felt a sense of pleasure and privilege to be on the island, the experience of observing physical offerings, stunning views, ecosystem or socialising with others in the leisurely environment.

"…There is no jetty so we just jump into the water and just walk to the island and walk around. It's really beautiful." (Jessy, 41)

Ephemeral Escapade 'Being Away' focuses on the motives and sentiments when participants visit TARP and participate in activities that are rejuvenating for example, hiking with a sea view.

4 Nurturing Sense of Place: Host Community Perspectives for Social Sustainability

> *"The overall feel that you are really isolated and away from everything. …Just getting away from everything, KK, and the traffic and everything" (Pizza, 32).*

'Seclusion' posed more in-depth SoP between participants and their favourite sites in TARP. For the regular visitors to the island, a sense of attachment to certain sites in TARP emerged. Inherently, participants identify with these sites and appear to be more protective of the ground which they consider as theirs. Beyond the need to be away, most participants also seek privacy and time to be alone when they are at TARP.

> *"… depends on where we were going. Sapi, Gaya then no problem. We all already have our own place. No one touches our own place. Our place. This is our place. We go to Sapi, we go there, we land, we go to the least crowded area, and then we set up our stuff and we try to make a barricade." (Akyu, 25)*

Being Host 'To Visitors' stems from the thoughts and a heart of hospitality grounded in the dynamic relationships between local and unfamiliar visitors, be it family, friends or strangers at TARP. Beyond friendliness, narratives showed a sense of care towards the welfare of other TARP visitors.

> *"I think personally I like meeting new people. I just go to random people. If I see like a tourist alone at the next table and I am alone… alright, do you want to join me?" (Ann, 29)*

'For Environment' focuses on the spectrum of the physical space within the marine park and the beliefs that the natural environment of a marine park needs protection. Participants showed a sense of care for the preservation of the reef.

> *"We were snorkelling and there were* Chinese tourists *standing on all the corals … I started shouting at someone as I was snorkelling. I was… "Get off the corals! [big hand movement]" … Because there were SO many people and they have no respect for the sea. … They have on their life jackets, they can't swim. They've got shoes like the… you know like, sea shoes? So they don't feel anything and they just stepped right on the corals. And they'll stand up to fix their mask or fix their life jacket… on the corals. It's really stressing me out [both hands hold close to chest]." (Haggis, 30)*

4.5.2 Negative Sense of Place

Crowdedness is the sense of metaphorical suffocation, cloudiness, and negative emotions, as a result of overcrowding due to number of visitors and their non-detachable behaviour. All participants indicated some form of negativity towards the issue of overcrowding on the islands of TARP. Notably, overcrowding is perceived differently, not just crowds of humans but also the expansive picnic areas for tourists.

> *"You've got all these extra tables they are just lying out there ready for more people coming and then you look at how many people are there already. Yeah, it looked so busy. Like you've got a beautiful beach and then you look up and there is just hell of a many tables filled with people and all their stuff. … you don't really want to see the setup where you see there is table everywhere and chairs. Yeah, it's so messy (Haggis, 30).*

Observing Island Changes relates to physical and economical changes experienced by the host community in the marine park due to tourism development such as increase of prices, losing their rightful place, garbage piled up and overdevelopment. Sadly, it seems the marine park has become more capitalistic and tourists-exclusive causing fear in that they might lose access.

> *"Usually when we go there. We go straight to the spot. Put tents and we relax. ... Now we got to wait until the Koreans leave the place and then we can set up. We don't mind them. But yes, I do feel that more and more of my own place has been taken over. Exclusiveness. Capitalism... ... Who knows maybe one day ... if you not with this company you cannot go. ... You can see this happening now. All the other side of the beaches will belong to these companies and then you can't go there unless you go with these [tour] companies. And then where do we go?*

Underwater Devastation refers to negative place experiences on land and in water. Marine life preservation and floating rubbish is of concern for host visitors. Participants who dived noted that compared with their first reef experiences, the underwater environment in TARP has deteriorated over the years.

> *"I remember well when I went back in the 90s you saw a lot more ... Corals were still colourful and there were many of them around. Fast forward till NOW, you got to go to like a secret place or behind the island or wherever there is no tourists if you want to see the good stuff." (Alan, 24)*

This section described participants' experiences of TARP which influenced their SoP. TARP is a special place for the host community, one that is shared with international tourists. Place meanings have been identified for future work to confirm.

4.6 Discussion and Conclusion

Host community SoP contributes to social sustainability for tourism development at national parks. We explored the host community and their perspectives of tourism at the national park through the SoP lens. Findings encourage a revision of the tourism business model at TARP. Since sustainability consists of three pillars, the social or 'people' pillar deserves greater attention. Particularly now at a time when the opportunity to reset allows us to re-consider what the future of tourism on TARP will look like. It is timely to reconsider how we evaluate a sustainable destination. The 'people' pillar should provide equity for residents of tourist destinations (Higgins-Desbiolles, 2018). Since access to recreation is connected to host community SoP, then social sustainability is the way forward. Higgins-Desbiolles (2020) suggests a community-centred tourism framework that aligns tourism based on the rights and interests of local communities. TARP is uniquely located in the vicinity of a capital city, an urban national park. Therefore, findings have implications for SDG 11 Sustainable Cities and Communities perspectives. SDG 11.7 specifically requires universal access to safe, inclusive, and accessible green and public spaces for city residents. The TARP host community place meanings themes could be translated into place-based indicators. Future tourism planning should test and apply these qualitative indicators to gauge social sustainability.

The TARP Host Meanings model identified specific experiences at a marine park which make it special for the host community. This supports the call to understand the experiences of place users to grasp intangible place meanings (Budruk et al., 2011; Christou et al., 2019). In effect, we refined the sustainability embedded place model proposed by Pearce (2005) by identifying components within the three place dimensions of activities, resources, and conceptions, albeit for hosts. Pearce only included positive elements within the place dimension and disregarded the negative attributes that should be improved or avoided. This essentially would create a *faux* reality of how users might experience place. The TARP Host Meanings model acknowledges that negative experiences do occur and need to be addressed to proceed sustainably. Findings provide park managers indicative areas for improvement. As Pearce's place model was tourist-based, its 'Conceptions' only focused on the SoP that park managers should portray to tourists. Specific attributes within each dimension were only implied. This study identified attributes of each dimension, was host-oriented; and 'Conceptions' result from recreation and social communication within the marine park. With a focus on social sustainability, our findings provide indicators of recreation experiences that are valued by the host community and influence their SoP. Negative experiences provide evidence of sharing public space with tourists and suggests it impact their quality of life (Helgadóttir et al., 2019).

Future work should evaluate the utility of this model to other contexts. Meanwhile, Sabah Parks could place more weightage in maintaining the positive attributes that intersect all three dimensions in the model (namely, Active Adventure, Experiences and Being Away) and work towards reducing the negative attributes among host community visitors (Crowdedness, Observing Island Changes and Underwater Devastation), although the pandemic has in effect played a role to reduce these. Sabah Parks could pay attention to the attributes under the Resource and Activities dimensions and consider these in policies, planning and tourism development.

For Malaysia, inbound tourism is still banned, and domestic travel restricted. TARP, once a prime international marine tourist destination in Sabah is left helpless with loss of international tourist receipts (Yusof, 2020). Reality insists that 'profit', or the economic viability of TARP is also given attention as presently, 70% of its main market has vanished with no clear return date. TARP, as a tourist destination and a marine national park, whilst having regulations in place, will need to balance its effort between marine conservation and the temptation of receiving high tourist receipts and high tourist arrivals. We suggest in the long run focusing on preserving the host community SoP will support sustainable tourism management and benefit the local economy. Locals should be willing to contribute more towards entrance fees and activities. Efforts should be made to encourage regular host visitors: (i) enlist through annual paid membership programmes; (ii) stewardship through regular beach clean-ups or nature activities; (iii) conservation campaigns to nurture topophilia for TARP. This corresponds to tourism marketers focusing on domestic tourism through the proposed Sabah Tourism Recovery Plan. It is time to shift the spotlight towards an understanding where hosts' SoP will ensure a sustainable cycle of domestic tourism support (Ferrari & Pratesi, 2012).

Understanding the bonds and values one has to a place would lead to an integrated approach to resource management and assist in planning for overall destination sustainability (Chapin & Knapp, 2015; Masterson et al., 2017; Jarratt et al., 2018; Ferrari & Gilli, 2018; Christou et al., 2019). Applying SoP as an indicator for social sustainability in tourism development would result in policies that consider the community first (Eusebio et al., 2018; Higgins-Desbiolles, 2018). Understanding the value of TARP as a site of recreation, a place that generates positive emotions in effect contributes to the well-being of the host community. In conclusion, our study suggests that for TARP to remain sustainable, nurturing host community SoP is the way forward to truly reflect it as an Asian tourist destination that protects local perspectives to share with all visitors and is key to ensuring place longevity.

References

Ashworth, G. J. (2003). Heritage, identity and places: For tourists and host communities. In S. Singh, D. J. Timothy, & R. K. Dowling (Eds.), *Tourism in destination communities* (pp. 79–88). CAB International.

Braun, V., & Clarke, V. (2013). *Successful qualitative research: A practical guide for beginners.* SAGE.

Bricker, K. S., & Kerstetter, D. (2006). Saravanua ni vanua: Exploring sense of place in the rural highlands of Fiji. In G. Jennings & N. Nickerson (Eds.), *Quality tourism experiences* (pp. 99–109). Routledge.

Budruk, M. S. A., Stanis, W., Schneider, I. E., & Anderson, D. H. (2011). Differentiating place attachment dimensions among proximate and distant visitors to two water-based recreation areas. *Society and Natural Resources, 24*(9), 917–932.

Christou, P. A. (2020). *Philosophies of hospitality and tourism: Giving and receiving.* Channel View Publications.

Chapin, F. S., & Knapp, C. N. (2015). Sense of place: A process for identifying and negotiating potentially contested visions of sustainability. *Environmental Science & Policy, 53*, 38–46.

Christou, P. A., Farmaki, A., Saveriades, A., & Spanou, E. (2019). The "genius loci" of places that experience intense tourism development. *Tourism Management Perspectives, 30*, 19–32.

Eusébio, C., Vieira, A. L., & Lima, S. (2018). Place attachment, host–tourist interactions, and residents' attitudes towards tourism development: The case of Boa Vista Island in Cape Verde. *Journal of Sustainable Tourism, 26*(6), 890–909.

Exel, J., & Graaf, G. D. (2005). *Q methodology: A sneak preview.* http://qmethod.org/articles/vanExel.pdf. Accessed 17 Jan 2016.

Ferrari, S., & Prates, C. A. (2012). National Parks in Italy – Sustainable tourism marketing strategies. *Matkailututkimus (Finnish Journal of Tourism Research), 8*(1), 7–23.

Ferrari, S., & Gilli, M. (2018). Sustainable tourism in natural protected areas: The points of view of hosts and guests in Sila National Park. In I. Azara, E. Michopoulou, A. Clarke, D. Taff, & F. Niccolini (Eds.), *Tourism, health, well-being and protected areas* (pp. 39–55). CABI.

Goeldner, C., & Ritchie, J. R. B. (2012). *Tourism: Principles, practices, philosophies* (12th ed.). Wiley.

Goh, H. C. (2015). Nature and community-based tourism (CBT) for poverty alleviation: A case study of lower Kinabatangan, East Malaysia. *Geografia-Malaysian Journal of Society and Space, 11*(3), 42–52.

Halpenny, E. (2010). Pro-environmental behaviors and park visitors: The effect of place attachment. *Journal of Environmental Psychology, 30*(4), 409–421.

Hamzah, A., & Mohamad, N. H. (2012). Critical success factors of community based ecotourism: Case study of Miso Walai Homestay, Kinabatangan, Sabah. *The Malaysian Forester, 75*(1), 29–42.

Henn, M., Weinstein, M., & Ford, N. (2006). *A short introduction to social research.* SAGE.

Helgadóttir, G., Einarsdóttir, A. V., Burns, G. L., Gunnarsdóttir, G. Þ., & Matthíasdóttir, J. M. E. (2019). Social sustainability of tourism in Iceland: A qualitative inquiry. *Scandinavian Journal of Hospitality and Tourism, 19*(4–5), 404–421.

Higgins-Desbiolles, F. (2018). Sustainable tourism: Sustaining tourism or something more? *Tourism Management Perspectives, 25*, 157–160.

Higgins-Desbiolles, F. (2020). Socialising tourism for social and ecological justice after COVID-19. *Tourism Geographies, 22*(3), 610–623. https://doi.org/10.1080/14616688.2020.1757748

Hutton, W. (2010). *Kota Kinabalu and surrounding areas.* Opus Publications.

Institute of Development Studies. (2007). *Sabah development corridor blueprint 2008–2025.* IDS.

Jarratt, D., Phelan, C., Wain, J., & Dale, S. (2018). Developing a sense of place toolkit: Identifying destination uniqueness. *Tourism and Hospitality Research, 19*(4), 408–421.

Kuhlman, T., & Farrington, J. (2010). What is sustainability? *Sustainability, 2*, 3436–3448.

Kunjuraman, V., & Hussin, R. (2017). Challenges of community-based homestay programme in Sabah, Malaysia: Hopeful or hopeless? *Tourism Management Perspectives, 21*, 1–9.

Kyle, G., & Chick, G. (2007). The social construction of a sense of place. *Leisure Sciences, 29*, 209–225.

Masterson, V. A., Stedman, R. C., Enqvist, J., Tengo, M., Giusti, M., Wahl, D., & Svedin, U. (2017). The contribution of sense of place to social-ecological systems research: A review and research agenda. *Ecology and Society, 22*(1), 49. https://doi.org/10.5751/ES-08872-220149

McClinchey, K. A. (2017). Social sustainability and a sense of place: Harnessing the emotional and sensuous experiences of urban multicultural leisure festivals. *Leisure/Loisir, 41*(3), 391–421.

Miwil, O. (2020). *Sabah tourist spots ready to welcome domestic visitors.* https://www.nst.com.my/news/nation/2020/06/598877/sabah-tourist-spots-ready-welcome-domestic-visitors. Accessed 4 Feb 2021.

Mowforth, M., & Munt, I. (2009). *Tourism and sustainability: Development, globalisation and new tourism in the third world* (3rd ed.). Routledge.

Nair, P. K., & Thomas, T. K. (2013). Sustainable tourism in Malaysia: Policies and practices. *Mondes du Tourisme, 8*, 60–69.

Pearce, P. L. (2005). *Tourist behaviour: Themes and conceptual schemes.* Channel View Publications.

Sabah Parks. (2021). *Sabah Parks official website.* https://sabahparks.org.my/about-us. Accessed 20 May 2021.

Scannell, L., & Gifford, R. (2010). Defining place attachment: A tripartite organizing framework. *Journal of Environmental Psychology, 30*(1), 1–10.

Sharpley, R. (2014). Host perceptions of tourism: A review of the research. *Tourism Management, 42*, 37–49.

Spait, M. (2001). *Marine park management: Issues and challenges.* Paper presented at the 6th SITE Research Seminar, Universiti Malaysia Sabah, Kota Kinabalu, 13–14 September 2001.

Stedman, R. C. (1999). Sense of place as an indicator of community sustainability. *The Forestry Chronicle, 75*(5), 765–770.

Stedman, R., Amsden, B. L., & Kruger, L. (2006). Sense of place and community: Points of intersection with implications for leisure research. *Leisure/Loisir, 30*(2), 393–404.

Stedman, R., Beckley, D., Wallace, S., & Ambard, M. (2004). A picture and 1000 words: Using resident-employed photography to understand attachment to high amenity places. *Journal of Leisure Research, 36*(4), 580–606.

Sullivan, L. E., Schuster, R. M., Kuehn, D. M., Doble, C. S., & Morais, D. (2009). Building sustainable communities using sense of place indicators in three Hudson river valley, NY, tourism destinations: An application of the limits of acceptable change process. In C. E. J. Watts & C. J. Fisher (Eds.), *Proceedings of the 2009 Northeastern recreation research symposium* (pp. 173–179). U.S. Forest Service Northern Research Station.

Tourism Malaysia – Malaysia Tourism Promotion Board. (2018). *Malaysia tourism key performance indicators.* http://mytourismdata.tourism.gov.my/wp-content/uploads/2019/10/key-performance-indicators-2018-pdf.pdf. Accessed 2 Feb 2021.

United Nations World Tourism Organization (UNWTO). (2005). *United Nations Environment Programme and the World Tourism Organization, Madrid.*

Yusof, A. (2020) *'Help us get back our jobs': Rebuilding tourism sector a hot button issue in Sabah state election.* https://www.channelnewsasia.com/news/asia/sabah-state-election-covid-19-tourism-revival-jobs-13123246. Accessed 3 Feb 2021.

Zaei, M. E., & Zaei, M. E. (2013). The impacts of tourism industry on host community. *European Journal of Tourism Hospitality and Research, 1*(2), 12–21.

Paulin Poh Lin Wong, born in Peninsular Malaysia, Dr Paulin P.L. Wong spent the last 10 years in Sabah, Malaysian Borneo obtaining her Bachelors of Business in Tourism Management with First Class (Hons) and a doctoral degree in Tourism. While doing so, she explored (almost!) every nook and cranny of Kota Kinabalu, a touristic city home to the highly visited Tunku Abdul Rahman marine national park. As a travel enthusiast academic who sees the world from the eyes of those forming the basis of a destination, she cannot imagine a destination without 'seeing' the host community. Currently a Senior Lecturer and Head of Programme at Quest International University, Ipoh, Malaysia, Dr. Paulin passionately continues her academic pursuit in advocating for understanding and incorporating host community Sense of Place in tourism destination development.

Balvinder Kaur Kler is Senior Lecturer in Tourism at the Faculty of Business, Economics and Accountancy, Universiti Malaysia Sabah. Her research explores people-place relationships specifically the meanings and attachments to place from both a resident and tourist perspective. She has authored articles and chapters on sense of place, niche tourism markets and destination image. She received her Ph.D in Tourism from the University of Surrey.

Chapter 5
Sustainability and the Tourist Wall: The Case of Hindered Interaction Between Chinese Visitors with Malaysian Society

Fei Long and Can-Seng Ooi

Abstract Many tourists want to travel in a more socially sustainable manner, which may mean that they have to engage more meaningfully with the host community. Tourists however inadvertently travel in bubbles. Tourist bubbles reduce tourist anxiety but they also build tourist walls between them and the host society. The wall seems to prevent tourists from a deeper comprehension of the host society. We use China's outbound tourists in Malaysia as our case. Including Malaysia, destinations and businesses are catering to Chinese tourists by providing more conveniences and comforts to them. Tourism promotion agencies are adopting China's social media platforms to disseminate relevant information. Consequently Chinese tourists may not have to use other platforms to communicate and interact with the world. Served with largely Chinese content and perspectives, host-guest appreciation may remain shallow, with few encounters that truly promote mutual respect and understanding to enhance a more socially sustainable tourism. This exploratory study looks at how Chinese tourists publicly review Malaysia on two top Chinese travel-sharing websites (i.e. Mafengwo.com and Qyer.com). It is found that there is a conspicuous silence on the discriminatory policy against Malaysian Chinese in those reviews even though the manifestations of that policy is omnipresent. Thus, we discuss how a Chinese tourist wall is constructed, how tourist businesses are inadvertently strengthening that wall, and how the wall limits the attainment of social sustainability goals. In addition, we are also suggesting the importance of acknowledging silence in data analysis. This paper makes contributions to the tourism literature on Chinese tourists and the complexity of the host-guest relations with regard to social sustainability of tourism.

F. Long (✉)
UKM-Graduate School of Business, National University of Malaysia (UKM), Bandar Baru Bangi, Malaysia

C.-S. Ooi
School of Social Sciences, University of Tasmania (UTAS), Hobart, Australia
e-mail: canseng.ooi@utas.edu.au

© The Author(s), under exclusive license to Springer Nature Singapore Pte Ltd. 2022
A. Selvaranee Balasingam, Y. Ma (eds.), *Asian Tourism Sustainability*, Perspectives on Asian Tourism, https://doi.org/10.1007/978-981-16-5264-6_5

Keywords Tourist bubble · Chinese outbound tourists · Ethnic discrimination · Malaysia · Social sustainability

5.1 Introduction

Malaysia seems to be the perfect destination for visitors from China. Because of its significant Chinese population, interaction between hosts and guests would be more seamless. A more meaningful understanding of the local community by visitors would also emerge. In the wider context, such a deeper engagement is promoted and encouraged by champions of sustainable tourism, as the visits are not merely commercial, superficial and economically exploitative. Hosts will not only be more welcoming, the visitors are also seen to be part of the community. However that deeper appreciation seems to remain elusive between hosts and guests in Malaysia and its Chinese visitors. This chapter highlights a set of social dynamics that prevent greater understanding of the host by Chinese visitors. We will: (1) highlight the inadvertent construction of the tourist wall that blocks communication and understanding; and (2) point to the importance of reading silence or omissions when understanding how tourists describe their experiences. By doing so, we will accentuate another factor that hinders host-guest interaction and understanding, and will also initiate a discussion on the research of silence in tourism studies.

As advocated, for tourism to be sustainable, the interlocking concerns of the economy, the society and the environment must be addressed (Budeanu et al., 2016). The overwhelming focus on economic sustainability has resulted in many scholars and activists to call for tourism to be more environmentally and socially responsible and sustainable (Jamal, 2019). There are also increasing demands for regenerative tourism, that is, for tourism to create social and environmental values (Higgins-Desbiolles, 2018). As much as tourists bring economic benefits to the community, tourists may also bring about social benefits, in terms of establishing dialogues of cooperation, of affirming common values and of generating mutual respect and understanding. Visitors will also mutually avow positive social and environmental values in the host society.

Also in a more sustainable tourism manner, visitors should not be ethnocentric but instead visitors can also be agents of change that can contribute to desired and positive changes in host societies (Ooi, 2021). Supporting the community to stand up against worker exploitation, environmental destruction and racial discrimination, for instance, provide not only social moral solidarity with but also economic support to local communities (Jamal, 2019). To accept the status quo in the host community may mean supporting and perpetuating the agendas of the established economic and political elites, ignoring the resistance and the activists in these places that demand justice, equality and fair opportunities. Visitors may reaffirm common values of the host society, and challenge injustices and corruption. For example, in gay tourism, LGBTQI+ visitors to China inevitably support and offer solidarity with the marginalized group in society, albeit this group is not formally discriminated against but nonetheless widely ostracized (Ooi, 2021).

In 2018, about 150 million Chinese tourists travelled outside of mainland China, which makes mainland China the largest source market for international outbound tourism (UNWTO, 2019). Given the noticeable economic benefits, overseas destinations and related businesses are catering to Chinese tourists' needs and expectations (Long & Aziz, 2021), such as providing Mandarin-speaking personnel and accepting UnionPay. In addition, tourism promotion agencies are using a range of Chinese social media platforms (e.g. WeChat and Qyer.com) to communicate with Chinese tourists (Ma et al., 2020). By doing so, authorities in destinations attempt to guide how Chinese tourists perceive places, alleviate tourist anxiety, and protect tourists from awkward encounters with local social issues that could shock or scare them. As a result, Chinese tourists do not need to seek travel information from other platforms and they don't even need to interact much with the locals during their trips. In serving the comfort needs of Chinese visitors, the economic benefits may be maximized.

The emphasis on providing a pleasing experience to Chinese visitors may also result in ignoring the environmental and social aspects of sustainability. We focus on social sustainability in this chapter. Tourists, including Chinese ones, may build their own "tourist bubbles" to avoid potential conflicts between their cultural assumptions and a foreign culture, and to view the host society through their own accustomed lenses and beliefs. For instance, Chinese tourists are very concerned about friendliness of locals, so they have created a supportive and friendly social environment for themselves by traveling with family, friends and other Chinese (Ye et al., 2012a, b; Moy & Phongpanichanan, 2014; Nielson, 2018). Therefore, Chinese tourists may inadvertently or otherwise travel in "tourist bubbles", and observe the host society through Chinese lenses. However, it does not mean that Chinese tourists are "close-minded" as studies have shown that they are keen to seek authentic travel experiences (Ma et al., 2018), and many of them are indeed adventurous (Cai, 2018). Due to the convenience of "tourist bubbles", Chinese guest-host interactions remain selective, which will be demonstrated by the case of Chinese tourists visiting Malaysia in this chapter.

Malaysia is one of the most popular destinations for mainland Chinese tourists. 3.11 million visited Malaysia in 2019, which makes China the 3rd largest source market for Malaysia, following Singapore and Indonesia (Tourism Malaysia, 2020). Meanwhile, Malaysia has been publicly implementing an official discriminatory policy against its own citizens with Chinese-heritage (Malaysian Chinese) and other ethnic minorities for decades (Harris & Han, 2020). In 2015, Dr. Huang Huikang, the then-Chinese ambassador to Malaysia, criticized this policy and showed support to the local Chinese community (Reuters, 2015). As will be shown, although ethnonationalistic sentiments are growing along with China's economic rise, it seems that the vast majority of Chinese tourists either are ignorant of or have ignored the ethnic tension in their understanding of Malaysia. In contrast, many of them have portrayed Malaysia as an ethnically harmonious society in their online travel reviews.

Thus, there is an apparent tourist wall between the Chinese tourists and the host society. The woke Chinese tourists seem to keep silent with regard to this discrimination.

In this context, the tourist wall is defined as the selectively manifested barriers and obstacles that prevent tourists from interacting and connecting with the host society. The barriers may be social, cultural and even technological, and are not necessarily insurmountable. More significantly, a tourist wall may hinder the social sustainability of tourism with regard to promoting amicability, understanding and trust among people from every corner of the world. Our reading of Chinese tourist view of ethnic discrimination in Malaysia is based on their omission of or silence on this topic in their travel reviews on this topic. So with regard to silence, it refers to Chinese tourists' inaction or passive response towards the unfair treatment of Malaysian Chinese and even themselves when they are traveling in Malaysia (Paltemaa et al., 2020). In the present research, the characteristics of China's outbound tourists and the ethnic issue of Malaysia are briefly discussed. Then, the focal analysis lies on the construction of the tourist wall in the case of Chinese tourists visiting Malaysia, and the tourist wall's impacts on bringing social benefits to the local community.

Tourism and Social Sustainability

The concept of sustainability has become a buzzword since the release of the Brundtland Report in 1987 (Higgins-Desbiolles, 2018). In tourism, it is defined as a development process, involving social, economic and environmental dimensions, that satisfies the present needs of tourists and hosts without compromising their future needs and prosperity (UNEP & UNWTO, 2005). Specifically, social sustainability emphasizes positive social effects of tourism and tourists to the local community, such as initiating meaningful social contacts and improving host-guest relations (UNEP & UNWTO, 2005). In fact, tourism's benefits to social sustainability, such as breaking down barriers among people, have been acknowledged by various governmental and international organizations (e.g. WTO and EU) (Farmaki, 2017). Unfortunately, today's tourism development is largely focused on economic benefits, and social values are often overlooked (Higgins-Desbiolles, 2010). For example, a lot of destinations are moving towards being "China-ready" by providing facilities/services that Chinese tourists are accustomed to and subsequently transforming these efforts to get Chinese tourists to feel comfortable and spend money (Arlt, 2013). There is little effort in deepening meaningful host-guest interaction; such loose host-guest relations do not support any social sustainability goals (Higgins-Desbiolles, 2018; Van der Zee & Go, 2013). Locals are predominantly just service providers or props in the destination.

Tourism is often imagined as a catalyst for promoting mutual understanding and global peace (Scheyvens & Biddulph, 2018). Jafari (1989) cited Mark Twain, "travel is fatal to prejudice, bigotry, and narrow mindedness" (p. 439). Many researchers argue for tourism's contribution to bringing about global social values. For instance, Edgell et al. (2008) argue that peace is the foundation of tourism, tourism leads to cultural understanding, cultural understanding results in mutual respect and trust, and a higher level of mutual respect and trust further promotes peace (Pedersen, 2020). Similarly Scheyvens and Biddulph (2018) state that tourism brings people together, then people gain a chance to empathize each other. With a better mutual understanding, inter-group hostility reduces. Based on these hopes and explanations, tourism is supposed to deliver laudable social benefits that are key factors for tourism's contribution to social sustainability in local communities and the world (Edgell et al., 2008; Higgins-Desbiolles, 2018). However, Khalilzadeh (2018) suggests that social values arising out of guest-host interaction, such as fostering inter-group harmony, remain inconclusive, and tourism's position for cultivating social sustainability is merely an ideal (Farmaki, 2017). Some studies have questioned the hope of tourism capability of contributing to international peace and harmony (Farmaki, 2017; Pedersen, 2020). There are also insufficient studies examining the barriers of generating these social values (Higgins-Desbiolles, 2020; Qiu Zhang et al., 2017). This chapter contributes to the latter.

Malaysia and Chinese Tourists

Compared to their western counterparts, Chinese tourists are generally less experienced in international travel (Fugmann & Aceves, 2013). As a result, they may easily overlook negative aspects of the destinations and accept the favorable images presented by the local tourism industry (Adiyia et al., 2015; Fan et al., 2017; MacCannell, 2001; Van der Zee & Go, 2013). Although more Chinese tourists are doing free and independent travel (UNWTO, 2019), their social contacts with the local community remain limited; despite their pursuits for the "authentic" experience, they are still dependent on information from various Chinese social media platforms (Lian, 2014; Wu & Pearce, 2016; Xiang, 2013). They may only visit spaces (e.g. attractions, hotels and restaurants) listed on well-prepared itineraries available on influential social media platforms, such as Mafengwo.com. Therefore, Chinese tourists would probably view the host society through rose-tinted glasses created by marketing authorities from the destination and industry, and many of these tourists will internalize and perpetuate these images (Fugmann & Aceves, 2013).

Tourists bring their own cultural background with them (Ooi, 2002). So in terms of ethnic relations, many Chinese tourists habitually interpret another multicultural host society from their own experiences in China, and through information from their own China news channels and social media platforms (Jaakson, 2004). Moreover, information on some topics is filtered, if not censored, in China. This includes news on tense ethnic relations in China (Paltemaa et al., 2020). Such sources of information will colour the Chinese perception of the host society. Officially, Chinese authorities claim that they have implemented preferential policies for minority groups (Zang, 2016). Impacts of these preferential policies remain controversial but regardless many Han Chinese (officially, 91.5% of the total population) think that the minority groups in China are privileged (Wu & He, 2016; Zang, 2016). Therefore, many Chinese believe that being a minority has privileges, and they may wrongly perceive the same for Malaysia (Ye et al., 2012a, b).

Significantly, Chinese tourists are more or less political subjects of China-Malaysia relations. Tourism is closely related to a country's soft power, so it is an indispensable but insidious component of the geopolitics matrix (Ooi, 2016). Many countries intend to enhance their soft power through tourism for gaining preferred outcomes in global scenarios, and Malaysia is no exception (Hussin, 2018). According to Ooi (2016), tourism authorities are assigned the task to glorify the positive images and counter the negative ones of the destination. In addition, both Chinese and Malaysian governments are willing to promote their people's mutual understandings through tourism in a directed method for either economic or political reasons (Yeoh, 2019; Yeoh et al., 2018). For example, 2020 was initially scheduled as *Visit* Malaysia *Year* and *Malaysia-China Cultural* Tourism *Year*, and many related campaigns were already arranged in China and Malaysia before the outbreak of the COVID-19 pandemic (Teoh, 2020). Under the current amicable bilateral relations, Malaysia has been highlighting racial harmony and multiculturalism concerning its own Chinese community to convey an explicit message that Chinese tourists are welcomed in Malaysia (Hussin, 2018). Meanwhile, China's state-owned media rarely report Malaysia's racial politics (Paltemaa et al., 2020). In short, how Chinese tourists, especially those with limited international exposure, perceive Malaysia is largely shaped, if not manipulated, by both Chinese and Malaysian governments out of their mutual and shared agendas.

5.2 Malaysia – The *bumiputera* context

Malaysia gained its independence in 1957. The way Malaysia is governed and organized reflects its diverse past. Parts of Malaysia had been occupied by different European powers since the sixteenth century. Like in other former colonies, residents and migrants in Malaysia were broadly identified according to their ethnic heritage (e.g. Malay, Chinese and Indian). Upon independence, the Malaysian government has been using the salad bowl rather than the melting pot model to manage its multicultural society (Gabriel, 2015). Although national pride is promoted, individuals are very cognizant of their ethnic identity in the social political system (Liu et al., 2002; Yashaiya & Noh, 2019). For a Malaysian, their ethnic identity sits comfortably and sometimes also uncomfortably with their national identity.

One of the prominent features of Malaysia's social political system is the *bumiputra* policy. In the country's attempt at wanting to level up the majority Malay population (67%) economically, this "son of the soil" policy explicitly discriminates against the Chinese (25%) and Indian (7%) populations. These minorities are not given equal access to school and university, government jobs and business support. While Malaysia is seen as a multicultural and harmonious society, there is dissatisfaction and disdain for that policy (Harris & Han, 2020). The unequal treatment is felt in everyday life for the minorities, for example, the occasional banning of the display of lanterns during Chinese New Year celebrations (NST, 2020). While local ethnic Chinese residents face discrimination, and their scorn for the situation is communicated frequently in the media, during election campaigns and privately, we however observe that visitors from China do not seem perturbed by the situation. It is debatable if there is an ethnic bond or affinity between Chinese Malaysians and Chinese visitors but regardless, the local Chinese population in Malaysia is seen as a drawcard in the outbound market of China. The sizable Chinese population is deemed to help alleviate some anxiety of travels for visitors from China.

5.3 Methodology

This research adopted an interpretive paradigm by reviewing travelogues posted on Mafengwo.com and Qyer.com, and the two websites are considered the equivalent of Lonely Planet in China (Cohen & Cohen, 2015). Unlike positivism, interpretive research assumes that reality is constructed intersubjectively in complexity, and attempts to gain empathetic understanding of conscious individuals (Goulding, 1999; Rossman & Rallis, 2003). Angen (2000) argues that the world is understood through meaningful interpretation, and our subjective experience is "an integral part of our understanding of ourselves, of others, and of the world around us" (p.385). One researcher in the study is a mainland Chinese citizen who has been living in Malaysia for over 4 years, and another one is a Chinese Singaporean citizen who has been doing research on Chinese tourists for a couple of decades, which allows both researchers to obtain deeper insights from travel stories shared by Chinese tourists visiting Malaysia (Rossman & Rallis, 2003).

Compared to structured questionnaires or in-depth interviews, online travelogues, as a form of user-generated content (UGC), are free of interference from researchers (Qi et al., 2018). In addition, Tussyadiah and Fesenmaier (2008) state that scholars and marketers could receive first hand information on how tourists perceive destinations from travel stories written by tourists. These travelogues reveal a wide variety of information that may be neglected by pre-designed questionnaires, which facilitates researchers capturing psychological and cognitive activities of informants, and forming a more holistic and comprehensive insight on the topic (Wong & Qi, 2017).

As a case study, the scope of the research is mainland Chinese tourists visiting Malaysia. Therefore, a keyword "Malaysia" was used to search travelogues from the two travel community websites. The authors found tens of thousands of relevant travelogues, and sorted out these travelogues chronologically. Then, the authors saved the latest 150 travelogues with at least 10 paragraphs posted in 2019 as Microsoft Word documents with an assigned number. These collected documents contained texts and photos, and some of them were very detailed. To analyze these travelogues comprehensively and efficiently, the authors conducted data pre-processing, selecting and transferring relevant information to an Excel sheet after reading, including contributor's nickname, website user rank, city of residency, post title and important extracts from the travelogues. Meanwhile, photos and short videos were excluded for analysis despite they may contain some relevant information (Wong & Qi, 2017).

The authors read the documents line by line. Besides, some key words, such as discrimination, unfair treatment, multi-culturalism, cultural diversity and ethnic harmony, are utilized to locate the important extracts from the travelogues. During the pre-processing, the authors deleted a few travelogues because they were not written by tourists from mainland China or they were identified as advertisements posted by travel operators. Beside extracts with key words, the authors also revisited paragraphs adjacent to the identified extracts or even the whole travelogue for perceiving the contributors' stance on certain issues related to the study (Van Laer et al., 2018), which facilitated us comprehending Chinese tourists' attitudes and sentiments towards the matter of Malaysia. The logic behind the content revisiting is to search for possibly hidden information without clear markers (Scott, 2017). As per archeology of knowledge, untold and unseen contents of a narrative discourse are important to form a better understanding on described issues, so it is necessary to make hidden information visible through reasonable analysis (Rajchman, 1988).

Thematic analysis was conducted manually to search for shared meanings from Chinese tourists' thoughts, experiences and behaviors reflected by their travelogues with regard to social sustainability and the tourist wall (Kiger & Varpio, 2020; Nowell et al., 2017). Chinese tourists' way of thinking and how they view overseas destinations are shaped by their own cultures and life experiences (Goulding, 1999). Thus, the lead researcher, as a Chinese national, introspects his own experiences traveling and living in Malaysia to search common themes and interpret the collected travelogues. The process may generate a certain degree of bias, but it facilitates the study to gain a deep understanding of Chinese tourists that is less likely to be achieved by a non-native Chinese researcher (Denzin & Lincoln, 2003). To increase the accuracy and credibility of data analysis, some important extracts were translated into English and integrated with the findings part (Mukminin, 2019). With regard to the quality of the translation, the lead researcher used to work as a professional translator, and the translated extracts were also checked by another researcher. The identified three themes are presented and discussed in the following sections.

5.4 Chinese Visitor Perceptions: Ethnic Diversity and Multiculturalism

During the fourteenth and eighteenth century, many businessmen from China, India and the Middle East arrived and settled in the Malay peninsula (Harris & Han, 2020). Then, the British colonists came with Western influences, making Malaysia a unique place where 'East meets West'. To promote its tourism to the global audience, Malaysia implements a branding strategy emphasizing ethnic and cultural diversity, which could be reflected by its national tourism slogan 'Malaysia, Truly Asia'. The slogan sends a clear message to the international audience that Malaysia is a melting pot of Asian cultures (e.g. Malay, Chinese and Indian cultures).

From the travelogues, Chinese tourists generally accept Malaysia's branding message. Many of them are impressed with the cultural diversity and ethnic harmony being manifested by some external symbols, such as food and architecture in Malaysia (Cetin & Bilgihan, 2015). Meanwhile, these symbols reinforce the perception of multiculturalism among Chinese tourists. Sample No. 55 is one typical example, and she saw a culturally diverse country with ethnic harmony through coexistence of different food and architecture. In her own words,

> Malaysia *is a multicultural country where Malay, Chinese and Indian keep their own ways of life and customs. In Penang,* Malaysia, *we can experience visiting the architecture of 5 different countries/regions, and tasting authentic food from different countries/regions.*

Such a perception is not only limited to Penang, some travelogues contain similar information describing Kuala Lumpur, Melaka and East Malaysia. In sample No. 13, the contributor wrote about his feeling when he and his spouse were traveling in Kuala Lumpur, that 'we have never before walked from Chinatown to Little India, and they [of different cultures] were only one road apart [in Kuala Lumpur]. We gained a deep understanding of multicultural tolerance in Malaysia......Chinese, Malays and Indians don't disturb each other, and live in harmony.' Meanwhile, similar comments were found in travelogue No. 11 to describe her experience in Melaka, in her own words,

> Melaka is the oldest ancient town of Malaysia. In the past hundreds of years, Chinese, Indian and Javanese came here one after another, and [their] cultures, languages, stories blended and grew together. There are Chinese-styled houses, Dutch-styled buildings with red roofs, and Portuguese style villages. Although (they are in) diverse styles, they exist in perfect harmony. It seems that this is the natural way how Melaka is supposed to look.

Some Chinese tourists also noticed some negative aspects of Malaysia, including its unreliable public transport, visibility of motorbike gangs, prevalence of tourist scams and pollution. However, these issues are visible. In samples No. 16 and 44, both contributors shared their travel experiences in Semporna which is well-known for its crystal clear water and marine diversity in East Malaysia. In the travelogues, they mentioned their encounters with tourist scams and marine ecological degradation. Nevertheless, many Chinese visitors highlighted the multiculturalism of Malaysia through physically displayed cultural symbols, which inevitably affirms the official narrative of ethnic harmony. Chinese tourists seemed largely to have ignored the issue of ethnic discrimination.

5.5 Cognizance of Discrimination Against Chinese Malaysians

The majority of the reviewed travelogues did not mention anything related to ethnic discrimination. On the contrary, many contributors gave their praises to the cultural diversity and ethnic harmony of Malaysia. In our study, most travelogue contributors visited Malaysia for relaxation with friends or family members. Fan et al. (2017) argue that this type of tourist does not desire to have deep interactions with locals (Qi et al., 2018). In addition, less inexperienced tourists are likely to face difficulties in cross-cultural communication and encounter unwanted tensions with local residents (Fan et al., 2020). To avoid that, they would embrace or even create tourist bubbles that separate them from the host community (Unger et al., 2019). Travelogue No. 50 is a clear example. The contributor wrote extensively on her interactions with her family members, and none on her contact with the locals. She explained why she revisited Malaysia:

> This was my second time visiting Malaysia. I truly love it. Last time, I went to Sipadan with my husband for honeymoon……I can't stop thinking of the bluish green sea of Semporna from my last trip. Xiaomenger [her son] was 3 years old, I think that I would take him to see the world. My grandma looked forward to the sea, and grandpa's legs recovered well from surgery. My thought [of revisiting Malaysia] coincided with theirs, so we booked flight tickets during Air Asia's annual promotion.

The focus of the trip for the writer of No. 50 was to spend time with her family. The destination was just a prop. Even if she knew of the discrimination in Malaysia, knowing the country better was not the main motivation of her trip.

However, a few contributors did write that Malaysian Chinese are not equally treated. By comparison, these contributors seem to share some common features: (1) they usually traveled alone in Malaysia; (2) they had a higher website rank; (3) they had traveled to other countries/regions before Malaysia; (4) they had more social interactions with the locals, such as taxi drivers, business owners and service staff. Arguably, all these characteristics indicate that these contributors are likely to be experienced international travelers. According to Pearce and Caltabiano (1983), experienced tourists emphasize more on higher order needs of Maslow's hierarchy, which may explain why they sought higher involvement with the locals, and subsequently noticed the institutionalized discrimination towards the local Chinese community (Fan et al., 2017).

The contributor of travelogue No. 11 is one of the clearest examples. Her homepage at Mafengwo.com contained 25 travelogues covering destinations in 10 different countries in Asia, Europe, Africa and Oceania since 2010. With regard to discrimination, she wrote that 'I am impressed how this magical country maintains the balance: the Malay [community] is clearly dominant, but the local Chinese preserve their culture and gain a firm foothold despite the fact that the government suppresses and restrains them.'

Similarly, the contributor of sample No. 101 visited 32 countries/regions, and she traveled to Malaysia alone. As an experienced traveler, she even compared Malaysia with Singapore to explain why Malaysian government imposes affirmative action policy (Liu et al., 2002). She immersed herself to the host society by communicating with Malaysian Chinese, so she gained a deeper understanding of the discrimination issue. Consequently, the official ethnic harmony bubble burst, and her anxiety level increased. In her own words,

> Kuala Lumpur (KL) deserves to be the capital: high buildings, government agencies, big mosques. However, what impressed me more is the endurance of Malaysian Chinese. On my first day in KL, I met my taxi driver, a middle-aged [Malaysian] Chinese at a busy metro entrance. He poured out all his [negative] experiences as a [Malaysian] Chinese living in KL after he knew that I am from China. His stories shaped my impressions of KL.

The contributor above perceived the existence of discrimination against local Chinese mainly by chatting with local Chinese taxi drivers, small business owners and service staff. Beside this travelogue, samples No. 6, 13, 28, 36, 47 and 103 all mentioned that the contributors heard stories of unequal treatment from Malaysian Chinese who were in the service sectors. Meanwhile, most Malaysian Chinese expressed that their situation was improving in recent years because China became stronger, which may work as a buffer to alleviate the tourists' anxiety triggered by the cognizance of discrimination against Malaysian Chinese.

In travelogue No. 101, the taxi driver said that 'China is strong now, and Malaysia relies on China for trade……'. When the contributor asked whether she herself would be discriminated against in Malaysia, the driver replied that 'no, young lady. It's different because you are an international tourist. Malays may have biases against minorities [Malaysian Chinese and Indians], but it doesn't mean that they are bad. The vast majority of Malays are friendly to international tourists. No worries.' There is context. The driver's answer suggests a more layered understanding of the issues, and Chinese tourists are seen primarily as an economic opportunity (Homans, 1958; Rasoolimanesh et al., 2015; Yow, 2016).

5.6 Reflections on the Wall and the Silence

As expected, there is a wide range of contrasting and contradicting travelogues. The positive comments mentioned above reflect the huge majority of the posts. They indicate that many Chinese tourists accept the official views and perceive Malaysia as a multicultural society with ethnic harmony. The Malaysia tourism authority seems to be successful in its destination branding via its 'Malaysia, Truly Asia' campaign, and the tourism industry provides much comfort to Chinese tourists for reducing their anxiety regarding possible discrimination (Ooi, 2002). In addition, many Chinese tourists rely heavily on social media platforms of China for travel-related information, and they are unlikely to find much information about Malaysia's affirmative action policy from these platforms (Paltemaa et al., 2020). Furthermore, they may not gain relevant local knowledge from very limited social contacts with the host community (Fan et al., 2017; Fan et al., 2020; Lajevardi et al., 2020).

As expected the posts did not constitute a body of coherent views, perspectives and opinions. Instead there was a cacophony of voices, pointing to the range of ways Chinese visitors appreciate Malaysia. There was however a silence on how Chinese Malaysians are discriminated against in Malaysia. Silence is a complex phenomenon to capture. It is an absence. It is an indirect discourse (Bindeman, 2017). Linguists and philosophers, for instance point to the limits of linguistic structures (Wittgenstein, 1980). Language may prevent or restrict us from articulating certain phenomena because there is no word or that the grammatical structure frames reality in particular ways. Silence can only be described by its effects and how it affects our lives (Bindeman, 2017). Silence also carries tacit knowledge or taken for granted notions (Polanyi, 1958). But silence and omission reveals the politics of how knowledge is articulated, and what is considered irrelevant, assumed away or intentionally marginalized (Foucault, 1972). According to Foucault (1972), silence limits discourse and oppresses. In tourism, marketing a place highlights what is considered attractive and distinctive about the place while marginalizing the ugly and tenuous. For instance, George Town and Melaka are UNESCO inscribed world heritage sites in Malaysia. Their heritage status is widely promoted but the social tensions entrenched in the politics of selecting what heritage to celebrate and what to sideline is ignored in their destination promotion (Lai & Ooi, 2015).

The tourist also omits things. Urry's (1990) tourist gaze, for instance, suggests that visitors pick up sights that are different from their everyday life. We do not give attention to what we consider mundane; and are thus omitted or ignored by us. Mediators are at hand to select, accentuate and dramatize the taken for granted into attractions, such as in Malaysia. In our case of Chinese visitors in Malaysia, the general omission of ethnic discrimination in Malaysia in Chinese visitor description of their experiences seems odd because it is relatively conspicuous.

Some complained about ethnic bias only when they suffered from ethnic discrimination themselves. The contributor of travelogue No. 32 wrote that one (Malay) immigration officer denied his and his spouse's request for a transit visa rudely, and without a proper explanation. Eventually, they got their transit visa with the assistance of another immigration officer. Nevertheless, their first impression of Malaysia was negative. In sample 102, it is even written that '*(airline) check-in staff was not friendly, most probably he deliberately made things difficult......Malaysia, I am very disappointed. I don't think I will come back again.*'

Chinese tourists, like many other tourists, have a certain degree of tolerance towards encounters with social injustice. Even confronting alleged ethnic discrimination, they may respond mildly and modestly. They may prefer to complain through their personal travelogue, rather than to report to the media or to the authorities. For many tourists, it is not worth the effort, they do not want to be further inconvenienced and/or they do not know how to go about complaining. Chinese tourists who travel with family and friends have to consider how their actions will affect those around them as well, especially all of them have committed time and money to enjoy themselves during the trip (Weber et al., 2017). Therefore, many Chinese tourists may choose to keep silent after they perceive or even encounter discrimination. They may also choose not to focus on negative encounters to have a more pleasant trip. Similarly, many may also choose to ignore the unpleasant to portray a more positive image of their travels. Regardless, research on what is not spoken deserves more attention.

5.7 Conclusion

Most tourists travel in bubbles, as their needs are specially catered to by tourism businesses. These bubbles also inevitably build tourist walls that prevent guests and hosts from having more meaningful and deeper interaction. The walls are social, cultural and even technological obstacles. Without deeper engagement, their tourism activities are shallow, and locals are treated merely as service providers and props for their enjoyment. This does not bode well for enhancing social sustainability in the industry. By analyzing various reactions of Chinese tourists towards the official narrative of ethnic harmony of Malaysia, we attempt to gain a deeper understanding of the complexity of host-guest relations and the role of tourism that can play in social sustainability.

It seems that the Chinese tourists either consider the issue of ethnic discrimination irrelevant or are not aware of the overt discrimination that they may have already encountered while in Malaysia, which alludes to a tourist wall disconnecting the tourists and the host society. Only a small portion of Chinese tourists in our data mentioned ethnic discrimination against Malaysian Chinese from a bystander's view. Nevertheless, the fraught silence and absence are possibly the passive responses of the Chinese tourists towards this issue, and such responses reflect the complexity of how guests view, behave and treat the host society.

There are at least four interrelated reasons why the vast majority of Chinese tourists keep silent towards the tacit ethnic discrimination in Malaysia. First, many Chinese tourists are inexperienced in outbound travel, and they are satisfied with the convenience, comfort and enjoyment within tourist bubbles (Ye et al., 2012a, b). Second, many of them are walled out from the host society because they only search for information from social media platforms and other news channels of China that do not say much about the discrimination issue of Malaysia probably because of China's censorship towards certain sensitive topics, such as ethnic minorities (Lajevardi et al., 2020; Paltemaa et al., 2020). Third, some Chinese tourists are not interested in politics and find the issue irrelevant to their travels in Malaysia. Fourth, many of them may not feel right to voice their opinions as outsiders (Fox & Holt, 2018).

No matter what the reason is, many Chinese tourists are traveling in cognitive bubbles that filter out unfavorable bits of a host society towards them. They are walled out from the host society, and the wall contributes to the indecisive relationship between tourism and social values. In other words, Chinese tourists are not likely to gain a holistic understanding of some local social issues, especially negative ones, which may lead to a hindered social interaction. As a result, Chinese tourists are not likely to bring social benefits, such as promoting inter-ethnic understanding, to the local community. In the case of Malaysia, Chinese tourists may not become a progressive force to mitigate the ethnic tension between the minorities (e.g. Chinese and Indian Malaysians) and the majority (i.e. the Malays). Furthermore, shallow host-guest encounters could even result in potential conflicts due to different social norms (Pedersen, 2020). Without dedication to social sustainability, tourism may not generate much social benefits to the local community as a benign social force (Higgins-Desbiolles, 2018).

Besides, silence is highlighted in the research so as to truly understand China's outbound tourists and their relations with overseas destinations. Tourists' ostensible silence may carry much hidden information that is neglected by previous tourism studies. What is not spoken probably reveals the loose host-guest relations between

Chinese tourists and a host society, and indicates that Chinese tourists carry a range of social, cultural, psychological and even technological spaces along with them during their trips abroad. Apparently, there is a tourist wall that limits tourists' interactions with the host society. Destinations and businesses' desire to cater to Chinese tourists, such as using social media platforms of China, inadvertently contributes to the construction of that wall. Moreover, the tourist wall is a major constraint for tourism to deliver considerable social benefits to the local community and eventually achieve social sustainability of tourism development.

With regard to practical implications, resorts and tourist places are encouraged to provide physical and psychological comforts to Chinese tourists. Although such a practice may build up a tourist wall, it reduces tourists' anxiety (Ooi, 2019). As a matter of fact, many Chinese tourists do not have sufficient local knowledge about destinations where they visit due to lack of international exposure (Fugmann & Aceves, 2013). Therefore, they may experience too much strangeness or even conflicts between their native culture and a host culture. A certain level of comfort is necessary to minimize cultural shocks and other uncertainties (MacCannell, 2001). However, resorts and tourist places must keep a balance between familiarity and authenticity. In addition, tourism stakeholders are suggested to interpret and understand Chinese tourists' behaviors from their values and beliefs. More importantly, tourism authorities and marketers need to analyze unmarked information and passive inactivities of Chinese tourists for comprehending a layered host-guest relations for managing the relations accordingly. Meanwhile, destinations should be prepared to explain unpleasant social issues of local society to Chinese tourists. Chinese tourists gradually mature, and will probably search closer social interactions with the host society and local residents (Pearce & Lee, 2005). Then, they may ask questions related to awkward social issues of host places. Without proper answers from overseas destinations, inter-group hostility may increase rather than decrease, and consequently tourism fails to achieve social sustainability as a benign social force. The authors speculate that the institutionalized discrimination against Malaysian Chinese are not likely to be terminated in the coming years, and Malaysia is not ready to explain the issue to tourists from China. Inevitably, Chinese and other international tourists remain political subjects of Malaysia's ethnic policy.

5.8 Limitation

Possible limitations of the study mainly come from the research methodology. At first, the research collected and analyzed data from user generated travelogues on two major online travel communities, and these travelogues were written by individuals who care about sharing travel stories. Besides, we don't know how Malaysia is perceived among Chinese citizens who have never visited the country. It is also possible that some Chinese tourists may refuse to visit Malaysia because they know

Malaysia's ethnic discriminatory policies against its own Chinese community. Thus, samples of the study may not represent the entire population of Chinese tourists. Secondly, the travelogues are interpreted based on the authors' knowledge and personal experiences. Researchers think in different ways, and they probably have different interpretations on the same "truth". Therefore, the results of the study may not be generalized. Therefore, the issue of the tourist wall with regard to host-guest relations and social sustainability needs further discussion in future research.

References

Adiyia, B., Stoffelen, A., Jennes, B., Vanneste, D., & Ahebwa, W. M. (2015). Analysing governance in tourism value chains to reshape the tourist bubble in developing countries: The case of cultural tourism in Uganda. *Journal of Ecotourism, 14*(2–3), 113–129.

Angen, M. J. (2000). Evaluating interpretive inquiry: Reviewing the validity debate and opening the dialogue. *Qualitative Health Research, 10*(3), 378–395.

Arlt, W. G. (2013). The second wave of Chinese outbound tourism. *Tourism Planning & Development, 10*(2), 126–133.

Bindeman, S. L. (2017). Introduction. In *Silence in philosophy, literature, and art* (pp. 1–4). Brill Rodopi. https://doi.org/10.1163/9789004352582_002

Budeanu, A., Miller, G., Moscardo, G., & Ooi, C. S. (2016). Sustainable tourism, progress, challenges and opportunities: An introduction. *Journal of Cleaner Production, 111*, 285–294. https://doi.org/10.1016/j.jclepro.2015.10.027

Cai, W. (2018). Donkey friends in Europe: A mobile ethnographic study in group orientation of Chinese outbound backpackers. In *Asian youth travellers* (pp. 79–95). Springer.

Cetin, G., & Bilgihan, A. (2015). Components of cultural tourists' experiences in destinations. *Current Issues in Tourism, 19*(2), 137–154. https://doi.org/10.1080/13683500.2014.994595

Cohen, E., & Cohen, S. A. (2015). A mobilities approach to tourism from emerging world regions. *Current Issues in Tourism, 18*(1), 11–43.

Denzin, N. K., & Lincoln, Y. S. (2003). Introduction: The discipline and practice of qualitative research. In N. K. Denzin & Y. S. Lincoln (Eds.), *The landscape of qualitative research: Theories and issues* (2nd ed., pp. 1–46). Sage Publications.

Edgell, D. L., Allen, M. D., Smith, G., & Swanson, J. (2008). *Tourism policy and planning: Yesterday, today, and tomorrow*. Routledge.

Fan, D. X. F., Zhang, H. Q., Jenkins, C. L., & Tavitiyaman, P. (2017). Tourist typology in social contact: An addition to existing theories. *Tourism Management, 60*, 357–366.

Fan, D. X. F., Qiu, H., Jenkins, C. L., & Lau, C. (2020). Towards a better tourist-host relationship: The role of social contact between tourists' perceived cultural distance and travel attitude. *Journal of Sustainable Tourism*. https://doi.org/10.1080/09669582.2020.1783275

Farmaki, A. (2017). The tourism and peace nexus. *Tourism Management, 59*, 528–540.

Foucault, M. (1972). *The archaeology of knowledge*. Routledge.

Fox, J., & Holt, L. F. (2018). Fear of isolation and perceived affordances: The spiral of silence on social networking sites regarding police discrimination. *Mass Communication and Society, 21*(5), 533–554. https://doi.org/10.1080/15205436.2018.1442480

Fugmann, R., & Aceves, B. (2013). Under control: Performing Chinese outbound tourism to Germany. *Tourism Planning & Development, 10*(2), 159–168.

Gabriel, S. P. (2015). The meaning of race in Malaysia: Colonial, post-colonial and possible new conjunctures. *Ethnicities, 15*(6), 782–809.

Goulding, C. (1999). Consumer research, interpretive paradigms and methodological ambiguities. *European Journal of Marketing, 33*(9/10), 859–873.

Harris, A., & Han, A. (2020). 1Malaysia? Young people and everyday multiculturalism in multiracialized Malaysia. *Ethnic and Racial Studies, 43*(5), 816–834. https://doi.org/10.1080/01419870.2019.1580379

Higgins-Desbiolles, F. (2010). The elusiveness of sustainability in tourism: The culture-ideology of consumerism and its implications. *Tourism and Hospitality Research, 10*(2), 116–129.

Higgins-Desbiolles, F. (2018). Sustainable tourism: Sustaining tourism or something more? *Tourism Management Perspectives, 25*, 157–160. https://doi.org/10.1016/j.tmp.2017.11.017

Higgins-Desbiolles, F. (2020). Socialising tourism for social and ecological justice after COVID-19. *Tourism Geographies, 22*(3), 610–623.

Homans, G. C. (1958). Social behavior as exchange. *American Journal of Sociology, 63*(6), 597–606.

Hussin, H. (2018). Gastronomy, tourism, and the soft power of Malaysia. *SAGE Open, 8*(4), 1–11.

Jaakson, R. (2004). BEYOND THE TOURIST BUBBLE? Cruiseship passengers in port. *Annals of Tourism Research, 31*(1), 44–60.

Jafari, J. (1989). Tourism and peace. *Annals of Tourism Research, 16*(3), 439–443.

Jamal, T. (2019). Tourism ethics: A perspective article. *Tourism Review, 75*(1), 221–224. https://doi.org/10.1108/TR-05-2019-0184

Khalilzadeh, J. (2018). Demonstration of exponential random graph models in tourism studies: Is tourism a means of global peace or the bottom line? *Annals of Tourism Research, 69*, 31–41.

Kiger, M. E., & Varpio, L. (2020). Thematic analysis of qualitative data: AMEE Guide No. 131. *Medical Teacher, 42*(8), 846–854.

Lai, S., & Ooi, C. S. (2015). Branded as a World Heritage city: The politics afterwards. *Place Branding and Public Diplomacy, 11*(4), 276–292. https://doi.org/10.1057/pb.2015.12

Lajevardi, N., Oskooii, K. A. R., Walker, H. L., & Westfall, A. L. (2020). The paradox between integration and perceived discrimination among American Muslims. *Political Psychology, 41*(3), 587–606. https://doi.org/10.1111/pops.12640

Liu, J. H., Lawrence, B., Ward, C., & Abraham, S. (2002). Social representations of history in Malaysia and Singapore: On the relationship between national and ethnic identity. *Asian Journal of Social Psychology, 5*(1), 3–20.

Lian, H. (2014). The post-1980s generation in China: Exploring its theoretical underpinning. *Journal of Youth Studies, 17*(7), 965–981.

Long, F., & Aziz, N. A. (2021). Travel abroad for face gaining or face saving? A comparison between Chinese Gen Y male and female tourists in a context of Chinese culture. *Journal of International Consumer Marketing.* https://doi.org/10.1080/08961530.2021.1899882

Ma, Y., Ooi, C. S., & Hardy, A. (2018). Chinese travelling overseas and their anxieties. In *Asian cultures and contemporary tourism* (pp. 201–220). Springer.

Ma, Y., Hardy, A., & Ooi, C. S. (2020). Researching Chinese tourists on the move. *Journal of China Tourism Research, 16*(2), 214–229. https://doi.org/10.1080/19388160.2019.1607794

MacCannell, D. (2001). Tourist agency. *Tourist Studies, 1*(1), 23–37.

Moy, L. Y. Y., & Phongpanichanan, C. (2014). Does the status of a UNESCO world heritage city make a destination more attractive to mainland Chinese tourists? A preliminary study of Melaka. *Procedia-Social and Behavioral Sciences, 144*, 280–289.

Mukminin, A. (2019). Acculturative experiences among Indonesian graduate students in Dutch higher education. *Journal of International Students, 9*(2), 488–510.

Nielson. (2018). *Outbound Chinese tourism and consumption trend.* Retrieved from https://www.nielsen.com/wp-content/uploads/sites/3/2019/05/outbound-chinese-tourism-and-consumption-trends.pdf

Nowell, L. S., Norris, J. M., White, D. E., & Moules, N. J. (2017). Thematic analysis: Striving to meet the trustworthiness criteria. *International Journal of Qualitative Methods, 16*(1), 1–13. https://doi.org/10.1177/1609406917733847

NST. (2020). *Politicians hit out at Putra over CNY decorations issue*. https://www.nst.com.my/news/nation/2020/01/554737/politicians-hit-out-putra-over-cny-decorations-issue

Ooi, C. S. (2002). *Cultural tourism and tourism cultures: The business of mediating experiences in Copenhagen and Singapore*. Copenhagen Business School Press.

Ooi, C. S. (2016). Soft power, tourism. In J. Jafari & H. Xiao (Eds.), *Encyclopedia of tourism* (pp. 1–2). Springer.

Ooi, C. S. (2019). Asian tourists and cultural complexity: Implications for practice and the Asianisation of tourism scholarship. *Tourism Management Perspectives, 31*, 14–23.

Ooi, C. S. (2021). Gay tourism: A celebration and appropriation of queer difference. In O. Vorobjovas-Pinta (Ed.), *Gay tourism: New perspectives* (pp. 15–33). Channel View Publications.

Paltemaa, L., Vuori, J. A., Mattlin, M., & Katajisto, J. (2020). Meta-information censorship and the creation of the Chinanet Bubble. *Information, Communication & Society*. https://doi.org/10.1080/1369118X.2020.1732441

Pearce, P. L., & Caltabiano, M. L. (1983). Inferring travel motivation from travelers' experiences. *Journal of Travel Research, 22*(2), 16–20.

Pearce, P. L., & Lee, U. (2005). Developing the travel career approach to tourist motivation. *Journal of Travel Research, 43*(3), 226–237.

Pedersen, S. B. (2020). A passport to peace? Modern tourism and internationalist idealism. *European Review, 28*(3), 389–402.

Polanyi, M. (1958). *Personal knowledge: Towards a post critical philosophy*. University of Chicago Press.

Qi, S., Wong, C. U. I., Chen, N., Rong, J., & Du, J. (2018). Profiling Macau cultural tourists by using user- generated content from online social media. *Information Technology & Tourism, 20*(1–4), 217–236.

Qiu Zhang, H., Fan, D. X., Tse, T. S., & King, B. (2017). Creating a scale for assessing socially sustainable tourism. *Journal of Sustainable Tourism, 25*(1), 61–78.

Rajchman, J. (1988). Foucault's art of seeing. *October, 44*, 89–117.

Rasoolimanesh, S. M., Jaafar, M., Kock, N., & Ramayah, T. (2015). A revised framework of social exchange theory to investigate the factors influencing residents' perceptions. *Tourism Management Perspectives, 16*, 335–345.

Rossman, G. B., & Rallis, S. F. (2003). *Learning in the field: An introduction to qualitative research* (2nd ed.). Sage.

Reuters. (2015). *China defends envoy to Malaysia after comments on racism*. https://www.reuters.com/article/us-china-malaysia-idUSKCN0RS0V520150928

Scheyvens, R., & Biddulph, R. (2018). Inclusive tourism development. *Tourism Geographies, 20*(4), 589–609.

Scott, S. (2017). A sociology of nothing: Understanding the unmarked. *Sociology, 52*(1), 3–19. https://doi.org/10.1177/0038038517690681

Teoh, P. Y. (2020, January 19). Malaysia, China toast 2020 year of culture and tourism. *New Straits Times*. https://www.nst.com.my/news/nation/2020/01/557974/malaysia-china-toast-2020-year-culture-and-tourism

The United Nations Environmental Programme (UNEP) & The United Nations World Tourism Organization (UNWTO). (2005). *Making tourism more sustainable: A guide for policy makers*. UNWTO.

Tourism Malaysia. (2020). *MyTourismData Portal*. http://mytourismdata.tourism.gov.my/?page_id=232#!range=year&from=2019&to=2020&type=558762c48155c&destination=34MY&origin=32CN,34SG

Tussyadiah, I. P., & Fesenmaier, D. R. (2008). Marketing places through first-person stories—An analysis of Pennsylvania roadtripper blog. *Journal of Travel & Tourism Marketing, 25*(3–4), 299–311.

Unger, O., Fuchs, G., & Uriely, N. (2019). Beyond the "tourist environmental bubble": Encounters with locals and destination experiences of business Travelers. *Journal of Travel Research, 59*(8), 1493–1505. https://doi.org/10.1177/0047287519884656

Urry, J. (1990). *The tourist gaze: Leisure and travel in contemporary societies*. Sage Publications.
Van der Zee, E., & Go, F. M. (2013). Analysing beyond the environmental bubble dichotomy: How the 2010 World Cup case helped to bridge the host–guest gap. *Journal of Sport & Tourism, 18*(3), 161–183.
Van Laer, T., Escalas, J. E., Ludwig, S., & van den Hende, E. A. (2018). What happens in Vegas stays on TripAdvisor? A theory and technique to understand narrativity in consumer reviews. *Journal of Consumer Research, 46*(2), 267–285.
Weber, K., Sparks, B., & Hsu, C. H. C. (2017). Moving beyond the Western versus Asian culture distinction. *International Journal of Contemporary Hospitality Management, 29*(6), 1703–1723. https://doi.org/10.1108/IJCHM-12-2015-0679
Wittgenstein, L. (1980). *Philosophical remarks*. University of Chicago Press.
Wong, C. U. I., & Qi, S. (2017). Tracking the evolution of a destination's image by text-mining online reviews – the case of Macau. *Tourism Management Perspectives, 23*, 19–29.
World Tourism Organization. (2019). *Guidelines for the success in the Chinese outbound tourism market*. UNWTO. https://doi.org/10.18111/9789284421138
Wu, M. Y., & Pearce, P. L. (2016). Tourism blogging motivations why do Chinese tourists create little "lonely planets"? *Journal of Travel Research, 55*(4), 537–549.
Wu, X. & He, G. (2016). *Ethnic Autonomy and Ethnic Equality: An Empirical Assessment of Ethnic Policy in Urban China*. Paper presented at the International Sociological Association-Research Committee on Social Stratification and Mobility (RC28) Biannual Meeting (spring), National University of Singapore. May 26–28, 2016.
Xiang, Y. (2013). The characteristics of independent Chinese outbound tourists. *Tourism Planning & Development, 10*(2), 134–148.
Yashaiya, N. H., & Noh, A. (2019). Persistence of bureaucratic over-representativeness or under-representativeness: Experience of the civil service in Malaysia. *Asia Pacific Journal of Public Administration, 41*(4), 203–216. https://doi.org/10.1080/23276665.2019.1696592
Ye, B., Zhang, H. Q., & Yuen, P. P. (2012a). Perceived discrimination in the context of high and low interactions – Evidence from medical and general tourists. *Asia Pacific Journal of Tourism Research, 17*(6), 635–655.
Ye, B. H., Zhang, H. Q., & Yuen, P. P. (2012b). An empirical study of anticipated and perceived discrimination of mainland Chinese tourists in Hong Kong: The role of intercultural competence. *Journal of China Tourism Research, 8*(4), 417–430.
Yeoh, E. K. K. (2019). Malaysia: Perception of contemporary China and its economic, political and societal determinants. *The Pacific Review, 32*(3), 395–418.
Yeoh, E. K. K., Chang, L., & Zhang, Y. (2018). China–Malaysia trade, investment, and cooperation in the contexts of China–ASEAN integration and the 21st century Maritime Silk Road construction. *The Chinese Economy, 51*(4), 298–317.
Yow, C. H. (2016). The Chinese diaspora in China–Malaysia relations: Dynamics of and changes in multiple transnational "scapes". *Journal of Contemporary China, 25*(102), 836–850.
Zang, X. (Ed.). (2016). *Handbook on ethnic minorities in China*. Edward Elgar Publishing.

Fei Long is currently pursuing his PhD at the National University of Malaysia (UKM) after 6 years of corporate experiences in marketing and communications. His industrial career spans over different regions, including East, South, Southeast Asia and South America, which has been shaping and reshaping his research interests. His research focuses on China's outbound tourism, cross-cultural communications, social justice and ASEAN studies. In the past few years, he joined some research projects involving consumer behaviors, digital marketing and organizational adoption of big data analytics. He is an invited author of Business Times (China). Besides, he was a visiting researcher at the University of Tasmania (UTAS) in November 2019.

Can-Seng Ooi is an anthropologist/sociologist. He is also Professor of Cultural and Heritage Tourism at the School of Social Sciences, University of Tasmania. His research career, in and outside the university system, spans over three decades. Singapore, Denmark, Australia and China are some of the countries he has conducted investigations. Besides tourism studies, he has contributed significantly to theories and understanding of art worlds, cross-cultural management, the experience economy, and place branding. His personal website is www.cansengooi.com.

Chapter 6
Sustainable Tourism in Emerging Regional Destinations in China: Stakeholder Participation in Genhe

Yue Ma and Lin Yang

Abstract Much of the attention in tourism related to China has been focusing on Chinese outbound tourists and their behaviour. What appears to be under investigated is the tourism industry within China, especially regional tourism development and its sustainability during industrial transition period. Based on preliminary research, this chapter presents a study which showcases regional areas pursuing sustainable tourism growth in recent years. Drawing largely from the data on the events and activities developed by an emerging natural tourism destination (Genhe, China) throughout a four-year span, the chapter provides a snapshot of how the region has evolved from a forestry industrial area to an innovative tourism destination. This chapter describes how the different stakeholders participate in achieving the region's development goals – environmental, social and economic sustainability. By analysing their tourism development initiatives, this chapter contributes to the understanding of tourism sustainability in Asia, particularly in the emerging regions. It also provides implications and recommendations for the future of the tourism development in the pursuit of sustainability in the regions that are not yet exploited.

Keywords Sustainable tourism · Chinese tourism · Regional tourism · Emerging destinations · Tourism stakeholders · Sustainability

Y. Ma (✉)
School of Social Sciences, University of Tasmania, Sandy Bay, Australia
e-mail: yuem@utas.edu.au

L. Yang
Tasmanian School of Business and Economics, University of Tasmania, Sandy Bay, Australia
e-mail: l.yang@utas.edu.au

6.1 Introduction

Much of the attention in sustainable tourism has been focusing on Western societies. What appears to be under investigated is the tourism and its sustainability within developing nations where tourism has increasingly been used as a mean to boost or diversify the economy. Prior to COVID-19, one of the most-watched markets is China's inbound and outbound tourism markets (Ma, 2020). It is reported that over 6 billion domestic trips were made in China in 2019 and the expenses of domestic tourism reached 5.73 trillion Yuan (Ma, 2020). As the domestic travel booms, a number of regions in China have geared up to promote tourism under the "Beautiful China' umbrella, but with a different theme for each area. However, sustainability has not been the top priority for some developments, such as Xinyang tea tourism (Cheng et al., 2012).

Although a significant income discrepancy exists between inland and coastal regions, some effort has been made to improve regional economic development and lesson such inequalities. Many inland regions possess natural advantages but have experienced difficulties in developing them in a balanced and sustainable way. To support the development of these regions, national policies provided some directions in tourism development, such as poverty alleviation through tourism, industrial transition plans and sustainable development agendas. Regional destinations in this chapter refer to areas that are usually underdeveloped and peripheral, with common characteristics of geographical remoteness, lack of innovation, underdeveloped infrastructure, slow socio-economic development, and receive far fewer tourists than national tourism icons and popular touristic destinations (Lemky, 2006; Zhang & Murphy, 2009). This chapter provides an analysis of the development of such regions with the focus of Genhe as a natural tourism destination.

Genhe, a county-level city of Inner Mongolia Autonomous Region, is located at the Greater Khingan Range of the north-eastern China. The region has the highest forest coverage rate (87.36%) in China. The city administers the largest native coniferous forest in the frigid zone in China. The destination management organisation (DMO) of Genhe Holiday Tourism Co. Ltd. (Genhe HTCL) will be used as an example to showcase the development of sustainable tourism in an emerging regional destination of China during the industrial transition time. This chapter is based on a desk-based research, investigating the participation of different stakeholders in developing a regional rural tourism destination by reviewing existing activities undertaken by the DMO. The case will be analysed based on the Triple Bottom Line framework for sustainable tourism development (Stoddard et al., 2012). This framework emphasises the economic growth for a tourism organisation, as well as considers less quantifiable indicators that measure social and environmental impacts. Guided by the framework, the analysis and discussion will centre around the three pillars, i.e., profit, people and planet.

6.2 Sustainable Tourism in Regional China

Since China's economic reform in 1978, tourism has been uplifted and played an important role in its socio-cultural diversification and economic development (Sofield & Li, 2011). Tourism has been elevated and integrated into the transition from a centrally planned economy to a socialist market economy through implementing specific government policy and planning (Li et al., 2020; Sofield & Li, 2011). Analysing recent Five-Year Guidelines for National and Economic and Social Development of China, Li et al. (2020) found that tourism has been used as one of the means of balancing regional disparity between the interior west and coastal east. In addition, the development of tourism has been utilised to maintain national unification, and to build state image and soft power (Li et al., 2020; Wang et al., 2019). Like many countries in the world, tourism in China is now advocated as a way to diversify the economy in underdeveloped regional areas by providing alternative sources of employment and income in times of downturn in traditional industries such as forestry, mining and agriculture.

Tourism industry attributes its rise to China's cultural and political heritage, and the value systems which have powerful influence in decision-making in tourism planning (Sofield & Li, 2011). Sofield and Li (2011) has explored macro-level tourism governance of China's evolving regime of planning for tourism and focused on the role of the state and its governance systems. The state government has highlighted the importance of product diversification and differentiation in achieving the sustainability of the tourism industry, and accordingly, the four key areas – rural tourism, *Hongse* (red) tourism, eco-tourism and cultural tourism the focus of development. Sofield and Li (2011) claim that the sustainable tourism development in China has shown to have had positive influences on transport, wildlife and natural heritage conservation and regional development. However, tourism resources and levels of development among different regions throughout the country are highly unbalanced. Furthermore, although efforts have been made to reduce the nation's ecological footprint, the environmental problems brought by the economic growth is still a critical issue faced by the country, which consequently affect the tourism industry (He et al., 2018, 2020).

Since the early 2000s, tourism has been emphasised by Chinese government to revitalise the development of the north-eastern industrial based provinces, as well as the development of West China (Li et al., 2020). Compared to the wealthy eastern and southern coastal regions of China, these places are regarded as underdeveloped and disadvantaged regions which suffer from labour leakage, lacking investment and infrastructure, lower educational level and vulnerable environmental situation. The development of the tourism industry has been used as an intervention by the government to raise living standards in the comparatively poorer provinces (Sofield & Li, 2011). Tourism is a tool to alleviate poverty in many inland regions (Zeng & Ryan, 2012). For instance, the policy on cessation of logging of natural forests allows eco-tourism to be adopted as one of the potential major sources of income by forestry departments all over the country. Other revenue streams have also been explored, such as e-commerce development for agricultural products (Cui et al., 2017; Huang et al., 2020).

6.3 Tourism Sustainability from Stakeholders' Perspectives

Stakeholder is referred to as "any person or group with an interest in the procedural and/or a substantive aspect of the organisation's activity" (Donaldson & Preston, 1995, p. 67). Literature in business management and public administration laid the foundations for studying the current concepts on stakeholders in tourism and the roles of stakeholders in tourism development (Byrd & Gustke, 2007). One of the earlier works in stakeholder theory is based on Freeman's model (1984). In his work in strategic management, Freeman emphasises the importance of stakeholders to the success of business organisations. His work has been further extended within the tourism studies focusing on the relationship and management of stakeholders within a destination (e.g. Sautter & Leisen, 1999; Waligo et al., 2013).

Sustainable tourism aims to achieve tourist satisfaction and long-term economic growth with minimised environmental and cultural damage to the region (Lane, 1994). When a destination adopts such philosophy, it tends to use a stakeholder approach to "conserve and preserve natural resources, protect local culture, satisfy demands of industry, provide improved living standards of residents" (Theobald, 2012, p. 231). Sustainable tourism addressed different issues and interests of a range of actors (e.g. industry, guests, communities). In a broader sense, tourism literatures have focused on four major stakeholders, including tourists, residents, business owners, and local governmental officials (Goeldner & Ritchie, 2007). Much research investigating the relationship between stakeholders and tourism has focused on the perceptions and attitudes of individual stakeholder groups in destination development (Andereck & Vogt, 2000; Pizam et al., 2000). From a slightly different angle, Timur and Getz examined the network of inter-relationship of critical stakeholders (government, community, and tourism and hospitality industry) in their studying of sustainable urban tourism development (Timur & Getz, 2008).

The relationship among different stakeholders has been found inconsistent in empirical studies. Cheng and her colleagues highlight that consideration should be given to each stakeholder/group without one being given priority over others in their tea tourism investigation (Cheng et al., 2012). Interestingly, based on the empirical study in urban tourism by Timur and Getz (2008), it is found that local government and destination marketing or management organizations are perceived to hold the greatest legitimacy and power over others in destination development, but there is a lack of 'bridges' between the three clusters of industry, government, and community. In a similar but more specific context, Theobald found that the industry could be the dominant player in urban destinations whereas the local authorities might be dominant in rural and peripheral areas (Theobald, 2012). Therefore, power imbalances do exist in managing all types of destinations. This is consistent with

Mitchell's proposition on power legitimacy in the management environment (Mitchell et al., 1997).

In the tourism context, the DMO needs to appreciate all the stakeholders who have interests in the operation of the destination management, from planning, process, delivery to the outcomes of the tourism service (Sautter & Leisen, 1999). Different stakeholders may have different levels of interest in a DMO, as well as levels of power and influence on the decision-making process of the DMO. Because of the inevitable involvement of stakeholders, it is important to identify multiple tourism stakeholder groups and their participation.

There are various stakeholder models being proposed in tourism studies. In the study of film tourism, Sautter and Leisen (1999) provide a simplistic example for identifying stakeholders of tourism planning. The key stakeholders in their study include DMOs, the local community, tourists, tourism businesses and the film industry. However, these stakeholders are not homogenous entities and there are significant overlaps between them. For example, local community residents own local businesses, and local communities are involved in the management of the destination.

Upon examining various frameworks, Wheeler's work, although initially developed in a European context, is widely adopted in tourism research and is considered to resemble to the case at hand to a greater extent (Wheeler, 1992). Wheeler's stakeholder model is based on an empirical research and is illustrated in Fig. 6.1. She identified a number of stakeholders with which a tourism marketeer faces in the local government environment (Wheeler, 1992). It provides a comprehensive list of stakeholders and demonstrates the issues existing among them. For the purpose of

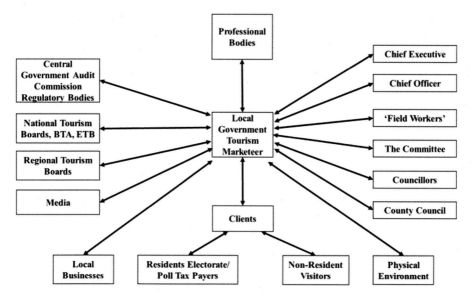

Fig. 6.1 The stakeholder concept in relation to the local government tourism marketeer (Wheeler, 1992, p. 228)

the following discussion, not all stakeholders are investigated in depth in our context. The focus here lies in the key stakeholders that cooperate closely in achieving each of the three pillars of sustainability tourism.

6.4 Destination Management Organisation (DMO) in Context

DMOs play a central role in sustainable tourism development as among their key roles is the management of relationships between stakeholders and the marketing and promotion of a destination. DMO in this case refers to Genhe Holiday Tourism Co. Ltd. (Genhe HTCL). Genhe HTCL is essentially a government invested entity with the headquarter located in Genhe. It was established with the strategic alliance of Inner Mongolia Forest Industry Refco Group Ltd. and six Forestry bureaus in Genhe, Jinhe, Alongshan, Mangui, Derbur and Mordoga. Genhe HTCL manages the north region of Greater Khingan Range in Inner Mongolia which includes multiple state-level tourism scenic attractions. These areas are also the key to the regional nature/ecotourism development. Currently Genhe HTCL operates with two major subsidiaries – Genhe Wetland Park and Genhe Tour Operator. The entity was formed with two main objectives: to preserve the natural environment and to gain economic benefit through promoting the nature/ecotourism in the region. Genhe Wetland Park presents the most intact and typical temperate wetland eco-system (Genhe-Government, 2020a). It is also known as the 'Qomolangma of China's Environmental Education' and the 'China's Cold Pole Wetland Natural Museum' thanks to its diverse collection of wetland vegetation, plantation and wildlife. The Wetland Park management is particularly responsible for conservation, environmental monitoring and protection of the biosphere within the region.

DMOs have a high interest and high power in influencing the development of a tourism destination because it represents a new opportunity. Different from DMOs in many Western tourism destinations, Genhe HTCL is essentially a profit-driven entity, yet is liable for conserving the region which they promote as a tourism product. Genhe HTCL has been involved in investing and developing a wide range of tourism products, such as RV self-driving camping site, conference centre, wildlife watching tour, white-water rafting, golf course, wild fruit picking, outdoor sports training, and science education walkway. Tours were organised in themes of Alpine Ski Orienteering (a well-known novel on which the story of movie The Taking of Tiger Mountain is based) in Greater Khingan Range, leisure and ethnic cultural experience, extreme cold challenges, etc.

The establishment of Genhe HTCL is different from most Western DMOs which are essentially non-profit organisations. Its unique position in the development of this regional tourism could be traced back to some historical and regulatory events. The development of the Greater Khingan Range in the past 60 years is a showcase of responding to China's move to modernisation as a priority over environmental considerations (Sofield & Li, 2011). From 1952 to 2015, the Greater Khingan Range forestry of Inner Mongolia was primarily used for commercial logging. It provided 200 million cubic meters of timbers and contributed 20 billion Yuan to the country's economy. However, the commercial logging of natural forests officially stopped since April 2015 following the call by President Xi under the campaign 'Green water and green mountains are golden and silver mountains'. Tourism has since come into play in the forestry-run reserves, and gradually replaced logging as the main source of income in the region.

6.5 Research Method

A desk-based research was used for this exploratory study. Secondary textual data related to the development of sustainable tourism in the region was used to accommodate this research. Data used for this analysis comprised of activities and events (documented as memorabilia) undertaken by the DMO – Genhe HTCL at a four-year span from 2016 to 2019. Informal conversations with staff at Genghe HTCL were also used as data to support the analysis of this study. This particular timeframe was selected due to the ban on commercial logging imposed in 2015 when tourism started to be accentuated in the policymaking of the area. It also excludes the potential impact of COVID-19 pandemic on the domestic tourism market. Desk-based research has been used previously by Heitmann (2010) when exploring stakeholders and mapping out their interrelationships in her study of film tourism for sustainable planning and development.

The first step was the use of content analysis to identify major stakeholder groups that the Genhe HTCL engages, by adapting to Western stakeholder's theories and frameworks (Freeman, 1984; Wheeler, 1992). Operationally, the data documents were collected directly in its original Chinese language format. The two bilingual authors translated the data into English for analysis. The translationed data were reviewed separately, and the discrepancies were discussed to ensure the quality of the data. At the second stage, the activities and events were categorized according to the stakeholders they involved. The three pillars of sustainability were then added to the analysis as the third dimension. As an illustration, Table 6.1 provides a snapshot of the analysis.

The analysis reveals that many stakeholders have participated in these activities differently, even though they belong to the same stakeholder group, such as community and decision-makers (as categorised in Western literature). Particularly, the role of the state government and its tourism governance system are worth further research. In the next section, we will discuss the key stakeholders and their participation in achieving the environmental, social, and economic sustainability in the region, as well as the relationships between different stakeholders and the DMO – Genhe HTCL.

Table 6.1 Illustration of data analysis

Year	Activity examples	Sustainability pillar	GOV	BUS	COM	NGOs	Media
2016	Genhe Wetland Park organising wetland themed seminars at the Genhe No. 2 Primary School	Social Environmental			X		
2016	Global Environmental Facility (GEF) regional conference, fieldtrip, experts/consultants visiting Wetland Park	Environmental	X			X	
2017	National Youth Chinese Wrestling Summer Camp	Social			X		
2017	Capital Normal University (Beijing) fieldtrip to Genhe Wetland Park	Environmental				X	
2018	BMW Customer Test Drive experience event at Genhe Wetland Park	Economic		X			
2018	Genhe Forestry Bureau organising voluntary tree planting activity	Social Environmental	X		X		
2019	Hunan TV network filming the reality show 'Our Masters' at Genhe Wetland Park	Economic					X
2019	'Pole of Cold' branding series activities: Snow and Ice Festival	Economic Social	X	X	X		

Note: *GOV* Government, *BUS* Business, *COM* Community, NGOs Non-government organisations

6.6 Findings and Discussion

Focusing on the DMO, its stakeholders and their activities are analysed based on the Triple Bottom Line framework of sustainable tourism development (Stoddard et al., 2012). Guided by the framework, the analysis and discussion center around three pillars, i.e., environment (planet), social (people) and economic (profit) considerations of the Genhe HTCL. The participation of various stakeholders are explained with examples. The stakeholder groups are identified adapting Wheeler's model (Wheeler, 1992), illustrated in Fig. 6.2. This model does not imply any bilateral relationship or power which exists among them. The complexity of these relationships warrants a more comprehensively designed research requiring a variety of data sources, and it is beyond the scope of this chapter.

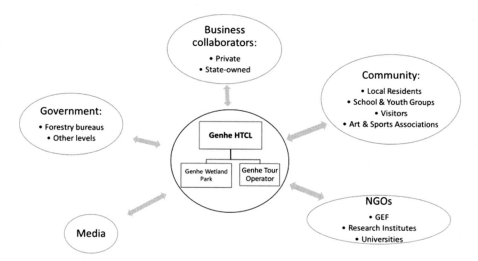

Fig. 6.2 Genhe HTCL stakeholder group model

6.6.1 Environmental Sustainability

Genhe HTCL has been focusing on further developing and conserving the natural environment as the core component of tourism in the region. Building on the wetland, Genhe HTCL initiated and invested in the development of the restricted camp site which offers three types of accommodation experiences– RVs, wooden sheds and tents. Unlike many other natural attractions suffering from over-crowding and over-commercialisation (Huang & Pearce, 2016), the development of Genhe wetland remains at a small scale with environmentally friendly operations. The site is built in a selected area with a design to minimize the impact and damage to the nature. Facilities such as tents and RVs were allocated sparsely in the wetland, adopting the concept of minimal ground contact and removable structure which allows recovery of the vegetation as facilities rotate over time. Fig. 6.3 illustrates an example of adopting such an environmentally friendly approach. The wooden sheds were constructed over removable supporting frames or panels using minimal ground space. In addition to that, within the Wetland park, a wildlife sanctuary is established to ensure breeding of wildlife from the Greater Kinghan Range.

As aforementioned, Genhe Wetland Park is mainly responsible for the environmental protection and conservation. For instance, the Park temporarily closes during the forest fire season in October. A uniqueness of the case is that the tourism operation of Wetland Park is managed by the Genhe HTCL (a commercial entity), but the Park is registered as a unit under the Genhe Forestry Bureau. Due to the top-down policy over the green development is implemented in the region, this triangle relationship among the three entities enables the activities and practices of the Park to be undertaken with collaborative effort from all parties. The Park has been developed and managed in an ecologically sustainable way which meets the national

Fig. 6.3 Genhe Wetland camp site wooden sheds illustration (Photos taken by the authors)

standards. Engaging other government stakeholders, Genhe Forestry Bureau has organised training courses to upskill their employees on the aspects of enhancing capabilities of ecological protection, improving service quality to the public, and workplace health and safety.

Non-government organizations (NGOs) are another stakeholder group that participated extensively in the development of the tourism in the region. NGOs play a significant role in the initial Wetland Park planning stage by working closely with the local forestry bureaus. For example, Global Environment Facility (GEF), an organization that helps tackle the planet's most pressing environmental problems, undertakes a project in the Great Khingan Range aimed at strengthening the management effectiveness of the protected wetland area, biodiversity and essential ecosystem services (GEF, 2020). During the five-year implementation of this GEF project, a range of exploratory and demonstrative projects were carried out around the themes of promoting biodiversity conservation, building capacity, improving protection and restoration technologies, enhancing publicity and education, and encouraging community co-management. The project has been reported as effectively improved the management capabilities of the forest management teams in this area, of which the environmental protection model has become replicable for other regions. Other NGOs such as public universities (e.g. Northeast Forestry University) and research institutes have acted as both collaborators and instructors, undertaking field investigations and providing monitoring and protection advice and guidance. This close collaboration could also be explained by the nature of the relationship between NGOs and the government bodies (here referring to Genhe Forestry Bureau), which is different from genuine NGOs in the Western context.

There appears to be very little initiatives involving communities of residents and visitors, particularly in the planning and development stage of the eco-tourism in the region. Although some tourist products were constructed for the use by this stakeholder group, Genhe HTCL has focused on educating the community on these initiatives as informational dissemination and encouraging participation than development.

6.6.2 Social Sustainability

The social dimension of sustainability represents the build of a wide range of social capital, which include improving trust, encouraging cooperation and collaboration, enhancing networks and supporting life-long learning (Stoddard et al., 2012). Some of the social sustainability indicators are "support for access and equity, pressure on services, pride and sense of belonging to the local area, support for cultural and artistic endeavours, regional showcase, and community health and safety issues" (Stoddard et al., 2012, p. 250). Different from environmental sustainability, Genhe HTCL involved the community more extensively in achieving social sustainability although mainly through participation. Genhe HTCL develops a variety of activities and events, yet the community has not been reported as providing input in the decision-making, such as consulting local residents or advocates in planning an activity. This aspect aligns with Xu and her colleagues' research on the evolving path of community participation in China which found that local residents lacked a channel to contribute to management and planning (Xu et al., 2019). Rather, in the case of Genhe, the communities are involved as participants who could potentially receive benefits from the sustainable development. Arguably, these actions build a closer relationship between the Genhe HTCL, local people and visitors.

One of the community groups is school children and youth groups. They are involved in the development of Genhe sustainable tourism as the beneficiaries. For instance, the staff from Genhe Wetland Park present public seminars and organise activities in a local primary school to educate students the knowledge on wetland. A few school Summer Camps catering to different hobbies such as sports and arts were organised in partnership with the Wetland Park so the students are plunged back into nature with these hobby-related activities. Largely attributed to its management of this natural environment, Genhe Wetland Park won the title of 'Hong Kong and Macau Youth Studying Base' in 2018. In an informal conversation, the director of Genhe Wetland Park points out that the Park priorities its contribution to the community through connecting with schools and engaging with them by raising awareness of wetland and enhancing their knowledge of the region. He states that,

> 'In the future, we will focus on building the Daxing'anling (i.e. Greater Khingan Range) nature educational projects for schools. We'll use the form of nature education to connect and integrate related resources surrounding the area.'

Consistent with literature in building social sustainability, the participation of such activities increases the environmental awareness and builds cultural capital for young people in the society (Shelley et al., 2019). Community participation is also seen in art, sports, literacy and festivals. The Genhe HTCL has co-organised photography competitions and tours targeting literacy and arts associations around the theme of the Wetland Park sceneries. These activities aim to provide a platform for the artists to showcase their work.

As the region is experiencing the transition from relying heavily on forestry logging to sustainable tourism, the history is an important component of its cultural capital. Genhe HTCL makes an effort in preserving local cultural heritage in order to improve the cultural value of this tourism destination. For example, the 'Logging Cessation Memorial' landmark was built in March 2015 as the commemoration of the officially ending forestry commercial logging. Its surrounding forestry settings have now become an iconic cultural attraction within the region. This cultural heritage asset is an important element of Genhe sustainable tourism product.

Looking at the internal stakeholder –L employees, Genhe HTC organises study tours for the employees to visit other peer institutions to learn the skills to improve the service standard and management. Trainings on tourism knowledge and service quality were also provided to the staff in between tourism peak seasons. In addition, Genhe HTCL staff participate in activities hosted by Forest Bureau (government stakeholder) such as 'Voluntary Tree Planting' project, and 'Forest Management Protection and Cultivation Knowledge Trivia'. This again highlights the intertwined relationship between Genhe HTCL and government stakeholders.

6.6.3 Economic Sustainability

Traditionally, financial performance is used as economic indicators in the tourism industry. It includes sales revenue, profit, return on investment (ROI), and heads in beds, etc. (Stoddard et al., 2012). Other scholars consider that financial leakage out of the community, employment rate and availability of local credit to local business should also be applied in measuring economic sustainability (Choi & Sirakaya, 2006). It is unclear from the data we use that how much Genhe HTCL activities and events have contributed to the local economy because the measurable economic indicators remain unpublished, such as hotel beds, ROI and direct employment. However, various collaborations among stakeholders have revealed that the Genhe HTCL as a DMO has the goal of raising the awareness of the region, marketing the destination, managing the supply side of the industry, and subsequently aims to gain profit through its tour operation subsidiary.

Place branding significantly contributes to tourism sustainability, and it especially activates the under-utilised tourism capacity during off-peak seasons. Being the officially labelled "the Coldest City" in China, Genhe recorded a temperature of −58 °C on its coldest day. Taking advantage of this fact, Genhe HTCL registered the brand 'China Pole of Cold'(中国冷极)'. A growing number of events and regular activities were hosted locally under the brand. The place branding and its subsequent marketing campaigns are able to attract more visitors and boost the destination awareness and economy (Ooi & Pedersen, 2010). Creative events such as 'Coldest Festival', 'Outdoor Hotpot', and snow and ice themed 'Winter Marathon' are organised. These events increased the livelihood and excitement among the local residents. Other events co-sponsored with Genhe HTCL also achieve similar results during off peak seasons, such as Summer Forest Marathon in Genhe Wetland Park which attracts over one thousand participants from interstate and local residents.

Stakeholders including businesses and enterprises have collaborated with Genhe HTCL in promoting and improving the destination. China Unicom Telecommunications Company, in achieving its smart tourism goal, provides a 5G platform for the Park. Luxurious car brands including BMW X3 and Aston Martin carried out customer test drive experience programs in the Park area in 2018 and 2019, taking advantage of the spacious landscape. Undoubtfully the awareness of the destination has increased, however, the impact of such activities on the natural environment and wildlife remain questionable. Apart from the business collaborations, Genhe HTCL has participated in several tourism product exhibitions at both regional and national levels to promote the Wetland Park. Another stream of marketing collaboration is through the engagement with the stakeholder of media. China Central Television network Channel 1 (CCTV 1) and Hunan TV network filmed reality shows in the Wetland Park featuring its scenery landscape. Genhe HTCL was responsible for forest fire control and environmental monitoring during the filming process. This emphasises the roles that Genhe HTCL play in both environmental protection and destination promotion.

Although the direct benefit cannot be assessed based on the scope of this study, the impact is ultimately targeted at economic enhancement. Indirect indicators such as the visitor number and income generated from tourism in the region can be used to assess its effectiveness of economic sustainability. The visitor number has increased from 1.05 million in 2017 to 1.35 million in 2019 with a growth rate of more than 13%. As a result, tourism income has also increased steadily from 1.46 billion Yuan in 2017 to 1.64 billion Yuan in 2019 with a growth rate of about 6% each year (Genhe-Government, 2020b).

Some activities were clearly developed to achieve both economic and social perspectives. In the transition time, the proliferation of tourism drives other sectors, as well as many other aspects in the society. For instance, many local artists, craftsmen and small businesses have gained economic benefit through entrepreneurship under the umbrella of local tourism initiatives such as local markets and souvenir shops. In the less developed northeast region of China, there are a large number of clusters of ethnic minorities. The diverse culture of the ethnic groups can become unique tourism resources if managed appropriately. In Genhe, the major indigenous group is the Ewenke ethnic tribe of Aoluguya which is recognised as 'the last hunting tribe and reindeer raiser of China'. Genhe HTCL creates ethnic cultural assets through building a 'Aoluguya Village' to preserve the indigenous culture as well as promoting the destination. The Village is now a major cultural attraction within the region. Local artists and craftsmen create artworks featuring indigenous themes and have them promoted/sold as souvenirs. Local businesses also produce reindeer products to profit from the expanded visitor market. Therefore, the development of tourism in the region enhances sustainability through the protected cultural heritage and increased environmental awareness and economic activities.

Based on this case in Genhe, it seems that tourism planning is mostly carried out in a top-down approach with imbalanced input from stakeholder groups, whereas non-government stakeholders contribute largely in the form of participation rather than development or decision-making. Collaborations exist between the tourism industry and other sectors, including forestry, sports, art and culture, education, media, research, wildlife protection, and commodities production. These interactions are an illustration of the coordinating power of centrally directed governance together with an effective market economy at work in China ((Sofield & Li, 2011). Our analysis uncovered the efforts in protecting ecosystems, indigenous environments, historical and cultural heritage.

6.7 Conclusion

This chapter provides a holistic view of how a regional tourism destination in China emerges and develops with the consideration of a variety of stakeholders. It uses the Triple-Bottom-Line framework for sustainable tourism development as a conceptual lens to evaluate the activities carried out in Genhe region. This case demonstrates the interventions by the government to use tourism as a major tool to raise living standards and livelihood in the comparatively poorer north-eastern regions through investment in tourism infrastructure and participation of the stakeholders. Genhe HTCL, as a government-owned DMO, is essentially a profit-driven entity, yet it is liable for conserving the region's environment. The nature of its entity ensures that the tourism actions undertaken align with the national sustainable directions. The function of the local government in tourism development in Genhe can be explained based on the centralised political system and administration-driven development approach in China. The government at different levels plays very important roles in regional development, as found in the study of tea tourism in Xinyang (Cheng et al., 2012). Infrastructure improvement can only be implemented with the leadership of the government and is mainly invested by the government. Demonstrated in this case, the establishment, planning and operation of the Wetland Park are seen to be led by the government-owned DMO.

Although the key decisions including the industrial transition from forestry to tourism are largely made based on the input from the different levels of the government bodies, other non-government stakeholders are also involved in the development process through various forms and levels of participation. These include private businesses, state-owned enterprises, research institutes and universities, international NGOs, residents, DMO employees, youth groups and schools, art and sport associations, visitors, and media. The community's involvement is implicit in the tourism activities implemented by the DMO, though their role in the development of the destination is demonstrated through participation rather than planning and assessment. In this case, their participation in the activities such as social events, educational activities and collective workplace activities contributes to the social sustainability, and indirectly to the environmental sustainability.

Since the COVID-19 Pandemic in 2020 and the worldwide border restrictions, domestic tourism growth is predicted to be a new priority in China under the 'dual circulation' development pattern (i.e. centering on the domestic economy and aiming at integrating the domestic and global economies) (Zhu, 2020). Consequently, tourism in regional emerging destinations will have tremendous potential in becoming an economic driver for the less developed regions in China. Still at the early stage of the destination tourism development life cycle, the regional DMOs may consider more engagement with other stakeholders, especially communities, in the development phase to achieve sustainable goals in the long run. The chapter also suggests that the research on Chinese sustainable tourism needs to consider context-specific issues and history of the region as they may present distinct opportunities and challenges.

While this chapter provides an overview of how various stakeholders participate in a regional destination development, it would be interesting to undertake in-depth research in the future to study the members of communities in terms of their perspectives on the tourism planning in the region. The current study is based on an exploratory desk-based research using the memorabilia of local DMO to provide a snapshot of Genhe tourism in the industrial transition time with the pursuit of growing sustainably. Future research should incorporate the dynamics of the relationships among the stakeholder groups, and their motivations. This may be achieved through a case study approach using a range of data sources such as interviews, observations and documents from different stakeholder groups. Such investigation will significantly contribute to the establishment of sustainable tourism in Asia.

References

Andereck, K. L., & Vogt, C. A. (2000). The relationship between residents' attitudes toward tourism and tourism development options. *Journal of Travel Research, 39*(1), 27–36.

Byrd, E. T., & Gustke, L. (2007). Using decision trees to identify tourism stakeholders: The case of two Eastern North Carolina counties. *Tourism and Hospitality Research, 7*(3-4), 176–193.

Cheng, S., Hu, J., Fox, D., & Zhang, Y. (2012). Tea tourism development in Xinyang, China: Stakeholders' view. *Tourism Management Perspectives, 2–3,* 28–34. https://doi.org/10.1016/j.tmp.2011.12.001

Choi, H. C., & Sirakaya, E. (2006). Sustainability indicators for managing community tourism. *Tourism Management, 27*(6), 1274–1289.

Cui, M., Pan, S. L., Newell, S., & Cui, L. (2017). Strategy, resource orchestration and e-commerce enabled social innovation in Rural China. *The Journal of Strategic Information Systems, 26*(1), 3–21.

Donaldson, T., & Preston, L. E. (1995). The stakeholder theory of the corporation: Concepts, evidence, and implications. *Academy of Management Review, 20*(1), 65–91.

Freeman, R. E. (1984). *Strategic management: A stakeholder approach*. Pitman.

GEF. (2020). *CBPF-MSL: Strengthening the management effectiveness of the protected area network in the Daxing'anling landscape*. Global Environment Facility. Retrieved from https://www.thegef.org/project/cbpf-msl-strengthening-management-effectiveness-protected-area-network-daxing-anling

Genhe-Government. (2020a). *Genheyuan Wetland Park attraction introduction of attractions*. http://www.genhe.gov.cn/Item/18050.aspx

Genhe-Government. (2020b). *Social economic development open database: Tourism industry*. http://www.genhe.gov.cn/Category_246/Index.aspx

Goeldner, C. R., & Ritchie, J. B. (2007). *Tourism principles, practices, philosophies*. Wiley.

He, P., He, Y., & Xu, F. (2018). Evolutionary analysis of sustainable tourism. *Annals of Tourism Research, 69,* 76–89.

He, L., Zha, J., & Loo, H. A. (2020). How to improve tourism energy efficiency to achieve sustainable tourism: Evidence from China. *Current Issues in Tourism, 23*(1), 1–16.

Heitmann, S. (2010). Film tourism planning and development – Questioning the role of stakeholders and sustainability. *Tourism and Hospitality Planning & Development, 7*(1).

Huang, C.-C., Jin, H., Zhang, J., Zheng, Q., Chen, Y., Cheung, S., & Liu, C. (2020). The effects of an innovative e-commerce poverty alleviation platform on Chinese rural laborer skills development and family well-being. *Children and Youth Services Review, 116,* 105189.

Huang, K., & Pearce, P. (2016). Insights about the commercialisation of religious tourism: Four great Buddhist mountains in China. *CAUTHE 2016: The Changing Landscape of Tourism and Hospitality: The Impact of Emerging Markets and Emerging Destinations, 100*.

Lane, B. (1994). What is rural tourism? *Journal of Sustainable Tourism, 2*(1–2), 7–21.

Lemky, K. (2006). Nature-based tourism in peripheral areas: Development or disaster? *Canadian Geographer, 50*(3), 411.

Li, M., Liu, T., & Qiu, S. (2020). Governance of sustainable tourism development in China. *Journal of China Tourism Research, 16*(2), 261–278.

Ma, Y. (2020). *Tourism industry in China – Statistics & facts*. Retrieved from https://www.statista.com/topics/1210/tourism-industry-in-china/

Mitchell, R. K., Agle, B. R., & Wood, D. J. (1997). Toward a theory of stakeholder identification and salience: Defining the principle of who and what really counts. *Academy of Management Review, 22*(4), 853–886.

Ooi, C.-S., & Pedersen, J. S. (2010). City branding and film festivals: Re-evaluating stakeholder's relations. *Place Branding and Public Diplomacy, 6*(4), 316–332.

Pizam, A., Uriely, N., & Reichel, A. (2000). The intensity of tourist–host social relationship and its effects on satisfaction and change of attitudes: The case of working tourists in Israel. *Tourism Management, 21*(4), 395–406.

Sautter, E. T., & Leisen, B. (1999). Managing stakeholders a tourism planning model. *Annals of Tourism Research, 26*(2), 312–328.

Shelley, B., Ooi, C.-S., & Brown, N. (2019). Playful learning? An extreme comparison of the Children's University in Malaysia and in Australia. *Journal of Applied Learning & Teaching (JALT), 2*(1), 16–23.

Sofield, T., & Li, S. (2011). Tourism governance and sustainable national development in China: A macro-level synthesis. *Journal of Sustainable Tourism, 19*(4–5), 501–534.

Stoddard, J. E., Pollard, C. E., & Evans, M. R. (2012). The triple bottom line: A framework for sustainable tourism development. *International Journal of Hospitality & Tourism Administration, 13*(3), 233–258.

Theobald, W. F. (2012). *Global tourism*. Routledge.

Timur, S., & Getz, D. (2008). A network perspective on managing stakeholders for sustainable urban tourism. *International Journal of Contemporary Hospitality Management, 20*(4), 445–461.

Waligo, V. M., Clarke, J., & Hawkins, R. (2013). Implementing sustainable tourism: A multi-stakeholder involvement management framework. *Tourism Management, 36*, 342–353.

Wang, R., Liu, G., Zhou, J., & Wang, J. (2019). Identifying the critical stakeholders for the sustainable development of architectural heritage of tourism: From the perspective of China. *Sustainability, 11*(6), 1671.

Wheeler, M. (1992). Applying ethics to the tourism industry. *Business Ethics: A European Review, 1*(4), 227–235. https://doi.org/10.1111/j.1467-8608.1992.tb00219.x

Xu, H., Jiang, F., Wall, G., & Wang, Y. (2019). The evolving path of community participation in toursim in China. *Journal of Sustainable Tourism, 27*(8), 1239–1258.

Zeng, B., & Ryan, C. (2012). Assisting the poor in China through tourism development: A review of research. *Tourism Management, 33*(2), 239–248.

Zhang, Y., & Murphy, P. (2009). Supply-chain considerations in marketing underdeveloped regional destinations: A case study of Chinese tourism to the Goldfields region of Victoria. *Tourism Management, 30*, 278–287.

Zhu, W. (2020, November 2). Have zest, will travel. *China Daily*. Retrieved from http://epaper.chinadaily.com.cn/a/202011/02/WS5f9f55fba31099a2343516f1.html

Yue Ma is currently a lecturer in tourism and society, and a member of the Tourism Research and Education Network (TRENd) at the University of Tasmania. She received her PhD in December 2019 from University of Tasmania. Her research has included: water-gender-tourism nexus; sustainable development of Chinese national parks; tourism education during pandemic, Chinese outbound tourism, Chinese culture and social media in research.

Lin Yang is a lecturer in Marketing at the University of Tasmania and an adjunct research fellow at Monash University Malaysia. She holds a PhD from Victoria University of Wellington. Her research areas lie in the field of consumer behaviour, specifically consumer green consumption, online engagement, and traveling behaviour in cross-cultural contexts. Her publications have appeared in International Journal of Consumer Studies, Journal of Travel and Tourism Marketing, Australasian Marketing Journal, Journal of Promotion Management, Journal of Studies in International Education, among others.

Part II
COVID-19 and Its Impact on Tourism Sustainability

Chapter 7
Re-negotiating the Future for Indonesian Tourism After COVID-19: Sustainability as the New Normal?

Mohamad Robbith Subandi, Karolina Doughty, and Rene van der Duim

Abstract The COVID-19 virus has brought tourism to its knees across the globe, so too in Indonesia. In the early period of the pandemic, between March and September 2020, the national debate in Indonesia (including the government, tourism businesses and academics) gradually saw the emergence of several competing discourses and narratives focused on short-term recovery of tourism, as well as potential long-term future developments. In this chapter we provide an analysis of the dominant discursive themes and their relation to the broader issue of sustainable tourism. The notion of the 'New Normal' clearly emerged as an overarching discourse that framed the debate throughout the period, with the notion of sustainable tourism gradually moving to the foreground as we entered the second half of 2020. Under the heading of the New Normal, three prominent issues prevailed: social distancing, health and hygiene protocols, and 'quality tourism'. Despite the growing significance of the notion of sustainability in the Indonesian tourism discourse, the interpretations and implementation of the concept itself remains indistinct and limited. As discourses will change as circumstances change, a continued monitoring of the developing discourse and its implementation is needed to assess whether the envisioned sustainability improvements will materialize or remain rhetorical.

Keywords Sustainable tourism · Post-Covid-19 tourism · Discourse analysis · New normal · Power-relations · Indonesia

---

M. R. Subandi (✉) · K. Doughty · R. van der Duim
Department of Environmental Sciences, Wageningen University & Research, Wageningen, The Netherlands
e-mail: robbith.subandi@wur.nl; Karolina.doughty@wur.nl

© The Author(s), under exclusive license to Springer Nature Singapore Pte Ltd. 2022
A. Selvaranee Balasingam, Y. Ma (eds.), *Asian Tourism Sustainability*, Perspectives on Asian Tourism, https://doi.org/10.1007/978-981-16-5264-6_7

7.1 Introduction

The COVID-19 pandemic has not only had a devastating impact on the tourism industry as it looks today, but is also predicted to substantially change the course of its future development (Gössling et al., 2020). The suspension of tourism activities caused by the crisis has not only forced tourism stakeholders to think of ways to cope with and survive this crisis, but also presents an opportunity for a range of stakeholders to re-negotiate the future of tourism (Brouder, 2020; Nepal, 2020). Within and outside academia we have seen lively debates about the probabilities of a return to 'business-as-usual' or to 'business-as-unusual', the latter scenario directing the discussion to a more fundamental reorientation of the way we have been travelling and have organized tourism. Although a general belief – or perhaps hope – of many is that tourism will rebound as it has from previous crises, there is also much evidence that COVID-19 will be different and transformative for the tourism sector (Gössling et al., 2020).

These debates have also been prominent in Indonesia, where a range of stakeholders have engaged in lively discussions about the prospects for Indonesia's tourism industry. Tourism in Indonesia was a growing sector before the pandemic, due to government policies placing tourism as one of the country's priority economic sectors. Tourism arrivals have increased over the last 5 years; in 2019 Indonesia attracted 16.1 million International tourists (Julita, 2020). Initially, this growth continued in 2020 with a strong 5.85% increase in January 2020 compared to the same period in 2019 (Kemenparekraf, 2020a) However, with the rapid onset of the global COVID-19 outbreak, the number of international tourists dropped drastically after January, as shown in Fig. 7.1 below:

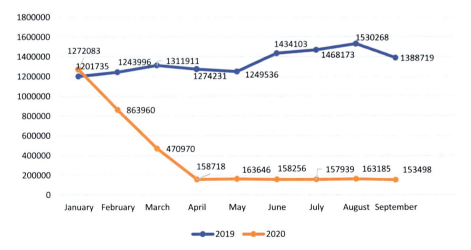

Fig. 7.1 January–September 2019–2020 international tourist arrivals comparison. (Source: Kemenparekraf, 2020a)

Figure 7.1 above clearly shows that the COVID-19 pandemic has had a devastating impact on Indonesian tourism, with a more than 80% drop in international visitors since April 2020 compared to 2019.

Since March, Indonesia, like many other countries, gradually saw the emergence of several competing discourses and narratives around the short-term recovery of tourism, as well as the potential long-term future development of the Indonesian tourism sector post COVID-19. Often these discourses included and reframed notions of sustainability. In this chapter we analyse the key discourses that emerged between March and September 2020, voiced by Indonesian tourism stakeholders, including the Indonesian central government and academics, to identify the dominant discursive themes and what they reveal about the impact of the current crisis on the evolving sustainability debate in Indonesia.

Our analysis of the construction of a post-pandemic New Normal in Indonesia contributes to broader examinations of how the global tourism sector is mobilizing ideas of 'responsible recovery' as an effort to move the industry in a more sustainable direction post COVID-19 (UNWTO, 2020b) by analysing how this plays out in the Indonesian context.

In the following section we briefly outline the pre-existing paradigm of sustainable tourism to contextualise the impact of the COVID-19 crisis on this evolving debate. The chapter then progresses with a methodological account followed by an in-depth discussion of the three key themes upon which the Indonesian New Normal discourse rests; (a) social distancing; (b) health and hygiene protocols, and (c) a shift from quantity to quality tourism. We argue that in Indonesia the New Normal discourse, which essentially pivots around the question of how to re-start tourism and only occasionally embraces sustainability language, so far has done little to re-imagine the future of tourism sustainability in the national context.

7.2 Literature Review

Worldwide, the notion of 'sustainable tourism' has become one of the most salient topics of debate within the field of tourism studies and scholarship since it was popularized following the 1987 publication of the World Commission on Environment and Development's (WCED) report, the so-called 'Brundtland report' (Ruhanen et al., 2015). In Indonesia, as around the world, the concept of sustainability has emerged as a prominent paradigm in tourism development, and has become part of the vernacular of governments, tourism-related industries, and tourism researchers. Indonesia's commitment to, and adoption of, this paradigm is recently exemplified by the 2016 issuing of a Ministerial Regulation on *Sustainable Destination Guidelines*, and the joining of the UNWTO International Network of Sustainable Tourism Observatories (INSTO) in the same year. However, despite the wide acceptance of this new paradigm of sustainable tourism – which developed alongside, but separate to, sustainable development projects, such as the Bali Sustainable Development Project (1989) – debates have continued over its conceptualization, and how to best interpret and implement its call for 'a more balanced approach to redressing the cumulative negative impacts of tourism activity' (Ruhanen et al., 2015, p. 517).

The considerable literature on sustainable tourism globally can be characterized by its ongoing and circular definitional debates (Gössling et al., 2008), its lack of progress (Bramwell & Lane, 2005), and the fact that the concept has still, to a large extent, not been adopted in practice (Ruhanen, 2013).

The global paradigm of sustainable tourism, which is dominated by the global North and often constructed in reaction to excess development and environmental degradation in the Western context, tends to prioritize environmental conservation over dealing with the sociocultural issues that local communities in the global South find more pressing (Cole, 2006; Wieckardt et al., 2020). In the global South, the emphasis may be on maintaining the balances of existing (but threatened) ways of life and resisting neoliberal policies that commoditize local natural (and cultural) resources with devastating consequences for both social equity and the environment. In the Indonesian context, sustainable tourism – despite being advocated as a means to boost local communities' benefits from tourism, especially in the form of Community Based Tourism and Ecotourism – has not been a central focus of tourism development in practice. Many tourism development projects are still focusing on building "mega projects" which favor large investors, despite their claims of sustainability, exemplified by the *Tirta Wahana* Bali *International* (TWBI) resort development project in Benoa, Bali (Warren & Wardana, 2018), and more recently the new development in Komodo National Park, dubbed as 'Jurassic Park' (Souisa, 2020). These developments draw concerns and fierce opposition from local communities, which often find themselves sidelined in processes of intense commodification (Warren & Wardana, 2018). On the part of the Indonesian government, the substantial contribution of tourism to the national economy seems to eclipse any concerns about the social sustainability of local communities, and their equitable participation in tourism destination development.

In relation with sustainable tourism development, crises in tourism can serve as opportunities for reassessment of the status quo, and the COVID-19 crisis is not an exception. The unprecedented impact of this crisis is touted as a chance to shift tourism development in a more sustainable direction (Ioannides & Gyimóthy, 2020; Romagosa, 2020), this sentiment is evident also in the Indonesian tourism debate. However, in the analysis that follows in this chapter, we examine to what extent the first 6 months the pandemic can truly be understood as 'transformative' for Indonesia's future tourism development, including its sustainability agenda.

7.3 Methodology

This chapter is based on a discourse analysis of the public debate in Indonesia concerning the impact of COVID-19 on its tourism sector. Discourse refers to a set of concepts that structure the contributions of participants in, for example, a public debate. It can be understood as an ensemble of ideas, concepts and categorizations which are co-created, and through which meaning is allocated to social and physical phenomena, and which is produced and reproduced in an identifiable set of practices (Hajer, 2006).

The text-based data comprised of newspaper articles, webinars (online seminars), and press releases and articles published on the official webpages of the Ministry of Tourism, with a date-range of the 1st of March 2020 to the 30th of September 2020. The newspaper articles were collected from the online editions of two of the most prominent news media outlets in Indonesia, targeting national and international audiences respectively; Kompas, published in Indonesian, and the English language newspaper, The Jakarta Post. Google search tool was used for keyword searches in the content of the websites to identify relevant articles published during the specified timeframe. The keywords used were "Pariwisata Indonesia" for Kompas, and "Indonesian Tourism" for The Jakarta Post. The searches resulted in 326 articles in Kompas, and 294 in The Jakarta Post. After a content-check, 81 articles (61 from Kompas and 20 from The Jakarta Post) were selected as relevant for further analysis.

The webinars selected for analysis were organized by a range of Indonesian tourism stakeholders, including tourism business associations, central government, academics/universities, and tourism consultants. Nine webinars were selected based on the relevance of their contents, and the accessibility of the recordings, which had been made publicly available on YouTube.

Five articles and 23 press releases from The Ministry of Tourism official webpages were also included in the analysis. For a breakdown of data sources, see Table 7.1.

7.3.1 Data Analysis

The analysis focused on the Indonesian tourism discourse as it was manifested in news media, governmental texts and verbal debates during webinars, in the early period of the COVID-19 pandemic (March–September 2020). The analysis drew inspiration from Foucauldian discourse analysis, which places power-relations at

Table 7.1 Data sources

Data type	Number
Newspaper articles Jakarta Post	20
Newspaper articles Kompas	61
Webinar transcripts	9
Ministry of Tourism press releases	23
Ministry of Tourism articles	5
Total number of texts analysed	108

the centre of its analysis (Sharp & Richardson, 2001). The 108 texts that comprised the final data sample (see Table 7.1) were manually coded to identify regularly occurring themes within the larger debate, with attention to how these key themes were constructed, what the mechanisms of dispersion were, and which voices were heard above others.

Through the analysis, it became clear that the dominant function of the debate was to discursively construct what can be termed 'the New Normal' for the tourism sector, and within this broader discourse a number of sub-themes could be identified. Given the focus on sustainability in this volume, we chose to include only the three most prominent sub-themes that most directly related to sustainability, but it should be noted that further themes were identified in the data, including digitalization and human resources.

7.4 The New Normal, Sustainability and Post COVID-19 Tourism

Our analysis of newspaper articles, webinars and government websites shows that the discussions on sustainable tourism in the early period of the COVID-19 pandemic in Indonesia were essentially part of a broader and more prominent discourse around the notion of the 'New Normal'. The New Normal and its subsequent impacts (including the opportunity of developing sustainable tourism) was by far the most salient and reoccurring narrative in the post COVID-19 pandemic discourse. It gradually became a central theme in the Indonesian tourism and COVID-19 discourse, especially after governments and some tourism destinations were planning to re-open their destinations and businesses from July 2020, despite the increasing number of COVID-19 cases in Indonesia.

This discourse on the New Normal fundamentally triggered almost every other discourse. Although increasingly articulated in the literature on post COVID-19 tourism, the New Normal as a term is not yet clearly defined, but it reflects a wish for society to regain a sense of 'normalcy' and to continue with their lives while also adapting to the restrictions and constrains dictated by COVID-19. This discourse is mostly proliferated by government officials and academics but to some extent it is also adopted and (re)produced by tourism business representatives. Below, we discuss the three key sub-themes of social distancing, health and safety protocols and quality tourism, and how these three themes reflect and reframe pre-existing paradigm of sustainable tourism.

7.4.1 Social Distancing

Social or physical distancing forms part of health protocols implemented to limit the transmission of COVID-19 and involves always keeping a distance of minimum 1–2 meters from other people. This topic is discussed in 18 newspaper articles and frequently discussed in the webinars as part of the New Normal "constraint" that limits the ability of the tourism industry to quickly recover, but at the same time it is also perceived as one of the underlying conditions of the 'New Normal' that will "force" the industry to shift in the direction of sustainability.

The practice of social distancing as a new and persisting international norm of social interaction has clear impacts on all aspects of daily life, including tourism. Based on our analysis, we found that stakeholders discussed several potential consequences of the new social distancing norm which were predicted to impact on tourist travel and holidaymaking. These consequences are described in Table 7.2 below.

Indonesian tourism stakeholders believed that this social distancing norm will have serious consequences for the way tourists travel and their choice of destination. Tourists were predicted to seek out more secluded, nature-based destinations which offer isolation away from the 'danger' of overcrowding:

> *As people get used to the "New Normal", tourists might also prefer to go to quieter* places *and opt for nature-based* tourism *and outdoor activities* (tourism practitioner cited in The Jakarta Post, (Rahman & Mufti, 2020))

> *If they [the tourists] were okay with going to packed and crowded* places, *they are not anymore. They will be more aware to the social and physical distancing concept* (government official cited in The Jakarta Post, (Rahman & Mufti, 2020))

The above shift in preference to more nature-based and remote destinations resonates with Carr's (2020) forecast from New Zealand, which predicted the increasing needs of tourists to re-connect with nature in the post-lockdown time. This new tendency itself may be associated with sustainability through its potential role in re-distributing the tourists from regularly overcrowded tourism hot-spots to the periphery, as tourists adhering to social distancing protocols look to avoid overcrowding, and subsequently seek lesser-known alternative destinations.

Table 7.2 Social distancing "sustainable consequences"

New normal	Consequences	Relation to sustainability
Social distancing	Tourists will prefer places that are natural, remote, and less crowded. Tourists will be vacationing closer to home and increasingly in small groups and using private cars (proximity tourism)	Reduce overcrowding in destinations and subsequently "slowing down" environmental degradation due to overtourism. Boosting local and domestic tourism

Source: Author's elaboration

Stakeholders also argued that tourists are more likely to choose destinations that are closer to home in favour of long-haul international trips. They will opt for short and 'safe' getaways, or visiting friends and relatives (VFR), boosting interest in domestic and regional tourism, as exemplified by these quotes below.

Tourism villages will be an option because our (domestic) guests won't risk going far, so the first thing to be tested is a (nearby) tourism village. (Academic in Webinar, 30 April 2020 (Institute, 2020))

So, people will do this when they are about to go out on a trip, visit their closest friends and relatives, or we Indonesians say "silaturahmi", this is what we will do first, then we will visit destinations that are close to home or domestic or one that is not too far. (Tourism practitioner in Webinar, 1 May 2020 (Sarungu, 2020))

This potential trend of vacationing near home in smaller groups also resonates with Huijbens' (2020) prediction that tourists see this as an opportunity to 'rediscover adventure opportunities' near home without having to 'jet off' to distant places halfway around the world, which – although not mentioned in the analysed transcripts – may ultimately reduce the tourism carbon foot print, especially if this trend persists beyond the COVID-19 crisis. This trend may also benefit local SME's and community-based destinations such as tourism villages, and galvanize domestic tourism, which is indeed considered as the potential main target market for Indonesian tourism in this recovery phase.

There will be a surge of emerging small-scale, community-based destinations in the future, as people would cease to go to popular destinations like Bali, the country's main tourism hub [...] *There will be more destination* diversification (academic, cited in The Jakarta Post (Mufti, 2020))

It is true that the recovery of domestic tourism *is something that is most instant and fast after this pandemic* (minister of tourism in Webinar, on 2 May 2020 (Ramidjal, 2020))

With the Indonesian central government's plan to still largely shut off access for International tourists until at least the end of 2020, regaining domestic tourism is seen as an essential first part of the recovery process of the Indonesian Tourism sector.

7.4.2 *Health and Hygiene Protocols*

The second prominent theme, constantly (re)produced by various tourism stakeholders, focused on health and hygiene protocols. 46 newspaper articles mentioned and discussed this health and hygiene protocols, and it was also discussed in the webinars and the ministry press release. Many of the discussions on these protocols are related to the Tourism Ministry program of launching a 'New Normal' and guidelines, which will be further discussed on the following page. Although this sub-theme clearly relates to the practical issue of re-starting tourism post (or in the midst of) a global health crisis, the link of these protocols with sustainability more likely emerged from the central government's effort to capitalize on the pandemic to simultaneously combining within one integrated program, the need of new rigorous health and hygiene protocols in the current COVID-19 pandemic with addressing Indonesia's poor performance on hygiene and environmental sustainability in the 2019 *Travel and* Tourism *Competitiveness Index (TTCI)*. Our analysis identified a uniform narrative, with repetitive messages in line with the central government narrative on the importance of implementing health and hygiene protocols in the New Normal era:

> *One of the important things in this* new normal *period, and this one can also be sustainable later in the post-vaccine period, namely the issues of health, hygiene, safety and security.* (Minister of tourism in Webinar on 11 June 2020 (Dynamics, 2020))

Another prediction came from a tourism practitioner:

> *If in the past we chose a 5-star hotel that offered extraordinary facilities with comfort, maybe in the future we will choose accommodation or a destination that says first they will provide health or safety procedures and maybe more importantly hygiene* (tourism practitioner in Webinar on 1 May 2020 (Sarungu, 2020))

This pattern also mirrors an international discourse on COVID-19 mitigation and recovery initiatives by UNWTO (UNWTO, 2020a, b) which encourages governments and other tourism stakeholders to link the growing needs of hygiene and safety protocols with sustainability (UNWTO, 2020b), which later was adopted and (re)produced by the Indonesian central government and other Indonesian tourism stakeholders respectively.

The (re)production of the discourse around these health and hygiene protocols into more concrete practices was beginning to take shape on the 10th of July 2020, when the central government through the Ministry of Tourism launched the Indonesia *Care (I do Care)* campaign to communicate the importance of health and hygiene protocols in tourism destinations (Prabawanti, 2020). This campaign also marked the official introduction of protocol guidelines labelled *Cleanliness, Health, Safety, Environmental sustainability* (CHSE), for a range of tourism and hospitality businesses and activities such as attractions, accommodation, transportation, restaurants (Kemenparekraf, 2020b).

7.4.3 Shifting from Quantity to Quality

The other prominent sub-theme related to sustainability is on Quality Tourism, despite only discussed explicitly in 10 news articles, Quality Tourism was extensively discussed in the webinars, where this form of tourism was discussed as an ideal and 'sustainable' way forward for post COVID-19 tourism. This discourse on shifting from quantity to quality is not new, nor it is a direct consequence of the New Normal, but it has resurfaced as part of the dominant discourse in the current pandemic era. This shift was also discussed in 2019 when Indonesia once again failed to meet its international tourist target of 20 million. This failure has provoked debates ever since, particularly on the pertinence of using tourist numbers (quantity) as a main indication of success in the first place.

Following the inability of his predecessor to achieve the 20 million international tourist target, in 2019 the newly appointed Minister of Tourism has opted for a different approach by focusing on 'quality' instead of 'quantity' in measuring Indonesian tourism progress and success:

Even before the COVID-19 pandemic, *we are somehow have been preparing to shift* Indonesia*'s* tourism *strategy from quantity to quality* (minister of tourism in Webinar on 11 June 2020 (Dynamics, 2020))

In the tourism recovery discourse, this shift from quantity to quality was also embraced and (re)produced by other tourism stakeholders:

The indicator of success in developing a tourism village is not only based on the number of tourists but should be based on quality tourism (academic in webinar on 30 April 2020, (Institute, 2020))

We all know that something which is zero waste or eco-friendly is not cheap, but Indonesia *should have go to that direction in order to attract quality tourism and not only mass tourism* (tourism practitioner in webinar on 1 May 2020, (Sarungu, 2020))

In relation with the above, our analysis also showed that the term 'quality tourism' in the Indonesian discourse was largely linked with sustainability and other terms such as *local wisdom, authenticity, uniqueness*, *participation* on the one hand and *high-spending*, *premium*, *revenue* on the other hand. Hence, based on the findings, the way that Quality Tourism is constructed has a lot to do with improving the quality of experiences to attract high-spending tourists who appreciate local culture and nature, and are 'less destructive' to the Indonesian cultural and natural resources, and at the same time bring more revenue to the economy. This narrative can be exemplified by the central government's proposition to develop 'super-priority' destinations, including 'premium' Labuan Bajo, which are also claimed to be more sustainable. A Ministry of Tourism representative in Labuan Bajo (Komodo National Park) makes this link between 'super-premium' developments and sustainability goals explicit:

We want to change the new governance (of destination), not make it mass tourism but exclusive so that it is sustainable (government representative cited in Kompas on 3 March, (Khairunissa, 2020))

However the relation between luxury consumption and sustainability is paradoxical, where luxury is deeply rooted in inequality, and thus inherently unsustainable (Moscardo & Benckendorff, 2010). The consequences of this paradox are to some extent also visible in the confusion around the central government tourism development plan on 'super premium' destinations such as Labuan Bajo. The proposed development does not necessarily directly involve reducing the number of tourists, but as a way to increase the economic gain through 'managing accesses' of tourists to different parts of the National park as explicitly stated by the Ministry of Tourism.

Super premium in Labuan Bajo, I see that the government is building an airport with a longer runway, and a lot of hotels are also built there. This means that there will definitely be more tourists and more income (minister of tourism cited in Kompas on 3 March, (Khairunissa, 2020)

The proposed shift to quality over quantity will not bring much of the desirable changes in terms of environmental conservation, social equality and justice if the conceptualization of what 'quality tourism' entails, and what its consequences might be, is not well understood by policy makers and tourism stakeholders in general.

7.5 Discussion and Conclusion

In this chapter we analysed the emerging discourses – from March to September 2020 – as voiced by Indonesian tourism stakeholders, including the government and academics, and examined to what extent these discourses included the notion of sustainability. Our analysis clearly identified the 'New Normal' as an overarching discourse which was consistently repeated and reproduced across the platforms we looked at. As part of this discourse the notion of sustainable tourism gradually moved to the foreground as we entered the second half of 2020. Under the heading of the New Normal, three issues prevailed: social distancing, health and hygiene protocols and Quality Tourism.

First, as part of the New Normal discourse and reflecting the environmental sustainability debate, it was argued that social distancing could lead to an increase in the desire for nature-based tourism; tourists were predicted to opt for more nature-based destinations as a consequence of the COVID-19 pandemic. This prediction resonates with Baillie (2020) who contended that social distancing has revitalized people's love for nature by giving them an opportunity to know and appreciate nature close to their home. The newly found, or re-invigorated, love for nature is also argued to lead to more support for nature conservation efforts in general. Alongside a rediscovery of nature, it was also argued, in reference to social sustainability, that social distancing measures (especially if continued for an extended period) may harm social interactions in tourism. A similar concern is also posed by others (Butcher, 2020; Huijbens, 2020) who fear that social distancing will undermine conviviality, which is one of the fundamental elements of tourism. Strict social distancing limits may discourage hosts and guests from engaging in meaningful interactions in a hospitable manner. These interactions may turn into brief and 'transactional' encounters around essential services, which could result in a serious set-back for mutual social and cultural exchange within tourism.

The second – and related – part of the New Normal discourse focused on health, hygiene and safety protocols. While the link between these protocols and the New Normal in the context of the pandemic was obvious, it is less clear how these protocols relate to furthering the sustainability agenda, except that the increased 'cleanliness' can contribute to overall environmental sustainability by reducing the waste problem which is currently a major tourism issue in Indonesia (Syaifullah, 2017).

Awan et al. (2020) further suggest that these protocols may also relate to 'economic sustainability' in the sense that implementing rigorous health, hygiene and safety protocols may restore touristic trust and confidence to re-visit and use certain tourism services again.

Thirdly, as part of the New Normal discourse, the notion of 'Quality Tourism' (re)appeared as an important means to achieve sustainability. To capitalize on the suspension of activity caused by the pandemic and to push the Indonesian tourism sector toward a more sustainable directions, some stakeholders proposed a shift from quantity to quality as a 'solution' for the poor performance of Indonesian tourism sector. However even though this terminology of quality tourism is not new to the tourism literatures, scholars have not been conclusive on the definition of quality tourism or quality tourism *experiences* (Jennings et al., 2009). Despite the lack of consensus of the meaning of quality tourism, the apparent inclination of the Indonesian tourism stakeholders to link quality with sustainability may mirror early literatures on sustainable tourism which have discussed this relation, exemplified in the following quote; 'if the overall goal of tourism development is to achieve economic, social, and ecological sustainability, it must provide a first quality visitor experience, conserve natural and cultural resources, and bring substantial benefits to local communities' (Hohl & Tisdell, 1995, p. 533). However, the concrete ways in which the notion of quality tourism – and its underlying benchmarks of 'local wisdom', 'authenticity', 'uniqueness', and 'participation' – will contribute anything new to the development of sustainable tourism after COVID-19 remains unclear.

In the dominant discourse outlining the New Normal, we have seen remarkably little evidence of including voices from the communities that presumably are billed to at least partly host the quality tourism revolution. They should, be heard on what their role might be in tourism post-COVID-19, and how an increased attention to sustainability may benefit them. Buzzwords such as 'local wisdom', 'authenticity' and 'uniqueness' abounded in the debate, but how these notions (as defined by whom?) would translate into practice, and how they would potentially further the sustainability agenda through so-called quality tourism, was unclear.

The central government retained a dominant role, not only in framing the discourse in terms of the New Normal, but also in promoting sustainability issues as part of it. For example, the Indonesian government's effort to push health, hygiene and safety protocols and an environmental sustainability agenda as part of central themes in the COVID-19 mitigation and recovery efforts did not come out of the blue, but likely emanated from the intention to align their policies with the global narratives on handling the COVID-19 crisis and sustainability in general. On one hand, Indonesia aspires to bring their policies into line with UNWTO guidelines on restarting tourism, expressed by the UNWTO Secretary-General Zurab Pololikashvili in June 2020;

> Sustainability must no longer be a niche part of tourism but must be the new norm for every part of our sector. This is one of the central elements of our *Global Guidelines to Restart Tourism*. It is in our hands to transform tourism and that emerging from COVID-19 becomes a turning point for sustainability (UNWTO, 2020b).

On the other hand, the Indonesian government's emphasis on health and hygiene protocols and the environmental sustainability improvement agenda in their recovery plan is also a result of the poor performance of Indonesian tourism on *Health and Hygiene* (rank 102th) and Environmental Sustainability (rank 135th) in the 2019 *Travel and Tourism Competitiveness Report* (WorldEconomicForum, 2019), which for the last few years has been a major reference-point for the Indonesian government in measuring tourism sector performance.

The emphasis of sustainability as part of the New Normal discourse was also supported and reinforced by tourism scholars which saw and took the opportunity to 'ride the wave', pushing the sustainable tourism agenda by – to some extent – re-aligning their stance to central government narratives on sustainability.

However, there was some reluctance from tourism businesses, which were less enthusiastic in embracing sustainability as part of the New Normal. Concrete steps for a significant business and operational overhaul towards sustainability were not noticeable in our data. Tourism businesses tended to discuss sustainability less in terms of operational changes and more in terms of marketing potential. Sustainability was identified as a potential post COVID-19 market trend, due to tourists being predicted to have gained a higher awareness of (cultural and environmental) sustainability issues and be likely to use this as one of the considerations when it comes to choosing destinations or activities. In our dataset, tourism businesses advocated for a return to 'business as usual', only now under the guise of sustainability.

We also observed a general reluctance to voice more daring visions for transformative change of the sector, as we have seen reflected in Western (academic) tourism debates, for example, in a special issue of Tourism *Geographies* published in June 2020, espousing visions of how 'the pandemic events of 2020 are contributing to a possibly substantial, meaningful and positive transformation of the planet in general, and tourism specifically' (Lew et al., 2020, p. 455). The dominant role played by the central government in shaping Indonesian tourism discourse is a likely reason for the absence of more lofty future visions for tourism and society.

These findings not only illustrate that sustainable tourism remains an 'open concept' (Kooij et al., 2014) that is prone to multiple interpretations, which further complicate its implementation (Cole, 2006; Mebratu, 1998), but also that the concept itself is not 'neutral' and thus susceptible to relations of power; also in this case particular interest groups have adopted and defended their own language of sustainability (Cohen, 2002; Mowforth & Munt, 2015). The concept of sustainability was brandished liberally in relation to almost anything, both by those with genuine interest in conserving nature and promoting social equality, and those more interested in simply promoting tourism growth. In reference to the latter, the discourse on sustainability remains part of a persistent 'growth' paradigm (Bianchi & de Man, 2020; Huijbens, 2020), the evident contradiction notwithstanding. Goals of sustainable tourism directly oppose the paradigm of unfettered growth which has been the central driving force of the industry (Bianchi & de Man, 2020), yet the same goals are utilized in promoting further tourism growth. Therefore, to accelerate the widespread acceptance and implementation of the notion of "sustainability" in post COVID-19 global tourism industry, any move toward a more sustainable form of tourism should not only mirror global concepts and perspectives but be deeply grounded in the local context. Further appreciation and effort should be given to recognize and distil local views on what sustainability means, how to achieve (and maintain) sustainability and what sustainable tourism has to gain from forms of 'local wisdom'.

Despite the breakthrough at the end of 2020 in the discovery of COVID-19 vaccines, and the subsequent vaccination effort across the globe in the beginning of 2021, the situation may not be improving anytime soon. Limited production capacity and distribution challenges make vaccines not yet within close reach of most of the world's population. Hence the future of tourism continues to be at a crossroads. It remains to be seen if – and if yes, in which ways – the New Normal will remain the dominant discourse in the period emerging after COVID-19 and to what extent 2021 will become a turning point for sustainability. As discourses will shift as broader influences and circumstances change, a continuous discourse analysis is needed to monitor whether the envisioned sustainability improvements will materialize or merely remain rhetorical.

Acknowledgement This research is funded by The Indonesia Endowment Fund for Education (LPDP).

References

Awan, M. I., Shamim, A., & Ahn, J. (2020). Implementing 'cleanliness is half of faith' in re-designing tourists, experiences and salvaging the hotel industry in Malaysia during COVID-19 pandemic. *Journal of Islamic Marketing*. https://doi.org/10.1108/JIMA-08-2020-0229

Baillie, R. (2020). How social distancing has renewed our love for nature, and what it means for a sustainable future. *Granite Journal, 4*(1), 27–36.

Bianchi, R. V., & de Man, F. (2020). Tourism, inclusive growth and decent work: A political economy critique. *Journal of Sustainable Tourism, 29*(2–3), 1–19. https://doi.org/10.1080/09669582.2020.1730862

Bramwell, B., & Lane, B. (2005). From niche to general relevance? Sustainable tourism, research and the role of tourism journals. *Journal of Tourism Studies 16*(2), 52–62.

Brouder, P. (2020). Reset redux: Possible evolutionary pathways towards the transformation of tourism in a COVID-19 world. *Tourism Geographies, 22*(3), 1–7. https://doi.org/10.1080/14616688.2020.1760928

Butcher, J. (2020). Let the good times roll (as soon as possible): Why we need a post COVID Convivial revolution. *ATLAS Tourism and Leisure Review*, 26–29.

Carr, A. (2020). COVID-19, indigenous peoples and tourism: A view from New Zealand. *Tourism Geographies, 22*(3), 491–502. https://doi.org/10.1080/14616688.2020.1768433

Cohen, E. (2002). Authenticity, equity and sustainability in tourism. *Journal of Sustainable Tourism, 10*(4), 267–276. https://doi.org/10.1080/09669580208667167

Cole, S. (2006). Information and empowerment: The keys to achieving sustainable tourism. *Journal of Sustainable Tourism, 14*(6), 629–644. https://doi.org/10.2167/jost607.0

Dynamics, H. (2020). Kebangkitan Pariwisata dan Ekonomi Kreatif di Era Normal Baru [Video] Youtube. Retrieved from https://www.youtube.com/watch?v=Q-9f0nzpn0Q&t=2827s

Gössling, S., Michael Hall, C., & Weaver, D. B. (2008). Sustainable tourism futures: Perspectives on systems, restructuring and innovations. In Gösling, S., Hall, M. & Weaver, D. B. eds. *Sustainable*

Tourism Futures: Perspectives on Systems, Restructuring and Innovations. London: Routledge, pp. 1-15 .https://doi.org/10.4324/9780203884256

Gössling, S., Scott, D., Hall, C. M., Gössling, S., Scott, D., & Pandemics, C. M. H. (2020). Pandemics, tourism and global change: A rapid assessment of COVID-19. *Journal of Sustainable Tourism, 29*(1), 1–20. https://doi.org/10.1080/09669582.2020.1758708

Hajer, M. A. (2006). Doing discourse analysis: Coalitions, practices, meaning. In van den Brink, M. & Metze, T. eds., *Words matter in policy and Planning - Discourse Theory and Method in the Social Sciences*. Amsterdam: Koninklijk Nederlands Aardrijkskundig Genootschap, pp. 65–74.

Hohl, A. E., & Tisdell, C. A. (1995). Peripheral tourism. Development and management. *Annals of Tourism Research, 22*(3), 517–534. https://doi.org/10.1016/0160-7383(95)00005-Q

Huijbens, E. H. (2020). Social distancing and the promise of tourism. In *ATLAS tourism and leisure review* (2nd ed., pp. 22–25).

Institute, D. W. (2020). Dampak COVID-19 terhadap Desa Wisata Di Indonesia [Video]. Youtube. Retrieved from https://www.youtube.com/watch?v=i3dLqTMragA&t=149s

Ioannides, D., & Gyimóthy, S. (2020). The COVID-19 crisis as an opportunity for escaping the unsustainable global tourism path. *Tourism Geographies, 22*(3), 624–632. https://doi.org/10.1080/14616688.2020.1763445

Jennings, G., Lee, Y. S., Ayling, A., Lunny, B., Cater, C., & Ollenburg, C. (2009). Quality tourism experiences: Reviews, reflections, research agendas. *Journal of Hospitality and Leisure Marketing, 18*(2–3), 294–310. https://doi.org/10.1080/19368620802594169

Julita, L. (2020). Turis Asing di 2019 Capai 16 Juta, Malaysia & China Terbanyak. *CNBC Indonesia*. Retrieved from https://www.cnbcindonesia.com/news/20200203121719-4-134730/turis-asing-di-2019-capai-16-juta-malaysia-china-terbanyak

Kemenparekraf. (2020a). *Data Kunjungan Wisatawan Mancanegara Bulanan Tahun 2020*. Retrieved from https://www.kemenparekraf.go.id/post/data-kunjungan-wisatawan-mancanegara-bulanan-tahun-2020

Kemenparekraf. (2020b). *Siaran Pers: Kemenparekraf Luncurkan Kampanye Penerapan Protokol Kesehatan 'Indonesia Care.'*

Khairunissa, S. N. (2020, March 3). Wisata Super Premium Pulau Komodo untuk Pariwisata Berkelanjutan? *Kompas.Com*. Retrieved from https://travel.kompas.com/read/2020/03/03/094423327/wisata-super-premium-pulau-komodo-untuk-pariwisata-berkelanjutan

Kooij, H. J., Van Assche, K., & Lagendijk, A. (2014). Open concepts as crystallization points and enablers of discursive configurations: The case of the innovation campus in the Netherlands. *European Planning Studies*. https://doi.org/10.1080/09654313.2012.731039

Lew, A. A., Cheer, J. M., Haywood, M., Brouder, P., & Salazar, N. B. (2020). Visions of travel and tourism after the global COVID-19 transformation of 2020. *Tourism Geographies, 22*(3), 455–466. https://doi.org/10.1080/14616688.2020.1770326

Mebratu, D. (1998). Sustainability and sustainable development: Historical and conceptual review. *Environmental Impact Assessment Review, 18*(6), 493–520. https://doi.org/10.1016/S0195-9255(98)00019-5

Moscardo, G., & Benckendorff, P. (2010). Sustainable luxury: Oxymoron or comfortable bedfellows? *Global Sustainable Tourism*, (January), 709–728. Retrieved from http://www.innotour.com/bestenBlog/wp-content/uploads/Sustainable-luxury-oxomoron-or-comfortable-bedfellows.pdf

Mowforth, M., & Munt, I. (2015). *Tourism and sustainability: Development, globalisation and new tourism in the Third World: Fourth edition*. https://doi.org/10.4324/9781315795348

Mufti, R. R. (2020, May 6). Hygiene, social distancing new priorities in post-pandemic tourism. *The Jakarta Post*. Retrieved from https://www.thejakartapost.com/news/2020/05/06/hygiene-social-distancing-new-priorities-in-post-pandemic-tourism.html

Nepal, S. K. (2020). Travel and tourism after COVID-19 – Business as usual or opportunity to reset? *Tourism Geographies, 22*(3), 46–650. https://doi.org/10.1080/14616688.2020.1760926

Prabawanti, M. A. H. (2020, July 11). Tingkatkan Kepercayaan di Sektor Parekraf, Kemenparekraf Kampanyekan "Indonesia Care." *Kompas.Com*. Retrieved from https://travel.kompas.com/read/2020/07/11/112141127/tingkatkan-kepercayaan-di-sektor-parekraf-kemenparekraf-kampanyekan-indonesia?page=all

Rahman, R., & Mufti, R. R. (2020, July 1). 'New normal' requires tourism players to shift focus. *The Jakarta Post*. Retrieved from https://www.thejakartapost.com/news/2020/07/01/new-normal-requires-tourism-players-to-shift-focus.html

Ramidjal, M. (2020). Diskusi ASITA dan Menparekraf RI Bapak Wishnutama [Video] Youtube. Retrieved from https://www.youtube.com/watch?v=e6tuSst-UWE&feature=youtu.be

Romagosa, F. (2020). The COVID-19 crisis: Opportunities for sustainable and proximity tourism. *Tourism Geographies, 0*(0), 1–5. https://doi.org/10.1080/14616688.2020.1763447

Ruhanen, L. (2013). Local government: Facilitator or inhibitor of sustainable tourism development? *Journal of Sustainable Tourism*. https://doi.org/10.1080/09669582.2012.680463

Ruhanen, L., Weiler, B., Moyle, B. D., & McLennan, C. lee J. (2015). Trends and patterns in sustainable tourism research: A 25-year bibliometric analysis. *Journal of Sustainable Tourism*. https://doi.org/10.1080/09669582.2014.978790

Sarungu, P. (2020). Bagaimana Dunia Travel Agent Setelah Pandemi COVID-19? Asita x Astindo @ Tourism Recovery Talk [Video] Youtube. Retrieved from Bagaimana Dunia Travel Agent Setelah Pandemi COVID-19 ? Asita x Astindo @ Tourism Recovery Talk.

Sharp, L., & Richardson, T. (2001). Reflections on foucauldian discourse analysis in planning and environmental policy research. *Journal of Environmental Policy and Planning, 3*(3), 193–209. https://doi.org/10.1002/jepp.88

Souisa, H. (2020, September 29). Indonesia's Jurassic Park-inspired tourist attraction worries Komodo dragon fans. *Abc*. Retrieved from https://www.abc.net.au/news/2020-09-29/indonesia-jurassic-park-inspired-tourist-site-worries-locals/12688876

Syaifullah, M. (2017, November 2). Sampah, Masalah Utama Sektor Pariwisata. *Tempo.Co*. Retrieved from https://bisnis.tempo.co/read/1029912/sampah-masalah-utama-sektor-pariwisata

UNWTO. (2020a). Global guidelines to restart tourism, (May).

UNWTO. (2020b). *One planet vision for a responsible recovery of tourism*. UNWTO. Retrieved from https://webunwto.s3.eu-west-1.amazonaws.com/s3fs-public/2020-06/one-planet-vision-responsible-recovery-of-the-tourism-sector.pdf

Warren, C., & Wardana, A. (2018). Sustaining the unsustainable? Environmental impact assessment and overdevelopment in Bali. *Asia Pacific Journal of Environmental Law, 21*(2), 101–125. https://doi.org/10.4337/apjel.2018.02.02

Wieckardt, C. E., Koot, S., & Karimasari, N. (2020). Environmentality, green grabbing, and neoliberal conservation: The ambiguous role of ecotourism in the Green Life privatised nature reserve, Sumatra, Indonesia. *Journal of Sustainable Tourism, 0*(0), 1–17. https://doi.org/10.1080/09669582.2020.1834564

WorldEconomicForum. (2019). *The travel and tourism competitiveness report 2019* [El Informe de Competitividad de Viajes y Turismo 2019]. Retrieved from http://www3.weforum.org/docs/WEF_TTCR_2019.pdf

Mohamad Robbith Subandi is currently a Ph.D. candidate at the Cultural Geography Research Group at Wageningen University & Research in The Netherlands. He is also a full-time lecturer at Sekolah Tinggi Pariwisata Bandung in Indonesia. He received his M.Sc in International Tourism & Hospitality Management from Leeds Beckett University in the United Kingdom. He also has profesional working experiences in the tourism and hospitality industry prior joining the academia. His current research focus lies in sustainable tourism development especially in the Post-COVID-19 Tourism recovery and political-economy dimension of tourism nexus.

Karolina Doughty is an Assistant Professor in Cultural Geography at Wageningen University & Research in the Netherlands. Her research explores the interactions between the environment, wellbeing, mobilities, and sensory experiences, with a particular interest in the relationship between the natural environment and wellbeing, alongside a broader focus on the role of soundscapes and auditory practices for wellbeing, conviviality, and belonging. Her work has primarily contributed to literatures on therapeutic landscapes, geographies of sound, and everyday mobilities. Her research utilizes qualitative and participatory modes of enquiry, especially audio-visual methods, to explore place-based experiences and interactions and their wellbeing-related outcomes.

Rene van der Duim is Emeritus Professor in Tourism and Sustainable Development at Wageningen University & Research in the Netherlands. He is a sociologist with special interest in actor-network theory and has executed research and educational projects in countries like Thailand, Nepal, Costa Rica, Tanzania, Namibia, Kenya, Uganda, Portugal and the Netherlands. In the last 15 years his research focused on tourism, conservation and development, especially in sub-Saharan Africa.

Chapter 8
Tourism Sustainability in Indonesia: Reflection and Reformulation

Fandy Tjiptono, Lin Yang, Andhy Setyawan, Ida Bagus Gede Adi Permana, and I. Putu Esa Widaharthana

Abstract Tourism has long been considered an important sector in Indonesia. Not only it has a significant contribution to the economy, the sector also has substantial impacts on the social, cultural, and environmental aspects of the nation. Just like in other emerging countries, sustainability is not an easy concept to implement, especially in the tourism industry. The trade-offs between short-term benefits (e.g., employment, revenue, contribution to GDP, economic growth, etc.) and long-term interests (e.g., environmental sustainability, protection of cultural heritage, etc.) are one of the most challenging issues faced by all relevant tourism stakeholders. This chapter aims to examine the emergence, development, and challenges of sustainable tourism thought and practices in Indonesia. It provides a brief reflection of what had been achieved up to a pre-COVID 19 period, followed by a description of how the pandemic has adversely disrupted the industry. The chapter also proposes several important potential directions and challenges for the future of tourism sustainability in the 'new normal' Indonesia.

F. Tjiptono (✉)
School of Marketing and International Business, Wellington School of Business and Government, Victoria University of Wellington, Wellington, New Zealand
e-mail: fandy.tjiptono@vuw.ac.nz

L. Yang
Tasmanian School of Business and Economics, University of Tasmania, Sandy Bay, Australia
e-mail: l.yang@utas.edu.au

A. Setyawan
Faculty of Business and Economics, Universitas Surabaya, Surabaya, Indonesia
e-mail: andhy@staff.ubaya.ac.id

I. B. G. A. Permana
Faculty of Economics and Business, Universitas Airlangga, Surabaya, Indonesia
e-mail: ibg.adipermana@feb.unair.ac.id

I. P. E. Widaharthana
Hospitality Business Program, Politeknik Pariwisata Bali, Bali, Indonesia
e-mail: iputuesa@ppb.ac.id

© The Author(s), under exclusive license to Springer Nature Singapore Pte Ltd. 2022
A. Selvaranee Balasingam, Y. Ma (eds.), *Asian Tourism Sustainability*, Perspectives on Asian Tourism, https://doi.org/10.1007/978-981-16-5264-6_8

Keywords Sustainable tourism · Indonesia · New normal · Reflection · Reformulation · Recovery strategy

8.1 Introduction

Tourism industry has played an important role in the Indonesian economy. It contributed about 4.13% to 5.25% to national GDP, attracted more than 10 million international tourists and 250 million domestic visitors per year, and employed between 10.36 and 12.9 million workers each year during the period of 2015–2019 (see Table 8.1). The Indonesian tourism sector has also grown significantly and become one of the national leading industries in terms of its contribution to foreign exchange, second to palm oil industry.

A recent report on biannual Bloom Consulting Country Brand Ranking for Trade and Tourism placed Indonesia among the Top 10 in Asia and number 31 in the world rank for country branding based on four criteria: economic performance, digital demand, country brand strategy (CBS rating), and online performance (Bloom Consulting, 2020). Indonesia's TTCI (Travel & Tourism Competitiveness Index) score has improved in the last decade: 3.80 (in 2009), 4.00 (2011), 4.03 (2013), 4.04 (2015), 4.16 (2017), and 4.30 (2019) (World Economic Forum, 2019). Its TTCI rank has also consistently increased from 81 in 2009 to 40 (out of 140 economies being analysed) in 2019. The rank was higher than Vietnam (ranked 63), Brunei Darussalam (ranked 72), and the Philippines (75), but lower than Singapore (17), Malaysia (29) and Thailand (31). The overall TTCI score of the Indonesian tourism sector in 2019 was 4.30 (on a scale of 1–7, where 1 being the worst and 7 being the best), with top 10 performance in two aspects, i.e. price competitiveness and prioritization of travel and tourism. However, several aspects still need significant improvement, such as tourist services infrastructure, ground & port infrastructure, air transport infrastructure, environmental sustainability, health & hygiene, and safety & security.

Table 8.1 The key performance indicators of the Indonesian tourism sector, 2015–2019

Indicator	2015	2016	2017	2018	2019
Contribution to national GDP	4.25%	4.13%	5.00%	5.25%	4.8%[b]
Foreign exchange (trillion Rupiah)	175.71	176.23	202.13	224	197[b]
Number of workers (million people)	10.36	12.28	12.6	12.7	12.9[b]
Travel & Tourism Competitiveness Index (World Economic Forum)[a]	#50	n.a.	#42	n.a.	#40[b]
International tourists (million arrivals)	10.41	12.02	14.04	15.81	16.1[b]
Domestic tourists (million visitors)	256.42	264.33	270.82	303.5	290[b]

Notes: [a]TTCI was provided only every 2 years; [b]estimation
Source: Ministry of Tourism and Creative Economy (2020)

As the Indonesian tourism sector grows in its importance and contribution to the national economy, the awareness and commitment to implement the principles of sustainable tourism development have also increased. The concept of sustainability has been incorporated in the Law Number 10 of 2009 on Tourism and several other relevant laws, such as Law Number 5 of 1990 on Conservation of Living Natural Resources and Their Ecosystem, Law Number 24 of 1992 on Spatial Planning, Law Number 5 of 1994 on Ratification of the United Nations Convention on Biodiversity, Law Number 41 of 1999 on Forestry, Law Number 25 of 2000 on National Development, Law Number 27 of 2007 on the Management of Coastal Zones and Small Islands, Law Number 32 of 2009 on Living Environment Protection and Management, and Law Number 11 of 2010 on Cultural Heritage Protection (Nurjaya, 2018).

In the Article 4 of the Law Number 10 of 2009 on Tourism, for instance, it is stipulated that tourism activities shall be intended to increase the economic growth, improve the people's welfare, eradicate poverty, overcome unemployment, preserve the nature, environment, and resource, promote the culture, raise the nation's image, foster a sense of patriotism, strengthen the national identity and unity, and strengthen international relationships. Furthermore, the Indonesian government issued Regulation of the Minister of Tourism of the Republic of Indonesia Number 14 of 2016 on guidelines for sustainable tourism destination. This regulation defines sustainable tourism as "tourism activities that take into account their current and future impacts on the economy, society and environment; meet the needs of tourists, industry, environment, and local community; and can be applied into all forms of tourism activities in all types of tourism destinations". In short, it is clear that the Indonesian government policies on tourism aim to create a balance of people, profit and planet (triple bottom line) or the 'Three Es' (environment, equity and economic dimensions) (Savitz & Weber, 2006).

However, since the first case of COVID-19 in Indonesia was confirmed on 2 March 2020, the Indonesian tourism ecosystem has been severely disrupted and fallen into crisis. Regional lockdowns, stay-at-home orders, mobility and travel bans, physical distancing, and quarantine policy have negative impacts on global, national, and regional tourism and hospitality industry. The accommodation sector is estimated to drop by 44.23% in the second quarter of 2020 compared to the same quarter of previous year and restaurant business is reported to decline by 16.81% during the same period (BPS, 2020b). The number of international tourist arrivals declined significantly from 1.39 million in September 2019 to 153,500 in September 2020, while hotel occupation rates dropped from 53.90% (April 2019) to 12.67% (April 2020) (BPS, 2020a).

This chapter aims to examine the emergence, development, and challenges of sustainable tourism in Indonesia. It begins with a brief reflection of what had been achieved up to a pre-COVID 19 period, followed by a description of how the pandemic has adversely influenced the industry. Finally, it proposes several important potential directions and challenges for the future of tourism sustainability in the 'new normal' Indonesia.

8.2 Methodology

The current research employed a qualitative approach to systematically and comprehensively examine the emergence, development, and challenges of sustainable tourism in Indonesia, the fourth most populous country in the world. Data were collected using a combination of archival document analysis and in-depth interviews. Available and accessible published materials (such as online newspaper articles, government websites, academic journal articles, and tourism-related reports) were used in the present study. The archival documents include publications in English and Bahasa Indonesia.

Interviews were conducted via Zoom with 13 representatives of 12 organisations that have been operating for at least 5 years. The average duration of the interviews was between 30 and 60 min. The interviewees consist of business owners, top-level managers and the head of the tourism management community. The organisations include three travel agents (Company A, Company B, and Company C), four hotels (Company D, Company E, Company F, and Company G), one villa management company (Company H), two restaurants (Company I and Company J), one tourism destination management (Company K), and one souvenir shop (Company L). The main objective of the interviews is to investigate how business players in the Bali tourism industry respond and adapt through the COVID-19 crisis. Specifically, the interviews focused on three issues: (1) the impact of COVID-19 pandemic on their businesses; (2) how they respond to the impact; and (3) strategy implemented in dealing with the 'new normal' situation. Both archival data and interview transcripts were content analysed to identify relevant themes or topics.

8.3 Reflection

Sustainable tourism refers to tourism development principles and practices with the purpose of making places better for people to live and visit. It aims to minimise the negative impacts and maximise the positive social, economic, and natural environment of tourism in destination communities (Saarinen, 2014). The concept and practice of sustainable tourism have been documented in Law Number 9 of 1990 covering the principles and objectives of Indonesia Tourism Development (Lemy et al., 2020). It is addressed in international scientific meetings and taught in tourism management courses and programs. However, a supportive national policy remained unclear until 2016 when the Regulation of the Ministry of Tourism Number 14 was announced (Lemy et al., 2020). The regulation consists of guidelines to build sustainable tourism destinations.

Only in recent years, Indonesian government recognise tourism as its leading primary sector. Indonesia has large and rich tourism resources in terms of natural environment and cultural resources of over one hundred ethnics (Nurjaya, 2018). There has been a major push in the government to support tourism development

(Lemy et al., 2020). Tourism industry is a key component of the national development in the country. The main purpose of the push to develop tourism in the country is to improve the national economy, to create business and job opportunities, to encourage regional development, and to empower tourism destinations and attractiveness (Nurjaya, 2018). However, the country's tourism development has been considered unbalanced and varied due to the lack of clear strategies (Lemy et al., 2020). One of the issues that the country faces is brought by the objective of increasing visitor numbers in the strategy (Indonesia-Investments, 2015). The government has made effort to promote destinations through a range of branding and marketing activities, for example, creating 10 new Bali destinations (Lemy et al., 2020). The goal is to ensure 20 million foreign tourists by 2019 (Indonesia-Investments, 2015). What has been criticised on these initiatives is on its lack of comprehensive tourism planning. The sole focus on massive sales and rising visitor numbers could distress the less-prepared destinations. Facilities and resources may be ruined and damaged through exceeding their carrying capacity. The local residents may reject tourism when they do not receive benefits from the sector, which lead to visitor dissatisfaction.

In 2016, the Ministry of Tourism published guidelines for sustainable tourism destination aligning with the three-pillar conception of (social, environmental and economic) sustainability. One of the highlighted areas is the value of national culture which is considered one of the tourism attractions. This is the main aspect in social sustainability for the sector to focus on in order to strengthen the national identity, pride and unity. Environmental element is specified in protecting biodiversity and natural resources in an integrated system of management protection which must be based on providing benefits for the economic and social development. Economic aspect focuses on generating economic benefits to local communities.

The scope of sustainable tourism destination development includes management of sustainable tourism destination, providing economic benefits to local communities, preserving culture for the community and visitors, and conserve the environment. The management of sustainable tourism destination has been given attention and the sector is advised to have short-term, mid-term and long-term tourism strategies covering issues such as access development to destination, tourism amenity, economic growth, social issues, cultural heritage, safety and security. Multiple destination management organisations are to be established involving both private and public sections with sufficient funding and clear tasks. It is worth noting that marketing activities has been given more weight in terms of tourism seasonality management focusing on identifying tourism opportunities and developing proper marketing strategy. In addition, destination promotion is encouraged, including promotion of products as well as services. Monitoring and reporting system is advised to ensure visitor satisfaction (Ministry of Tourism, 2016).

In its effort to optimise economic benefits for local communities, businesses at tourism destination are required to provide employments and training opportunities, work safety, and fair remuneration for all. The stakeholders from public and private sectors and local communities are encouraged to participate in the planning and decision making on the sustainable development of tourist destination. The Sapta

Pesona Program is developed to be applied regularly to local communities. This program intends to raise tourism awareness, educate the communities to improve their understanding of opportunities and challenges in the tourism development of the destinations, as well as to highlight the importance in maintaining sustainability (Ministry of Tourism, 2016). In addition, legislations and programs have been established to prevent exploitation, such as commercial and sexual exploitation and harassment, other form of violation to children, teenager, women, and minority groups.

To optimise cultural preservation, policies and systems are developed to assess the effort in preserving cultural heritage, such as historical buildings and archaeological sites (Aznar & Hoefnagels, 2020). Indonesia has very diverse ethnic and racial cultures, and guidelines are designed to minimise potential impact from visitors on sensitive tourism locations. In the similar vein, the information in such destinations are adjusted in accordance to the local custom and developed in consultation with the community (Ministry of Tourism, 2016). Environmental conservation has also been given attention such as establishing systems to assess environmental risks in the process of tourism development as well as to prevent and address damages to the environment. In the sector, much effort is put into protecting ecosystem, species and habitat conservation areas, and preventing from invasive species. Other schemes and systems focus on protection of wildlife, energy conservation, better water management system, waste reduction, as well as promoting low-impact transportation (Ministry of Tourism, 2016).

Based on the principles of sustainable tourism, the government has established a number of systems and attempted to address sustainable issues in tourism development in the country. Many initiatives are made to ensure the welfare of all stakeholders involved in the destination development at the strategic level or at the early stage of the process. However, sustainable tourism development requires resources and can be space and land-intensive. There are challenges and/or obstacles in implementing these principles and guidelines for sustainable tourism. For example, there are frequently conflicts emerging between local community and tourism entrepreneurs in regard to the land use and occupation and other access to natural resources of the local community (Nurjaya, 2018). Economic benefits were mostly gained by those who have capital to invest, as a result, equitable benefit of tourism is difficult to achieve as the case in Toraja, Indonesia (Junaid, 2015).

Furthermore, as the world's largest business sector and the most international in nature (Kotler et al., 2017), tourism is highly vulnerable to political, economic, socio-economic, security, and health risks. Despite the nation has shown resilience in bouncing back from several crises and outbreaks in the past (e.g., earthquakes, volcanic eruptions, terrorism, SARS, Ebola, influenza) (Novelli, et al., 2018), the unprecedented nature and effects of COVID-19 can have different yet significant long-term impacts on tourism industry (Sigala, 2020).

During the first 8 months of 2020, the number of international tourist arrivals was 700 million fewer than the same period in 2019, representing a loss of US$ 730 billion in export revenues from tourism, which is more than 8 times the loss due to the global economic crisis in 2009 (UNWTO, 2020). It was estimated that the international arrivals will drop by 70% globally in 2020, where Asia and the Pacific region recorded a 79% decrease in January–August 2020, while Africa and the Middle East both saw a 69% decline, Europe experienced a 68% decrease in arrivals and the Americas 65% (UNWTO, 2020).

The Indonesian tourism industry has been severely impacted by the COVID-19 pandemic. Both the total number of international tourist arrivals and the arrivals from each specific foreign country dropped dramatically (see Table 8.2). For instance, there were only about 3.5 million arrivals during January–September 2020, a 70.57% drop compared to the same period (12 million arrivals) in 2019 (BPS, 2020a). In September 2020, Indonesia recorded only 153,500 international arrivals. Half of them were from Timor Leste (76,800 arrivals—a 21.36% decline compared to September 2019), while about 35.3% (54,200 arrivals—a 76.35% decline) was from Malaysia (BPS, 2020a).

Hotels saw a dramatic decline in occupancy rates since the COVID-19 outbreak reached Indonesia. The occupancy rates of star-rated hotels were around 51.91–60.19% in 2018 and 43.53%–59.39% in 2019, but the figures dropped to as low as 12.67% in April 2020 (see Fig. 8.1). This was caused by the decline of both international and domestic travels, international border closures, physical/social distancing policy, regional lockdowns in several cities in Indonesia, and stay-at-home campaigns in response to the high level of COVID-19 community transmission cases in the country (516,753 total cases and 16,352 total deaths per 27 November 2020) (Worldometers, 2020).

The Indonesian Central Bureau of Statistics estimates that about 29.12 million people have been affected by COVID-19, where they lost jobs, fail to secure a temporary job or had working hours shortened (BPS, 2020b). In the accommodation and restaurant sectors, for instance, the employment rates grew from 5.2% in first quarter of 2018 to 6.41% in the fourth quarter in 2019 (see Fig. 8.2). However, it has been a significant drop since early 2020 and plummeted soon after. Following the trends in the tourism industry in general, most hotels and restaurants faced declining sales, which in turn forced them to take efficiency initiatives, including voluntary, temporary and/or permanent redundancies.

Bali, the most popular tourism destination in Indonesia, presents an insightful case of how COVID-19 pandemic has created the lowest point in its tourism history (Wibisono, 2020). Bali had experienced several tourism-related crises in the past, such as terrorism (Bali Bombings 2002 and 2005) and volcanic eruption (Mouth Agung in 2017). Despite some negative effects, such as 20%–60% decline in hotels' occupancy rates, tourism activities still took place during these difficult times (Sugiari, 2020). However, during the current COVID-19 outbreak, all tourism-related sectors in Bali have closed (Wibisono, 2020). The first confirmed COVID-19 case in Bali, a province with 40% contribution to the Indonesian tourism income (Susanto, 2020), was announced on 10 March 2020. The Governor of Bali, Wayan Koster, decided to take an unprecedented action by closing all tourism destinations in the province since 20 March 2020 to mitigate community transmission (Divianta, 2020; see Fig. 8.3 for some illustrations of the conditions). The economic impact of the closure is significant, where tourism in the province was predicted to lose about

Table 8.2 The number of international tourist arrivals in Indonesia, 2015–2020

Year	Jan	Feb	Mar	Apr	May	June	July	Aug	Sep	Oct	Nov	Dec	Total
2015	771,066	833,000	827,069	787,282	838,030	858,359	860,703	895,420	905,806	861,505	820,669	971,866	10,230,775
2016	814,303	888,309	915,019	901,095	915,206	857,651	1,032,741	1,031,986	1,006,653	1,040,651	1,002,333	1,113,328	11,519,275
2017	1,107,968	1,023,388	1,059,777	1,171,386	1,148,588	1,144,001	1,370,591	1,383,243	1,250,231	1,161,565	1,062,030	1,147,031	14,039,799
2018	1,097,839	1,197,503	1,363,426	1,302,321	1,242,705	1,322,674	1,547,231	1,511,021	1,370,943	1,291,605	1,157,483	1,405,554	15,810,305
2019	1,201,735	1,243,996	1,311,911	1,274,231	1,249,536	1,434,103	1,468,173	1,530,268	1,388,719	1,346,434	1,280,781	1,377,067	16,106,954
2020	1,272,083	863,960	470,970	158,718	163,646	158,256	157,939	163,185	153,498				3,562,255[a]

Note: [a]January–September 2020
Source: BPS (2020a)

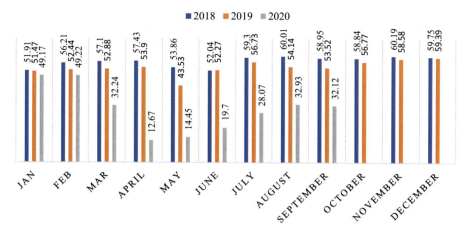

Fig. 8.1 Hotel occupancy rates, 2018–2020
Note: The 2020 data only covers January–September
Source: BPS (2020a)

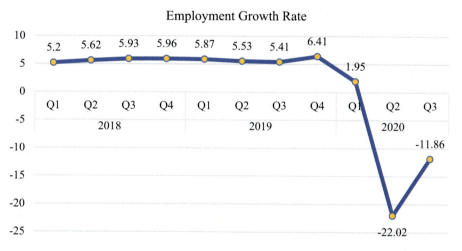

Fig. 8.2 Employment growth rate in the accommodation and restaurant sectors, 2018–2020
Note: The 2020 data only covers three quarters
Source: BPS (2020b)

Rp 9.7 trillion per month and almost 95% of the hotels were closed due to the airport closure (Sugiari, 2020). It shows that COVID-19 pandemic "is not only different but has profound and long-term structural and transformational changes to tourism as socio-economic activity and industry" (Sigala, 2020, p. 312).

At the time of writing this chapter, COVID-19 pandemic is ongoing and is very difficult to predict when it will be over. Vaccines are still under development. Many

Uluwatu (Before COVID-19)

Source: Personal Documentation

Uluwatu (During the Pandemic, 26 January 2021)

Source: Personal Documentation

Kuta Beach (Before COVID-19)

Source: Personal Documentation

Kuta Beach (During the Pandemic, 24 December 2020)

Source: Personal Documentation

Bedugul National Park (Before COVID-19)

Source: Personal Documentation

Bedugul National Park (During the Pandemic, 2 Oct 2020)

Source: Personal Documentation

Fig. 8.3 Tourism destinations in Bali: before and during the COVID-19. (**a**) Uluwatu (Before COVID-19). Source: Personal Documentation. (**b**) Uluwatu (During the Pandemic, 26 January 2021). Source: Personal Documentation. (**c**) Kuta Beach (Before COVID-19). Source: Personal Documentation. (**d**) Kuta Beach (During the Pandemic, 24 December 2020). Source: Personal Documentation. (**e**) Bedugul National Park (Before COVID-19). Source: Personal Documentation. (**f**) Bedugul National Park (During the Pandemic, 2 Oct 2020). Source: Personal Documentation. (**g**) Sanur Beach (Before COVID-19). Source: Personal Documentation. (**h**) Sanur Beach (During the Pandemic, 24 December 2020). Source: Personal Documentation

8 Tourism Sustainability in Indonesia: Reflection and Reformulation   149

Sanur Beach (Before COVID-19)   **Sanur Beach (During the Pandemic, 24 December 2020)**

Source: Personal Documentation   **Source:** Personal Documentation

Fig. 8.3 (continued)

countries still have borders closed. Health-related protocols (e.g., wearing face masks and/or face shields, providing hand sanitisers, using mobility tracking applications, maintaining physical distance, and others) are part of 'new normal' in many countries, including Indonesia. Now every stakeholder in tourism industry focuses on survival issues or figures out how to bounce back. In fact, survival is a basic goal for an institution or organisation and a prerequisite for success in other key performance indicators, such as profitability and market share (Cottrell & Nault, 2004; Suarez & Utterback, 1995). In short, it requires an integrated effort of survival strategies and sustainability concept for all relevant stakeholders in the Indonesian tourism sector.

8.4 Reformulation

An important question to ask regarding sustainable tourism during the pandemic is: is the COVID-19 a setback for the implementation of sustainable tourism policy or a transformative opportunity to recover, reimagine and reform the next normal and economic order (Mair, 2020; McKinsey, 2020; Sigala, 2020) under the sustainable tourism framework? This question is not only relevant to the Indonesian tourism industry, but also to tourism sectors in all other countries. Some reports during coronavirus lockdowns show the positive impacts on the environment, such as clearer Venice canals (McLaughlin, 2020), declines in carbon emission and improved air quality in China, the UK and the U.S (Monks, 2020), and liberated wildlife in Wales, Japan, Spain, Chile, Canada, and the UK (Child, 2020). Sigala (2020) argues that it is the moment to break through and reset the tourism practice by converting the COVID-19 crisis disruption into transformative innovation. She recommended crisis management should focus on three major stakeholders (tourism demand, tourism operators, destinations and policy makers) under three stages (respond, recovery, and restart).

In their strategic plan for 2020–2024, the Ministry of Tourism and Creative Economy (2020) identified several specific challenges in developing sustainable tourism, including climate change and natural disasters (Indonesia locates at 'the ring of fire' where there is a high risk of earthquakes, tsunamis, flood, forest fires, draught, and volcanic eruptions), weak connectivity and infrastructure at tourism destinations; lack of empowerment of local community, investment-related issues (e.g., bureaucracy and perceived difficulties in doing business in the country), weak integrated branding and marketing strategies; lack of synergies between relevant stakeholders in the tourism industry, and lack of commitment to social, natural, and cultural environments among tourism business players. These challenges are even more difficult to address during the COVID-19 pandemic as UNWTO (2020) predicts that the decreasing growth of tourism industry will continue for the next five to 7 years. However, the Ministry of Tourism and Creative Economy (2020) also acknowledges that the pandemic provides two opportunities for transformation and recovery: (1) changing the business model from traditional tourism management into digital tourism management; and (2) shifting the target market from international tourists to domestic travellers.

Similarly, McKinsey & Company (Lath et al., 2020) suggests that the Indonesian tourism industry could be rebuilt by expanding domestic tourism (e.g., promoting its lesser-known destinations to locals) and developing niche and nature-based tourism to respond to changing traveller's behaviours. Some pre-COVID tourism issues, such as waste (especially plastic trash) in many tourism destinations (e.g., Bali, Bunaken, Pulau Sempu, Ranu Kumbolo, and Gunung Gede Pangrango) (WowKeren, 2018), need to be handled effectively. For instance, it is important to accelerate initiatives for cleaning up the waste and increasing recycling, so both domestic and foreign tourists will have a better experience once it is safe to travel (Lath et al., 2020).

Indonesia is prone to natural disasters (e.g., volcanic eruptions, earthquakes, floods and tsunamis) and man-made disasters (e.g., forest fires) (Indonesia-Investments, 2018). Some notable disasters in Indonesia during the past 20 years include volcanic eruptions (Mount Merapi in 2010, Mount Agung in 2017), earthquakes (Lombok in 2018, Sumatra in 2004), tsunami (Aceh in 2004), and forest fires (Sumatra and Kalimantan in 2015). Despite its experience in managing and recovering from such crises (e.g., Gurtner, 2016; Liu-Lastres et al., 2020; Syamsidik et al., 2021), the country has been struggling in navigating the unprecedented detrimental effects of coronavirus outbreak (Aljazeera, 2020; Jaffrey, 2020; The Jakarta Post, 2020), such as unemployment, recession, and malnutrition. The global pandemic has caused severe global humanitarian problems, which was described by the United Nations as "the bleakest and darkest" time in the UN's history (Aljazeera, 2020). Many industries faced the risk of survival, which beg for support and compassion from the government or other members of society (Kadirov et al., 2020). Tourism industry, for instance, is severely affected by mobility restrictions and bans, lockdowns, self- and mandatory quarantines, and social distancing policy (Sigala, 2020; Ugur & Akbiyik, 2020), because travel is requisite for tourism activity (Yeh, 2020). With its reliance on tourism sector (about 60% of its Gross Domestic

Product before the COVID-19 pandemic), the economy of Bali province has been the hardest hit in Indonesia by the outbreak (Aljazeera, 2020).

Furthermore, Butler (1999, p. 11) argued that a proper definition of sustainable tourism is "tourism which is in a form which can maintain its viability in an area for an indefinite period of time". This definition suggests the importance of long-term survival (longevity) of a tourism destination, its ecosystems and its relevant stakeholders. In order to provide insights from business players in the Indonesian tourism industry, we conducted in-depth interviews with representatives (business owners, top-level managers, and head of local tourism management) of three travel agents, four hotels, one villa management company, two restaurants, one tourism destination management, and one souvenir shop in Bali. In terms of the impact of the COVID-19 outbreak on their businesses, all interviewees consistently reported that their organisations have faced difficult times during the pandemic. However, their specific responses to the impact varies between companies.

The three travel agents (Company A, Company B, and Company C) experienced a dramatic decrease in sales (down to zero sales) due to regional lockdown and the closure of international airports. The initial effort made by Company A was laying off some employees, imposing unpaid leave, implementing working from home policy, and reducing numbers of working days. The same strategy was adopted by Company B and Company C, but they did not reduce the number of employees. The difficult situation has forced the travel agents to make new breakthroughs to maintain their businesses. Among the initiatives are virtual tours, 50% discount rates, and special vouchers ('pay now, stay later'). They welcome the relaxation of restrictions under the 'new normal' policy set by the national and local government by implementing new health protocols (e.g., providing hand sanitizers and face masks) and shifting their focus at least temporarily from international markets to domestic markets.

The four hotels (Company D, Company E, Company F, and Company G) and the villa management company (Company H) faced a decrease in hotel occupancy rates by about 80% because many tourists decided to leave Bali and return to their home countries earlier during the regional lockdown. In response to this difficult situation, hotel managers had to implement redundancy policy, unpaid leave, working from home, and reduced working days. During the 'new normal' condition, where Bali was open to domestic travel only, both international and local hotel managers decided to shift their target market from foreign tourists to domestic ones. Health-based customer services were put in place to provide a sense of safety and comfort for hotel guests. Another income generating source initiated by hotels is offering hotel facilities, such as swimming pools and restaurants, to local people who want to enjoy these facilities without checking in as room guests.

Company I, whose main customers are domestic tourists who travelled in a large group, had to close its outlet and lay off their employees temporarily. Their remaining employees only worked for 15 days in a month. In contrast, Company J, which is a boutique restaurant with fewer employees compared to Company I, retained its all employees during the pandemic. These two restaurants came up with some breakthroughs to generate income. Company I, for instance, rents its open space for camping purposes, a unique offer for those who want to do outdoor activities in a safe environment. Company J opens some culinary courses to public and sells organic market (i.e. fresh vegetables).

Company K is one of the most popular tourism attractions in Bali. By using the concept of a tourist village, the manager (who is also the local community's leader) empowers the surrounding community to work at the company. During this pandemic, the manager followed the provincial government's instruction to close its services. As a result, almost no tourists visited the location during that time. The manager decided to reduce the number of working days for all employees to control its spending. However, no employees are dismissed, because they are members of the local community. In anticipating the new normal condition, they prepare new health protocols and design new attractions.

Company L is one of the biggest souvenir shops in Bali. Facing declining sales since mid-March 2020, the owner decided to close all outlets and offer temporary redundancy to its employees. Some initiatives were explored, such as using the owner's agricultural land for planting snow peas to support his employees and developing online marketing channels to expand its markets. The snow peas now become one of the company's new products. During the 'new normal' condition, the owner re-opens some outlets and provides COVID-19 health protocols (e.g., providing hand sanitizers, facilities for washing hands).

8.5 Survival and Recovery Strategies

The interview results revealed a pattern of survival and recovery strategies implemented by companies under study (see Table 8.3). These organisations have implemented a combination of the following strategies (4Rs: Restructuring, Realigning, Researching, and Retargeting). The first and most common strategy, *restructuring*, focuses on efficiency. Travel agents controlled their operational costs by reducing working hours, offering temporary and voluntary redundancies to their employees, discontinuing the contracts for casual workers, and offering unpaid leaves. While working from home (WFH) is adopted by all travel agents, it is impractical for restaurant business. Similar strategy but slightly different approach was employed by Company K, Company L, and Company H. Instead of laying off workers, Company K reduced and re-arranged tasks/activities. This initiative was chosen because all their employees are locals who need jobs. Company L re-arranged its working schedules by allowing its employees to work every other week. Company H changed its operational system from commercial into residential villas. Under the new system, the maintenance and service frequency provided to each villa had been reduced.

The second strategy, *re-aligning the business process*, reflects efforts and initiatives to comply with the new COVID-19 protocols set by the Indonesian government. Company C evaluated the readiness of its potential collaborators (e.g., restaurants and hotels) in meeting the new COVID-19 protocols. Company D limits meeting room capacity to only 50% and impose a digital invoice for staying guests.

8 Tourism Sustainability in Indonesia: Reflection and Reformulation

Table 8.3 Typology of survival and recovery strategies

No.	Strategy	Description	Examples	Company
1.	Restructuring the business	Initiatives and efforts to cut costs and focus on short-term and medium-term survival.	"... *working from home, taking unpaid leaves and also terminating casual workers....*"	Company A
			"... *they come to the office only twice a week...*"	Company C
			"... *all jobs have been centralized to the head quarter...*"	Company F
2.	Re-aligning business processes	Aligning the business processes in compliance to COVID-19 protocols.	*"Our Standard Operating Procedures were changed to comply with the new normal requirements... We reduced the meeting room capacity by 40-50% due to social distancing..."*	Company D
			"Company B is ready to implement CHSE (Cleanliness, Health, Safety, Environment) standards..."	Company B
			"When customers come, they must wash their hands... our employees must wear face masks and also hand gloves..."	Company L
3.	Researching and responding to new business opportunities	Exploring and exploiting potential business opportunities for short-term and long-term purposes.	*"Virtual tour is what we can do now."*	Company A
			".. if customers want to enjoy the restaurant, pool..."	Company E
			"We are preparing a sort of picnic area in Company I... Now we're learning how to do online selling."	Company I
			"We open an organic market."	Company J
			".. in this area we will build a man-made coral reef... that is for the future target... it's for diving..."	Company K
4.	Retargeting the market	Shifting the target market (from international travelers into domestic visitors).	*"Our focus now is staycation... We are switching from foreigners to domestic market..."*	Company G
			"We can't rely on tourists from China, so we have started targeting the domestic tourists..."	Company E
		Changing B2B to B2C market.	*"... since we have shifted to the domestic market, we move to B2C..."*	Company A

Company B chooses to only accept VIP guests, amounting to four people. The travel agents have begun to use digital marketing channels to attract tourists. Company L requires its guests to wash their hands and to have their body temperatures check. All Company L's employees are equipped with masks, gloves and face shields. Company H formed a special taskforce to clean all areas using disinfectants regularly.

The third strategy is *researching and responding to the new business opportunities*. In order to explore potential business opportunities, companies have initiated several market research activities, such as talking to suppliers, distributors, customers, and tourism-related associations (e.g., Indonesian Hotel & Restaurant Association, Association of the Indonesian Tours & Travel Agencies), attending webinars, and monitoring news on mainstream media and social media. Based on the insights and inspiration from best practices of other companies around the globe, the travel agents (Company A, Company B, and Company C) and hotels (Company D, Company E, Company F, and Company G) decided to explore virtual tours, hotel 'staycation', self-quarantine facilities, and online food delivery services to help them maintain their cash flow. In addition, Company A has started to offer corporate outing events to several large local companies, while Company B focuses on activity-based tourism and experiences in rural life. Utilizing its large area to attract local tourists who want to experience the sensation of camping on the beach while maintaining physical distance, a unique 'camping on the beach' package has been offered by Company I.

The last strategy in the typology, retargeting the market, involves shifting the target market segment(s) from international to domestic market. Driven by the closure of international airports, travel agents have retargeted domestic travellers or local Balinese tourists. Hotels have also turned to domestic market, including honeymooners and millennial travellers. Honeymooners tend to have more certain travel dates than other segments of holidayers/travellers. Company G serves millennials who are believed to seek for adventures, love new experiences, and look for value-for-money offers. Company G also targets tourists who plan for a long-term vacation (staycation). Company A, a big travel agent used to focus on B2B model, has changed its emphasis to B2C model amid the COVID-19 pandemic.

Interestingly, the two recovery opportunities (i.e. digital tourism management and domestic market focus) identified by the Ministry of Tourism and Creative Economy (2020) have been pursued by tourism business players in Bali. What seems to be the case during the COVID-19 crisis is that the top priority for most stakeholders in the tourism industry is survival and recovery. It is interesting to see how such priority can be further integrated with the sustainable tourism development policy from the government.

8.6 Concluding Remarks

In their 25-year bibliometric analysis of sustainable tourism research, Ruhanen et al. (2015) noted that most of such study was conducted in the North-West Europe, Oceania, and North America. A specific research on Southeast Asian context, including Indonesia, has been relatively limited. The current study fills the gap by focusing on the emergence, development, and challenges of sustainable tourism thought and practices in Indonesia, the largest economy in the Southeast Asian region. The findings show that there has been a growing awareness and commitment to adopt sustainable tourism development principles in the country. The government has issued several relevant policies and regulations to support the creation of a balance of social, economic, and environmental aspects of tourism activities. However, there are still many challenges in coordinating and implementing the policies effectively. While the COVID-19 outbreak has severely impacted the tourism industry, there are opportunities to survive and recover. At the micro level, those who innovate will have a higher opportunity to succeed. At the macro level, continuous support from the government and public is required to help the industry to bounce back, which in turn may transform into a more sustainable one.

Furthermore, ensuring business continuance and building resilience is an important implication of COVID-19 (Sigala, 2020). The present study offers important insights into how tourism and hospitality businesses in Bali respond and adapt during the COVID-19 pandemic and new normal. The experiences within the five sectors of tourism (travel agent, hotel, restaurant, tourism destination, and souvenir shop) show that all companies have faced the same critical conditions and they engage in three stages for overcoming the effects of the COVID-19 pandemic: response, recovery, and reset (Sigala, 2020). Although the specific responses varied across companies reflecting specific contexts, adaptability and flexibility of each player, the patterns of survival and recovery strategies can be classified into the 4Rs strategies. Companies have navigated and survived the crisis by restructuring the business to improve their efficiency, re-aligning business processes in compliance to COVID-19 health protocols, research and responding to new business opportunities, and/or retargeting the market. Interestingly, the strategies show that during the COVID-19 pandemic, which has been perceived as a 'death sentence' for many businesses, companies in the Indonesian tourism and hospitality industry have explored many innovative breakthroughs beyond survival. Such insights are relevant for other companies in the same and different industries as well as in different countries (e.g., Southeast Asian region) facing the COVID-19 crisis. Therefore, the typology of 4Rs strategies reflects the theoretical contribution of the current study to the business survival and recovery strategy literature, particularly in the context of sustainable tourism.

There are several practical implications of the current study's findings for the relevant industry stakeholders. First, the national and local governments need to involve and integrate community stakeholders and available resources in preparing, organising, implementing, and controlling a comprehensive tourism planning for post-COVID era. Partnerships with private sectors and non-government organisations (NGOs) are essential in providing continuous support and assistance for individuals and organisations affected by the COVID-19 crisis. Second, community engagement is crucial in making sustainable tourism a success. In times of crisis, community participatory approach based on good understanding of local culture and religion is essential for building resilience to recover (Liu-Lastres et al., 2020). The experience of Company K in the current research provides a good example of such local engagement. Third, tourism business players may consider adopting one or more of the 4R strategies in navigating the COVID-19 crisis. Technology and market orientation are two important factors for leaving the crisis stronger. Fourth, as tourists are adapting to the new normal, the government and tourism destination management may prepare more sustainable and responsible consumer practice guidelines once tourist traffic increases again. To summarize, it takes an integrated effort of all relevant stakeholders to develop tourism activities with "a suitable balance between the environmental, economic and socio-cultural aspects to guarantee its long-term sustainability" (UNEP & UNWTO, 2005, p. 11).

References

Aljazeera. (2020). *Bali struggles with 'Covid-poor' as Indonesian cases hit record*. Retrieved from: https://www.aljazeera.com/news/2020/12/4/covid-poor-emerge-in-bali-as-indonesian-cases-hit-new-records

Aznar, M., & Hoefnagels, H. (2020). Empowering small rural communities through heritage tourism. In P. L. Pearce & H. Oktadiana (Eds.), *Delivering tourism intelligence: From analysis to action* (pp. 49–60). Emerald Publishing Limited.

Bloom Consulting. (2020). *Bloom consulting country brand ranking 2019–2020 tourism edition*. Bloom Consulting.

BPS. (2020a). Inflasi: Perkembangan indeks harga konsumen. *Berita Resmi Statistik*, 80 (11/XXIII, 2 November).

BPS. (2020b). Pertumbuhan ekonomi: Produk domestik bruto. *Berita Resmi Statistik*, 85 (11/XXIII, 5 November).

Butler, R. W. (1999). Sustainable tourism: A state-of-the-art review. *Tourism Geographies*, 1(1), 7–25.

Child, D. (2020). The positive impacts on the environment since the coronavirus lockdown began. *Evening Standard*. Retrieved from: https://www.standard.co.uk/news/world/positive-impact-environment-coronavirus-lockdown-a4404751.html

Cottrell, T., & Nault, B. R. (2004). Product variety and firm survival in the microcomputer software industry. *Strategic Management Journal*, 25, 1005–1025.

Divianta, D. (2020). *Gubernur minta seluruh obyek wisata di Bali ditutup untuk meredam penyebaran COVID-19*. Retrieved from: https://www.liputan6.com/regional/read/4207548/gubernur-minta-seluruh-obyek-wisata-di-bali-ditutup-untuk-meredam-penyebaran-COVID-19

Gurtner, Y. (2016). Returning to paradise: Investigating issues of tourism crisis and disaster recovery on the island of Bali. *Journal of Hospitality and Tourism Management*, 28, 11–19.

Indonesia-Investments. (2015). *Analysts: Indonesia should attract 33 million foreign tourists by 2019*. Retrieved from: https://www.indonesia-investments.com/news/todays-headlines/analysts-indonesia-should-attract-33-million-foreign-tourists-by-2019/item6284?searchstring=20%20million%20foreign%20tourists

Indonesia-Investments. (2018). *Natural disasters in Indonesia*. Retrieved from: https://www.indonesia-investments.com/business/risks/natural-disasters/item243#:~:text=Being%20located%20on%20the%20Pacific,%2C%20earthquakes%2C%20floods%20and%20tsunamis.

Jaffrey, S. (2020). *Coronavirus blunders in Indonesia turn crisis into catastrophe*. Retrieved from: https://carnegieendowment.org/2020/04/29/coronavirus-blunders-in-indonesia-turn-crisis-into-catastrophe-pub-81684

Junaid, I. (2015). Sustainable tourism in Toraja: Perspective of indigenous people. *ASEAN Journal on Hospitality and Tourism, 14*(1), 45–55.

Kadirov, D., Tjiptono, F., & Sharipudin, M. N. S. (2020). Halal service research: Challenges of the COVID-19 pandemic. *Journal of Halal Service Research, 1*(2), 1–10.

Kotler, P., Bowen, J. T., Makens, J. C., & Baloglu, S. (2017). *Marketing for hospitality and tourism* (7th ed.). Pearson Education Limited.

Lath, V., Lee, T., Tan, K. T., & Wibowo, P. (2020). *With effort, Indonesia can emerge from the Covid-19 crisis stronger*. Retrieved from: https://www.mckinsey.com/featured-insights/asia-pacific/with-effort-indonesia-can-emerge-from-the-covid-19-crisis-stronger

Lemy, D. M., Teguh, F., & Pramezwary, A. (2020). Tourism development in Indonesia: Establishment of sustainable strategies. In P. L. Pearce & H. Oktadiana (Eds.), *Delivering tourism intelligence: From analysis to action* (pp. 91–108). Emerald Publishing Limited.

Liu-Lastres, B., Mariska, D., Tan, X., & Ying, T. (2020). Can post-disaster tourism development improve destination livelihoods? A case study of Aceh, Indonesia. *Journal of Destination Marketing & Management, 18*, 100510.

Mair, S. (2020). *What will the world be like after coronavirus? Four possible futures. The Stuff*. Retrieved from: https://www.stuff.co.nz/national/health/coronavirus/120728480/what-will-the-world-be-like-after-coronavirus-four-possible-futures

McKinsey & Company. (2020). *Beyond coronavirus: The path to the next normal*. Retrieved from: https://www.mckinsey.com/industries/healthcare-systems-and-services/our-insights/beyond-coronavirus-the-path-to-the-next-normal

McLaughlin, K. (2020). *Satellite images show just how much Venice's canals have cleared up since the city went under coronavirus lockdown*. Retrieved from: https://www.insider.com/satellite-images-venice-canals-clear-coronavirus-lockdown-2020-4

Ministry of Tourism and Creative Economy. (2020). *Rencana Strategis 2020–2024*. Ministry of Tourism and Creative Economy of the Republic of Indonesia.

Ministry of Tourism. (2016). *Regulations of the Minister of Tourism of the Republic of Indonesia: Number 14 of 2016 on guidelines of sustainable tourism destination*. Minister of Tourism of the Republic of Indonesia.

Monks, P. (2020). *Here's how lockdowns have improved air quality around the world*. World Economic Forum. Retrieved from: https://www.weforum.org/agenda/2020/04/coronavirus-lockdowns-air-pollution

Novelli, M., Burgess, L. V., Jones, A., & Ritchie, B. W. (2018). No Ebola… still doomed —The Ebola-induced tourism crisis. *Annals of Tourism Research, 70*, 76–87.

Nurjaya, I. N. (2018). Sustainable tourism development in Indonesia: Policy and legal political point of view. *Advances in Social Science, Education and Humanities Research, 282*, 199–203.

Ruhanen, L., Weiler, B., Moyle, B. D., & McLennan, C. L. J. (2015). Trends and patterns in sustainable tourism research: A 25-year bibliometric analysis. *Journal of Sustainable Tourism, 23*(4), 517–535.

Saarinen, J. (2014). Critical sustainability: Setting the limits to growth and responsibility in tourism. *Sustainability, 6*(1), 1–17.

Savitz, A. W., & Weber, K. (2006). *The triple bottom line: How today's best-run companies are achieving economic, social and environmental success—And how you can too*. Wiley.

Sigala, M. (2020). Tourism and COVID-19: Impacts and implications for advancing and resetting industry and research. *Journal of Business Research, 117*, 312–321.

Suarez, F. F., & Utterback, J. M. (1995). Dominant designs and the survival of firms. *Strategic Management Journal, 16*(6), 415–430.

Sugiari, L. P. (2020). *Dampak COVID-19 bagi pariwisata jauh lebih parah dari bom Bali*. Retrieved from: https://bali.bisnis.com/read/20200410/538/1225373/dampak-COVID-19-bagi-pariwisata-jauh-lebih-parah-dari-bom-bali

Susanto, V. Y. (2020). *Sepanjang 2019, devisa sektor pariwisata mencapai Rp 280 triliun*. Retrieved from: https://nasional.kontan.co.id/news/sepanjang-2019-devisa-sektor-pariwisata-mencapai-rp-280-triliun

Syamsidik, S., Oktari, R. S., Nugroho, A., Fahmi, M., Suppasri, A., Munadi, K., & Amra, R. (2021). Fifteen years of the 2004 Indian Ocean Tsunami in Aceh-Indonesia: Mitigation, preparedness and challenges for a long-term disaster recovery process. *International Journal of Disaster Risk Reduction, 54*, 102052.

The Jakarta Post. (2020). *Indonesian health system might collapse soon: Covid-19 task force*. Retrieved from: https://www.thejakartapost.com/news/2020/09/22/indonesian-health-system-might-collapse-soon-covid-19-task-force.html

Uğur, N. G., & Akbıyık, A. (2020). Impacts of COVID-19 on global tourism industry: A cross-regional comparison. *Tourism Management Perspectives, 36*, 100744.

UNEP and UNWTO. (2005). *Making tourism more sustainable: A guide for policy makers*. United Nations Environment Programme and World Tourism Organization.

UNWTO. (2020). *UNWTO world tourism barometer (Vol. 18, Issue 6, October 2020)*. UNWTO.

Wibisono, A. (2020). *Dampak COVID-19, pertumbuhan perekonomian Bali triwulan I-IV 2020 bakal terkoreksi*. Retrieved from: https://balitribune.co.id/content/dampak-COVID-19-pertumbuhan-perekonomian-bali-triwulan-i-iv-2020-bakal-terkoreksi

World Economic Forum. (2019). *The travel & tourism competitiveness report 2019: Travel and tourism at a tipping point*. World Economic Forum.

Worldometers. (2020). *Coronavirus cases*. Retrieved from https://www.worldometers.info/coronavirus/?utm_campaign=homeAdvegas1?#countries

WowKeren. (2018). *Miris banget, keindahan alam di tempat wisata ini rusak karena ulah manusia*. Retrieved from https://www.wowkeren.com/berita/tampil/00233873.html

Yeh, S. S. (2020). Tourism recovery strategy against COVID-19 pandemic. *Tourism Recreation Research*, 1–7. https://doi.org/10.1080/02508281.2020.1805933

Fandy Tjiptono holds a Ph.D in Marketing from the University of New South Wales (Australia) and is a Senior Lecturer at the School of Marketing and International Business, Victoria University of Wellington. His primary research interests are consumer behavior and marketing practices in emerging markets, consumer ethics, corporate social responsibility, and brand management. His work has been published in several top journals, including Journal of Business Ethics, European Journal of Marketing, Journal of Travel and Tourism Marketing, International Journal of Consumer Studies, Marketing Intelligence and Planning, Internet Research, Journal of Cleaner Production, and Journal of Retailing and Consumer Services.

Lin Yang is a Lecturer in Marketing at the University of Tasmania and an adjunct research fellow at Monash University Malaysia. She holds a PhD from Victoria University of Wellington. Her research areas lie in the field of consumer behaviour, specifically consumer green consumption, online engagement, and traveling behaviour in cross-cultural contexts. Her publications have appeared in International Journal of Consumer Studies, Journal of Travel and Tourism Marketing, Australasian Marketing Journal, Journal of Promotion Management, Journal of Studies in International Education, among others.

Andhy Setyawan is currently a Doctoral Candidate at the Faculty of Economics and Business, Universitas Brawijaya, Malang, Indonesia. He is a Lecturer at Department of Management, Faculty of Business and Economics, Universitas Surabaya, Surabaya, Indonesia. His primary research interests are consumer behavior and marketing practices in pro environmental behavior, emerging market, and responsible consumption. As an academic, he is actively presenting his research at several regional and international conferences, such as European Marketing Academy Conference (EMAC), International Social Innovation Research Conference (ISIRC), International Research Society for Public Management (IRSPM) Conference, and Asia Academy of Management.

Ida Bagus Gede Adi Permana is a Lecturer and Researcher at Faculty of Economics and Business, University of Airlangga, Surabaya, Indonesia. He holds a Master of Science in Human Resources Management from Universitas Gadjah Mada. His research areas are human resources management, organizational behavior, leadership, and change management. He is currently active in presenting his research at national and international conferences, such as European Marketing Academy Conference (EMAC), International Conference of Organization Innovation, International Conference on Entrepreneurship, and Asian Forum on Business Education. Several of his work have been published in journals, including International Journal of Psychosocial Rehabilitation, OPCION, International Journal of Organizational Innovation, and International Journal of Innovation Creativity and Change.

I. Putu Esa Widaharthana is Lecturer and Researcher at Bali Tourism Polytechnic (Politeknik Pariwisata Bali), Indonesia. He holds a Master of Science in Human Resources Management from Universitas Gadjah Mada. His research areas are human resources management, change management, and entrepreneurship. He is currently the Head of Entrepreneurship & Career Development at Bali Tourism Polytechnic. Several awards have been received, such as Bronze winner of entrepreneurial campus for vocational education, awarded by ICSB (Indonesia Council for Small Business) and Tri Founder of Philip Kotler Center of Asia (PK-CAM).

Part III
Issues of Sustainable Tourism in Asia

Chapter 9
Scenarios of Sustainable Tourism Development in Cambodia

Heidi Dahles

Abstract The aim of this chapter is to provide a critical assessment of the current tourism development in Cambodia from the perspective of the 'sustainable tourism development' narrative. As one of Cambodia's core industries, second only after the garment industry, tourism is a major source of income and an engine of economic growth. Despite the pivotal role of tourism in Cambodia's economy, the dimension of sustainability is largely absent from the country's current Tourism Development Strategic Plan. Outside the scope of this plan and largely ignored by the Cambodian government, myriad of pioneering initiatives are undertaken that have the potential to provide economic benefits to local communities. Commonly led by non-governmental organizations (NGO), such initiatives encourage the establishment of social enterprises that employ tourism as an instrument for creating sustainable livelihoods. But rarely are such enterprises developed and operated by local people. In this vein, this chapter will compare and contrast two scenarios that feature in Cambodia's tourism development: the government-driven growth scenario and the diversification scenario led by local initiatives that evolve under the banner of sustainable tourism. It will critically assess the extent to which local people are engaged in the development and management of such initiatives in order to achieve sustainable outcomes.

Keywords Sustainable development · Local community · Community participation · Tourism-based social enterprise · Cambodia

---

H. Dahles (✉)
University of Tasmania, Sandy Bay, Australia

Griffith University, Gold Coast, Australia

© The Author(s), under exclusive license to Springer Nature Singapore Pte Ltd. 2022
A. Selvaranee Balasingam, Y. Ma (eds.), *Asian Tourism Sustainability*, Perspectives on Asian Tourism, https://doi.org/10.1007/978-981-16-5264-6_9

9.1 Introduction

Cambodia is among those countries in Southeast Asia that have neglected the dimension of sustainability in their national tourism development strategy. Whilst Cambodia's current "Tourism Development Strategic Plan 2012–2020" promotes the country's traditional cultural tourism sites, a vision for sustainable development is lacking. Under this Strategic Plan tourism has become a major source of foreign income and an engine of economic growth. As Cambodia's core industry, second only to the garment sector, tourism has contributed US$ 7.2 billion, or 32.4% of GDP, in 2017 and, according to a pre-COVID-19 estimate, was expected to add US$ 13 billion, or 28.3% of GDP, to the national economy in 2028 – an increase of 6% per annum (WTTC, 2018, p. 1).

As critics have pointed out, tourism growth, if left unregulated, poses challenges that often outweigh the benefits, subjecting local communities to dispossession and dislocation, environmental degradation, and human trafficking (Carter et al., 2015; Mao et al., 2013). Perhaps less manifest, but no less corroding for local livelihoods and community development is the revenue leakage to overseas agents and investors that is commonly implied by growth-driven tourism development. Estimated at 40% in 2017, Cambodia's revenue leakage is one of the highest in Asia (World Bank Group, 2017, p. 52). Therefore, more effort has to be invested in searching for ways of ensuring that a greater share of benefits reaches the poorest segments of Cambodian society. In order to achieve this, approaches to tourism have to be advanced that contribute to sustainable development.

Outside the scope of the Tourism Ministry's strategic plan and largely ignored by the Cambodian government, myriad of pioneering initiatives are currently undertaken that have the potential to provide revenues to rural populations, alleviate poverty and diversify income opportunities. However, rarely are such initiatives developed and operated by local people (Biddulph, 2017; Mao et al., 2014). The emergence of social enterprises, on the other hand, often linked to ecotourism and community-based tourism, shows promising signs of change to the government's focus on growth in international visitor arrivals. Social entrepreneurship has come to play an increasingly important role in various segments of the Cambodian economy (Khieng & Dahles, 2015; Lyne et al., 2015). These enterprises often build on the knowledge, experience and networks of the well-established NGO sector that has been a major force in the economic and political recovery of the country since the ousting of the Khmer Rouge regime.

This chapter aims at contributing to a critical assessment of major tourism trends in Cambodia from the perspective of the 'sustainable tourism development' narrative, which has risen to great prominence in current tourism research across academic fields (Sharpley, 2000, 2020). This narrative embraces efforts to employ tourism as an instrument for providing economic benefits to local communities and create sustainable livelihoods. However, approaches designed to this purpose do not necessarily include the voice of the intended beneficiaries. In this vein, this chapter will compare and contrast two scenarios that feature in Cambodia's tourism development: the government-driven growth scenario and the diversification scenario led by local initiatives that evolve under the banner of sustainable tourism. In addition, some preliminary observations will be shared on how the COVID-19 pandemic, which unfolded at the time of drafting this chapter, affects Cambodian tourism development.

The body of data underlying this chapter is based on a decade of research on economic and social transformation in Cambodia and an extensive media analysis on Cambodia's tourism development as an engine of these transformations undertaken in 2019. Results of this longitudinal research, including a detailed account of the underlying methodology of data gathering and analysis, have been published in various academic journals (see for example Dahles et al., 2019, 2020; Khieng & Dahles, 2015). Together, these publications reiterate the need for a critical approach to claims of sustainable development both in government policies and new social enterprise initiatives.

This chapter is structured as follows. The next section reviews literature relevant to the narrative on sustainable tourism development in order to identify the key concepts used in the analysis of the Cambodian case. Then, the contextual background of Cambodia's tourism development will be briefly discussed, followed by an elaboration on, first, the growth scenario for Cambodia's mainstream tourism and, second, emerging initiatives in tourism-based social enterprises (TSEs). The final section will discuss and compare the two different scenarios of tourism development against the background of the sustainable tourism development narrative.

9.2 Literature Review and Key Concepts: Sustainable Tourism and Social Enterprise

The concept of sustainable tourism development has risen to great prominence in both academic literature and tourism policy documents and came to underlie the narrative on tourism as an instrument to provide economic benefits to local communities (Bramwell & Sharman, 2000; Sharpley, 2000, 2020; Tao & Wall, 2009). However, as more and more policy makers and developers claim to engage in sustainable tourism to legitimize tourism development at large, sustainable tourism has become a trope, devoid of meaning and packed with political correctness. Often defined in tourism-centric terms, this concept has come to promote the sustainability of tourism and the tourism industry as such, whilst a critical assessment of tourism as a development strategy for local economies is lacking (Sharpley, 2000).

As critics argue that sustainable tourism development is unachievable (Sharpley, 2020), the narrative has come to motivate new 'tourisms' that claim to offer livelihood opportunities for local communities. Among such new variants are ecotourism, community-based tourism, and responsible and sustainable tourism. In addressing a variety of social, economic and environmental issues, the new tourisms capture alternative ways in which tourism development differs from conventional tourism (see Sheldon & Daniele, 2017). There is growing awareness that the intended long-term effects of such new tourisms depend on the participation of local communities (Carter et al., 2015). Building on the work of Chambers and Conway (1992) and Tao and Wall (2009), the concept of sustainable livelihoods has come to represent another innovative strategy for development through tourism. A livelihood approach focuses on ways in which households strategically deploy their assets and capacities in order to satisfy current and future needs (Scoones, 1998). Tourism scholars have studied the contribution of tourism-related activities to local livelihoods in particular in developing countries where tourism often emerges as the single alternative to a loss of traditional livelihoods (e.g. Lasso & Dahles, 2018; Tao & Wall, 2009). However, as Biddulph in his study of rural Cambodia (2015, p. 99) points out, the impact of tourism, in particular mass tourism, may be overrated as tourism is "part of a broader process of rural income diversification" that local communities experience in the wider capitalist economy. The long-term effects of tourism largely depend on the engagement of local communities which, after all, are "not mere spectators in development but are active agents who cope and evolve with the challenges associated with tourism development" (Movono & Becken, 2018, p. 155).

This resonates with the literature on social enterprise in tourism. As Giang et al. (2017) argue, TSEs have the potential to offer pathways to innovations that may create sustainable solutions for all stakeholders in local tourism development (Giang et al., 2017). In the burgeoning literature on how to define social entrepreneurship (for a recent review of the relevant literature see Choi and Majumdar (2014), consensus is gathering that social enterprises undertake revenue generating strategies in order to achieve social and environmental goals and create secondary benefits such as the enhancement of social and human capital (DiDomenico et al., 2010). The dual mission of financial sustainability and social value creation being the defining characteristic of social enterprise, such ventures do not fit neatly into the conventional categories of private and public, profit and non-profit organizations. The quest for financial sustainability follows the logic of the market, whereas social objectives abide by the rule of community to create social value and advance social change (Mair & Martì, 2006). As hybrid organizations, social enterprises mobilize a wide range of financial resources and apply a variety of business models to accommodate both seemingly incompatible objectives (Peredo & McLean, 2006).

As recent research shows, there is rapid growth in TSEs, in particular in low- and middle-income countries where tourism is a key economic sector (Altinay et al., 2016). It is assumed that, due to their hybrid character, social enterprise is particularly well equipped to effectively mobilize financial resources and ensure the cooperation of multiple stakeholders. As TSEs preferably engage with tourisms that advance economic, social and environmental goals, they are committed to create value for local communities without jeopardizing the environment and contribute to sustainable regional development (Kline et al., 2014). In the context of low income countries such as Cambodia where the tourism industry is foreign-dominated creating income leakage (Mao et al., 2013), where local people lack financial resources and skills to operate business (Mao et al., 2014), and where government institutions are too weak to enforce appropriate regulations to support local communities, social enterprises may create the necessary infrastructure and mechanisms for local participation. An increasing number of case studies provide evidence of benefits accruing to local communities from social entrepreneurial initiatives (Dahles et al., 2020). Focusing on social enterprises in the Cambodia tourism sector, Biddulph (2017), for example, lists a wide variety of social benefits that became available to rural people, among which security and stability of employment, social insurance and health benefits, and participation in decision-making.

In summary, pushed by governments as an engine of rapid growth, tourism development can cause increased economic insecurity for local communities. Under such growth scenarios, local livelihoods transform into 'tourism livelihoods' characterized by an extreme, if not complete, dependence on tourism as the only source of income. Such tourism livelihoods are particularly vulnerable to visitor volatility and external events (Dahles & Susilowati, 2015; Lasso & Dahles, 2018). Sustainable tourism development does not revolve around the sustainability of tourism as such, but advances local development with tourism as one among other tools for economic diversification. In this vein, TSEs with their dual mission of income security and social value creation seem to offer a promising alternative. Whilst there is consensus in the literature that community participation is essential in achieving the aims set for sustainable development through tourism, it is yet to be seen whether these enterprises will contribute to social change beyond the tourism sector.

9.3 The Contextual Background of Cambodia's Tourism Development

Visitors arriving in Cambodia are presented with remnants of the glorious past of the great Khmer empire, the splendor of the colony reminiscent of the French rule (1863–1953), and the turmoil of the 1970s and 1980s that destroyed the country's vital institutions and social fabric. When in the early 1990s peace was restored, substantial development assistance from a variety of international sources poured into the country in order to facilitate the rebuilding of its economy and civil society. This marked the onset of a massive influx of international non-governmental organizations (NGOs) and, in their wake, the establishment of local NGOs operating in Cambodia (Khieng & Dahles, 2015). Whilst NGOs have played key roles as development agents and have contributed significantly to developing the economy and alleviating poverty (Lyne et al., 2015), their prominence in Cambodia's economy has resulted in an extreme level of persistent donor-dependence.

Yet, since Cambodia's heydays as a donor darling, the financial support for NGOs has undergone significant changes. Not only has international donor funding declined considerably, but also have concerns been raised about the effectiveness of NGO activities in a country with one of the highest economic growth rates in Asia (World Bank, 2009). As a consequence, NGOs have been forced to diversify their funding sources and many have since transformed into social enterprises as an alternative way to pursue their social mission (Khieng & Dahles, 2015; Lyne et al., 2015). As the tourism industry has become Cambodia's second engine of economic growth after the garment sector (Carter et al., 2015, p. 800), many NGOs have jumped on its bandwagon to compensate for the loss of donor income. In the process, some NGOs-turned-social-enterprises have come to lead initiatives in sustainable and community-based tourism.

Cambodia is largely a cultural tourism destination and dependent on a few key attractions (Reimer & Walter, 2013). The most prominent tourist attraction, the famous temple complex of Angkor Wat, a relic of the great Khmer empire, situated in the Angkor Archaeological Park in the province of Siem Reap, welcomed nearly 2.6 million international visitors in 2018 (42% of all international arrivals) generating over USD 100 million in revenue (Cheng, 2019). Beyond Angkor Wat, tourists commonly visit Phnom Penh, Cambodia's capital city, famous for its royal palace and pagodas, markets and genocide museums; and the seaside town of Sihanoukville with its beach-resorts and soaring casino industry. Underlying this limited repertoire of attractions is a government strategy that views tourism exclusively as a source of foreign exchange and GDP growth, and prioritizes an increase in international arrivals. Such a limited perspective has not only hampered investments in innovation, but has also failed to identify measures for poverty alleviation (Biddulph, 2015; Carter et al., 2015). As Biddulph (2015, p. 101) puts it"Cambodia is noted as a country where relatively little of tourists' spending finds its way into the hands of the poor." Moreover, this growth scenario leaves the sector exposed to fluctuations in international tourist arrivals as the dramatic collapse of the industry caused by the COVID-19 pandemic exemplifies.

The Cambodian Tourism Development Strategic Plan 2012–2020 (Ministry of Tourism, 2012) fails to explicitly commit to sustainable tourism development, an omission that was candidly pointed out by Prime Minister Hun Sen in his "Message of Support" on the first pages of this plan: "Cultural tourism is highly prioritized for Cambodia tourism development while ecotourism, a vision for sustainable development, needs to be improved and developed as a new tourist destination, responsibly contributing to mitigating against climate change and toward building up green economic development" (Ministry of Tourism, 2012, p. i–ii). As the tourism strategy for the next decade is due to be revealed to the public, the government has pledged to advance ecotourism as part of its 'green' economic development plan. Recently, the national policy on ecotourism has been approved by the Council of Ministers. Under this policy, the Ministry of Environment has initiated 22 ecotourism communities covering an area of 35,003 ha in 12 protected areas in order to spur local economic development providing employment and boost local incomes (Dara, 2020). Meanwhile the Ministry of Tourism has announced that 56 sites with ecotourism potential will be developed, most of which financed by Chinese investors (Cheng, 2018). This development is a powerful reminder of the significance of the economic aid and investments that Cambodia has been receiving from China over the past decades, as will be elaborated in the next section.

9.4 The Growth Scenario: Tourism as the Engine of Economic Success

Undeniably, the growth-driven government strategy has been rather effective as Cambodia, in less than 20 years time, has become one of the fastest-growing tourism destinations in South-East Asia. International arrivals show consistent expansion since the early 2000s. Between 2000 and 2010, tourist numbers surged from 450,000 to 2.5 million (Carter et al., 2015, p. 799) and to 6.2 million in 2018 with an average annual growth rate of 16% (WTTC, 2018, p. 1). In the next decade, international tourist arrivals are expected to grow by 5.2% per annum to about 8 million in 2028 (WTTC, 2018, p. 1). The majority of international visitors are from Asian countries with the Chinese topping the list of arrivals (Heng, 2018; Sorn, 2019). Cambodia welcomed some two million Chinese tourists in 2018, up more than 70% on the previous year (Sorn, 2019). According to pre-COVID-19 estimates, the country was expected to attract three million Chinese tourists in 2020 and five million in 2025 (Sorn, 2019).

In pre-Covid-19 Cambodia, however, tourism showed signs of stagnation in terms of value captured per tourist – from US$ 585 in 2005 to US$ 655 in 2016. While low-end businesses mushroomed, stays remained short with limited repeat visits, and destinations suffered from overcrowding and degradation (World Bank Group, 2017). To overcome these problems the Cambodian government set their eyes on more foreign investments and new markets. As for investments, the Kingdom's participation in China's Belt and Road Initiative (BRI) is of critical importance. Cambodia has embraced the BRI since its inception in 2013, as China has undeniably become Cambodia's most important economic partner. From infrastructure and connectivity development to cross-border trade and tourism, Cambodia has benefited significantly from cooperation with China under the BRI framework (Sok, 2019). Cambodia's vision of prosperity also entails a shift away from its overreliance on low-paid and low-skilled jobs currently provided by the (Chinese-owned) garment sector.

As for the new markets, the Cambodian government launched a strategic marketing plan in 2015 to woo more Chinese tourists through the China Ready initiative. This initiative, first launched in 2016, aims to foster trust between local tourism businesses and Chinese tourists (World Bank Group, 2017). In an effort to capitalize on the rapid growth in Chinese inbound tourism, Cambodia has established the China Ready Center (CRC) to cater to soaring numbers of Chinese tourists, as well as to improve the skills of local tourist operators working with Chinese clients. This resonates with the recently launched special tourism zoning plan designed to attract long-stay and repeat visitors and to advance property purchase in Cambodia. Tailor-made for Chinese visitors, this development is expected to resolve many challenges, including containing the spread of Covid-19 (Amarthalingam, 2020a). However, sustainable development is not among its priorities.

Chinese investments in Cambodia are soaring, especially in Sihanoukville. These investments include Chinese tour agencies entering the Kingdom, new hotels and entertainment venues being established and large-scale projects such as airports and dams being undertaken (Po & Heng, 2019). So far, the casino industry has provided the most tangible impetus in the tourism industry. The performance of Hong Kong-listed NagaCorp Ltd. which operates the NagaWorld gaming and hotel complex in Phnom Penh was boosted by the boom in arrivals from China. VIP gaming revenue totaled US$ 625.3 million, more than double the revenue brought in from mass market gambling, which came out to US$ 300.6 million (O'Byrne, 2018a). The NagaWorld Complex is changing the face of Phnom Penh. The complex is connected via an underground shopping mall known as the NagaCity Walk (Hor, 2018).

While gambling establishments and shopping precincts absorb the big-package tour groups from China, new tourist facilities are being designed to cater to higher-income Chinese visitors. Among such initiatives is the US$ 500.4 million Tourism, Ecological, Marine and International (TEMI) tourism project which is part of the Chinese-owned Dara Sakor Tourism Resort project and comprises a five-star hotel with 800 rooms, a commercial centre, a golf course, bungalows, villas, amusement parks, and a naval park among other attractions. Located in the coastal province of Koh Kong between Sihanoukville and the Thai border, the project is set to create more than 5000 jobs (Hin, 2019).

9.5 The Diversification Scenario: Emerging Initiatives in Tourism-Based Social Enterprise

As Chinese investments are bringing profound change to coastal resorts, cultural heritage sites and urban landscapes, a silent transformation is materializing in NGO-supported projects and local businesses in the Cambodian tourism and hospitality sector. The emergence of social entrepreneurial activities in this sector is overwhelmingly motivated by challenges in sustaining local NGOs due to diminishing donor funding (Khieng & Dahles, 2015). A variety of business models has been developed to accommodate such commercial ventures (Dahles et al., 2020). More and more NGOs organize their business activities in separate legal entities within their organization or in independently managed external social enterprises in order to generate revenues from tourism at large. Commercial activities in the tourism sector are commonly unrelated to the social mission of these organizations (Khieng & Dahles, 2015). Their involvement with tourism is money-driven and tourism itself is not seen as an area in need of development and empowerment. Instead, the local community is the designated beneficiary of the revenues generated by the tourism-related social enterprises that operate under these NGOs in that they offer employment and training to Cambodians recruited into jobs, development of infrastructure and cash donations to meet specific community needs. Whilst many of such projects do not engage with sustainable tourism in particular, NGOs are known for pushing the sustainable development agenda. As these NGOs provide advocacy on environmental protection, land rights and access to natural resources, they also encourage local community to become active agents in tourism development. Hence the emergence of initiatives in pro-poor tourism and community-based tourism where local community is not a passive recipient of benefits but an integral part of the tourist experience offered. In such projects, NGOs often provide skills training in hospitality, offer foreign language instruction and familiarize local people with foreign tourist expectations.

In the wake of NGO-based social ventures, independent social enterprises are emerging in Cambodia (Khieng & Dahles, 2015). Where such enterprises have sustainable tourism development in their mission statement, they have the explicit ambition to develop tourisms that address persistent social and environmental issues (Kline et al., 2014). This new generation of social enterprises attempts to meet a dual objective: to subject their commercial strategies to a social mission and, at the same time, to make tourism more inclusive. These tourism-based social enterprises (TSEs) offer a novel approach to development away from the persistent dependence on donor funding and alternatives to a foreign-dominated economy (Dahles et al., 2020). While some of these new TSEs are foreign-owned and managed, more and more young and well-educated Cambodians have the ambition to become a social entrepreneur. With their first-hand understanding of the major challenges in Cambodian society, they define the social impact of their enterprise in terms of its significance for social change in rural Cambodia, in particular advocating local ownership and grassroots-level empowerment. These objectives are pursued by including staff, tourists and local community. The centerpiece of the tourist experience provided is the engagement of villagers and the celebration of village life. The participation of local people may include the demonstration of particular skills, the trade in handicrafts and the supply of homestay accommodation (see Altinay et al., 2016; Dahles et al., 2019, 2020; Von der Weppen & Cochrane, 2012). Local communities engaging in such tourism development benefit in multiple ways, by gaining an income and employment, by improving the infrastructure in their village, by receiving training and education and, eventually, by obtaining (business)ownership and the support of multiple stakeholders.

9.6 Discussion and Conclusion

The recent surge in tourist arrivals from China is a consequence of the intensifying entanglement of Cambodia's fate with China. Growing Cambodia-China ties have seen the latter's influence sweep across the Kingdom through increased investments in tourism development. Tourist arrivals from China have spawned a vast increase in Chinese investment as China has become the leading source of foreign funds in Cambodia, fuelling the construction sector with huge casino and hotel projects (Po & Heng, 2019). However, the benefits to the economy have been lopsided as the returns largely remain with Chinese companies and fail to trickle down to local Cambodians (O'Byrne, 2018b) adding to the leakage of tourism revenues to overseas agents and investors. Chinese investment in Cambodia's real estate market is almost exclusively aimed at the Cambodian upper class, as well as Chinese tourists and businessmen. This is driving market prices up, making housing unaffordable for most Cambodians (Po & Heng, 2019). Despite the economic potential of hotels, casinos and increased tourism numbers, Cambodia's gambling industry has long maintained a murky reputation, with the coastal destination of Sihanoukville rarely earning positive headlines. Money laundering, illegal casino operations and human trafficking have become acute concerns (Po & Heng, 2019). While the BRI's Chinese investors have played a crucial role in the Cambodian economy, this injection of capital has exacerbated the weakness of Cambodia's regulatory environment. These Chinese investors have perpetuated the host country's socio-political culture of patron-client networks, partly entrenched by the Sino-Cambodian elites at the expense of local communities (Young, 2020).

Turning our attention to the opposite end of the tourism spectrum, we find that in the Cambodian tourism and hospitality sector the emergence of social entrepreneurship is largely motivated by challenges in sustaining local NGOs due to diminishing donor funding. Many TSEs continue to do what NGOs have been doing since the 1990s: providing goods and services to local community for the purpose of local development. Yet, local participation in the production, planning and management of tourism is still exceptional. Overall, local communities keep playing a passive role as the recipient of benefits accruing from the TSEs' social programs financed by tourism revenues. It is fair to conclude that mainstream Cambodian TSEs rarely offer pathways to innovation that may bridge the gap between the 'development first' and the 'tourism first' approach (Giang et al., 2017). Although TSEs have the potential to channel a greater share of tourism benefits to communities and reduce revenue leakage, investments in infrastructure, training and education, including basic business management, are called for before a meaningful participation can be established (Dahles et al., 2020).

TSEs operating under the responsible and inclusive model of tourism engagement, on the other hand, make laudable attempts at engaging local community by providing initial infrastructure and training to enable locals to benefit from tourism as owners of independently operated micro-businesses. However, it is yet unclear whether these enterprises will be able to "create sustainable solutions for all stakeholders involved" (Giang et al., 2017, p. 157). Notwithstanding the boundless goodwill and substantial contribution of this new generation of TSEs to sustainable tourism, it remains to be seen whether the model of engagement espoused by these enterprises will indeed transform the tourism sector and, in the end, society in Cambodia. The focus on alternative modes of tourism has to be carefully reviewed in view of the transformations that tourism in Cambodia is currently facing. As Carter et al. (2015, p. 808) rightly point out, there is an increasing mismatch between the tourism product developed by Western agents for Western consumers and the market which is impacted by increasing numbers of arrivals from East Asia and China in particular. Whilst the Cambodian government assumes that Chinese tourists prefer resort tourism – as echoed by the TEMI tourism project and the new zoning plan as developed by the Ministry of Tourism –, reliable data on Chinese consumer tastes is still lacking. Conversely, the new 'alternative' forms of tourism as being developed by TSEs may appeal to segments among the Chinese consumers for their 'clean and green' image. However, these innovative products may not satisfy Chinese consumer tastes at large and may, in the end, cater only to a shrinking, Western, market. The Cambodian government and the sector's tourism professionals are advised to undertake systematic market research among the various consumer segments in order to gain an understanding of consumer demand and align their marketing strategies with the need to develop more sustainable tourism products.

At the time of writing, in 2020, the COVID-19 pandemic has brought the tourism sector to its knees. As recent data released by the Cambodian Ministry of Tourism reveal, international tourist arrivals, due to travel restrictions and lockdowns, declined by 74% to 1.2 million between January and September this year from 4.8 million in the same period in 2019 (Amarthalingam, 2020a). In the first 6 months of 2020, an estimated 3000 tourism-related businesses have closed down and 45,400 jobs have been lost (Amarthalingam, 2020b). In Siem Reap, home of the Angkor Wat temple complex, over 80% of accommodations permanently or temporarily suspended business. Little is known about how this downturn affects local communities, small tourism-based businesses and Cambodians who lost their jobs. In similar cases, where the sector was hit by a sudden and persistent decrease in tourist arrivals, local people were left with very limited alternatives to sustain their livelihoods. Instead, they turned to subsistence strategies or left the tourist precinct to resume farming in rural areas (Dahles & Susilowati, 2015). Importantly, local people should be encouraged to diversify their business or trade with opportunities outside the narrow contours of the tourism industry to avoid the risks implied by a downturn in tourist arrivals. For the government, this crisis represents an opportunity to reboot the sector and create the conditions for a more sustainable tourism development in Cambodia.

References

Altinay, L., Sigala, M., & Waligo, V. (2016). Social value creation through tourism enterprise. *Tourism Management, 54*, 404–417.
Amarthalingam, S. (2020a). Relaxing policies, fixing quirks to rouse a sleeping tourism sector. *Phnom Penh Post.* Posted on 5 November 2020.
Amarthalingam, S. (2020b). Wither tourism? Can Cambodia resuscitate the sector post-Covid-19? *Phnom Penh Post.* Posted on 23 July 2020.
Biddulph, R. (2015). Limits to mass tourism's effects in rural peripheries. *Annals of Tourism Research, 50*(1), 98–112.
Biddulph, R. (2017). Social enterprise and inclusive tourism. Five cases in Siem Reap, Cambodia. *Tourism Geographies, 20*(4), 610–629.
Bramwell, B., & Sharman, A. (2000). Approaches to sustainable tourism planning and community participation: The case of Hope Valley. In G. Richards & D. Hall (Eds.), *Tourism and sustainable community development* (pp. 17–35). Routledge.
Carter, A. W., Thok, S., O'Rourke, V., & Pearce, T. (2015). Sustainable tourism and its use as a development strategy in Cambodia: A systematic literature review. *Journal of Sustainable Tourism, 23*(5), 797–818.

Chambers, R., & Conway, G. (1992). *Sustainable rural livelihoods: Practical concepts for the 21st century* (IDS discussion paper no. 296). Institute for Development Studies (IDS).

Cheng, S. (2018). Ecotourism policy draft approved. *Phnom Penh Post*. Posted on 20 November 2018.

Cheng, S. (2019). Angkor hosts 2.6M visitors. *Phnom Penh Post*. Posted on 02 January 2019.

Choi, N., & Majumdar, S. (2014). Social entrepreneurship as an essentially contested concept: Opening a new avenue for systematic future research. *Journal of Business Venturing, 29*(3), 363–376.

Dahles, H., & Susilowati, T. P. (2015). Business resilience in times of growth and crisis. *Annals of Tourism Research, 51*, 34–50.

Dahles, H., Verver, M., Khieng, M., Schellens, I., & N. (2019). Scaling up social enterprise: Predicament or prospect in a comparative perspective. *Journal of Social Entrepreneurship*. https://doi.org/10.1080/19420676.2019.1641136

Dahles, H., Khieng, S., Verver, M., & Manders, I. (2020). Social entrepreneurship and tourism in Cambodia: Advancing community engagement. *Journal of Sustainable Tourism, 28*(6), 816–833.

Dara, V. (2020). Eco-tourism gets gov't boost. *Phnom Penh Post*. Posted on 18 November 2020.

DiDomenico, M. L., Haugh, H., & Tracey, P. (2010). Social bricolage: Theorizing social value creation in social enterprises. *Entrepreneurship Theory and Practice, 34*(4), 681–703.

Giang, T. P., Whitford, M., & Dredge, D. (2017). Knowledge dynamics in the tourism SE nexus. In P. Sheldon & R. Daniele (Eds.), *Social entrepreneurship and tourism. Philosophy and practice* (pp. 155–172). Springer.

Heng, C. (2018). Chinese tourists make up bulk of arrivals. *Phnom Penh Post*. Posted on 16 October 2018.

Hin, P. (2019). TEMI tourism project approved by the CDC. *Phnom Penh Post*. Posted on 20 February 2019.

Hor, K. (2018). Naga announces $1B gaming revenue. *Phnom Penh Post*. Posted on 03 October 2018.

Khieng, S., & Dahles, H. (2015). Commercialization in the Non-Profit Sector: The Emergence of Social Enterprise in Cambodia. *Journal of Social Entrepreneurship, 6*(2), 218–243.

Kline, C., Shah, N., & Rubright, H. (2014). Applying the positive theory of social entrepreneurship to understand food entrepreneurs and their operations. *Tourism Planning & Development, 11*(3), 330–342.

Lasso, A., & Dahles, H. (2018). Are tourism livelihoods sustainable? Tourism development and economic transformation on Komodo Island, Indonesia. *Asia Pacific Journal of Tourism Research, 23*(5), 473–485.

Lyne, I., Khieng, S., & Ngin, C. (2015). *Social enterprise in Cambodia: An overview* (ICSEM working papers no. 05). The International Comparative Social Enterprise Models (ICSEM) Project.

Mair, J., & Martí, I. (2006). Social entrepreneurship research: A source of explanation, prediction and delight. *Journal of World Business, 41*(1), 36–44.

Mao, N., DeLacy, T., & Grunfeld, H. (2013). Local livelihoods and the tourism value chain: A case study in Siem Reap-Angkor Region, Cambodia. *International Journal of Environmental and Rural Development, 4*(2), 120–126.

Mao, N., Grunfeld, H., DeLacy, T., & Chandler, D. (2014). Agriculture and tourism linkage constraints in the Siem Reap-Angkor region of Cambodia. *Tourism Geographies, 16*(4), 669–686.

Ministry of Tourism. (2012). *Tourism development strategic plan 2012–2020*. Ministry of Tourism.

Movono, A., & Becken, S. (2018). Solesolevaki as social capital: A tale of a village, two tribes, and a resort in Fiji. *Asia Pacific Journal of Tourism Research, 23*(2), 146–157.

O'Byrne, B. (2018a). NagaWorld's profits soar in 2017. *Phnom Penh Post*. Posted on 09 February 2018.

O'Byrne, B. (2018b). Spike in Chinese visitors drives tourism boom. *Phnom Penh Post*. Posted on 25 January 2018.

Peredo, A. M., & McLean, M. (2006). Social entrepreneurship: A critical review of the concept. *Journal of World Business, 41*(1), 56–65.

Po, S., & Heng, K. (2019). Assessing the impacts of Chinese investments in Cambodia: The case of Preah Sihanoukville province. A working paper on China-Cambodia relations. Pacific Forum. *Issues & Insights Working Paper, 19*(4).

Reimer, J. K., & Walter, P. (2013). How do you know it when you see it? Community-based ecotourism in the Cardamom Mountains of southwestern Cambodia. *Tourism Management, 34*, 122–132.

Scoones, I. (1998). *Sustainable rural livelihoods a framework for analysis* (IDS working paper 72). Institute for Development Studies.

Sharpley, R. (2000). Tourism and sustainable development: Exploring the theoretical divide. *Journal of Sustainable Tourism, 8*(1), 1–19.

Sharpley, R. (2020). Tourism, sustainable development and the theoretical divide: 20 years on. *Journal of Sustainable Tourism, 28*(11), 1932–1946.

Sheldon, P., & Daniele, R. (2017). *Social entrepreneurship and tourism: Philosophy and practice.* Springer.

Sok K. (2019). In Cambodia, the BRI must benefit locals too. *East Asia Forum.* Posted on 18 May 2019.

Sorn, S. (2019). Chinese tourists soar to 2M. *Phnom Penh Post.* Posted on Fri, 1 February 2019.

Tao, T. C. H., & Wall, G. (2009). A livelihood approach to sustainability. *Asia Pacific Journal of Tourism Research, 14*(2), 137–152.

Von der Weppen, J., & Cochrane, J. (2012). Social enterprises in tourism: An exploratory study of operational models and success factors. *Journal of Sustainable Tourism, 20*(3), 497–511.

World Bank. (2009). *Cambodia – Sustaining rapid growth in a challenging environment: Country economic memorandum.* World Bank.

World Bank Group. (2017). Cambodia economic update, October 2017: Climbing up the manufacturing value chains. *The World Bank.* Posted on 22 November 2017. https://www.worldbank.org/en/country/cambodia/publication/cambodia-economic-update-october-2017. Accessed 28 Sep 2020.

WTTC. (2018, March). *Travel & tourism economic impact 2018.* World Travel & Tourism Council.

Young, S. (2020). China's belt and road initiative: Patron-client and capture in Cambodia. *The Chinese Journal of Comparative Law.* https://doi.org/10.1093/cjcl/cxaa025

Heidi Dahles (MSc & PhD, Radboud University, Netherlands) is adjunct professor at the School of Social Sciences, University of Tasmania, and at the Griffith Institute for Tourism (GIFT), Griffith University, Gold Coast, Australia. Prior to these appointments, she held academic leadership positions at Griffith Business School (Brisbane) and Vrije University Amsterdam (Netherlands). Her research interest is in local livelihoods, resilience and social enterprise, in particular in the tourism industry, in Southeast Asia.

Chapter 10
Sustainable Tourism and the Moral Limits of the Market: Can Asia Offer Better Alternatives

Can-Seng Ooi

Abstract Despite its entanglements with society, tourism is still an industry that uses the market for economic exchange, so as to price tourism goods, services and experiences. The market serves important functions in society but there are two moral limits. The first is on how market exchange may transform some products, services and experiences in ways that denigrate and even destroy their intrinsic values. The second is on the failure of the market in distributing benefits from economic exchange more equitably, and to those who need them more. This does not mean that the market is immoral, it just means that there are inherent limitations to how the market maximises or enhances the welfare of society. This chapter looks at four common sustainable tourism approaches, and argues that they all address the moral limits of the market, from local perspectives. And subsequently, can lessons be learned from the Asian experience in doing sustainable tourism? The answer is yes but with caveats.

Keywords Triple bottom line · Public-private partnerships · Community-led tourism · Market redesign · Regenerative tourism · Asian models of sustainable tourism · Moral limits of the market · Social justice · Social equity

10.1 Introduction

At the biggest United Nations (UN) conference ever, the 2012 Rio+20 UN conference on sustainable development affirmed the position that a comprehensive and holistic approach is needed if we are to have continuous global prosperity and growth. The diverse and overlapping needs of the community, the environment, workers and civil society must be integrated into economic development.

C.-S. Ooi (✉)
School of Social Sciences, University of Tasmania (UTAS), Hobart, Australia
e-mail: canseng.ooi@utas.edu.au

Globalization and international trade create competition, and opportunities for all countries to cooperate, to support each other and to benefit together. Tourism is one of many areas that should contribute to achieving various social development goals. Paragraphs 130 and 131 in the conference outcome report pertain specifically to sustainable tourism (Rio+20 United Nations Conference on Sustainable Development, 2012):

> 130. We emphasize that well-designed and managed tourism can make a significant contribution to the three dimensions of sustainable development, has close linkages to other sectors, and can create decent jobs and generate trade opportunities. We recognize the need to support sustainable tourism activities and relevant capacity building that promote environmental awareness, conserve and protect the environment, respect wildlife, flora, biodiversity, ecosystems and cultural diversity, and improve the welfare and livelihoods of local communities by supporting their local economies and the human and natural environment as a whole. We call for enhanced support for sustainable tourism activities and relevant capacity-building in developing countries in order to contribute to the achievement of sustainable development.

> 131. We encourage the promotion of investment in sustainable tourism, including ecotourism and cultural tourism, which may include creating small and medium sized enterprises and facilitating access to finance, including through microcredit initiatives for the poor, indigenous peoples and local communities in areas with high eco-tourism potential. In this regard, we underline the importance of establishing, where necessary, appropriate guidelines and regulations in accordance with national priorities and legislation for promoting and supporting sustainable tourism.

Sustainable tourism is part of the wider concern for more balanced development around the world. The subtext is that the current economic agenda has dominated development at the detriment to the environment and the community, and tourism is part of the problem. International tourism is sometimes viewed as an ongoing force of colonization and domination by rich Western countries over poorer ones (Chambers & Buzinde, 2015; Hales et al., 2018; Mietzner & Storch, 2019). Environmental destruction, worker exploitation and community suffering embedded in a set of lucrative and popular tourism activities generate worries because they confront our sense of justice, fairness and morality (Fennell, 2018; Jamal, 2019). If we do not address the ethical issues embedded in the impacts of tourism, the industry cannot stay viable as it will be resisted by civil society, workers and members of host communities. Tourism is beyond business, it is entangled socially, culturally and politically in society.

Many scholars, activists, politicians and even businesspersons are advocating alternatives to end exploitative tourism. One way of looking for alternatives is to look at non-Western methods of managing social and economic life, including tourism. So can Asian experiences offer local community-driven alternatives that bring about a more sustainable form of tourism globally? A so-called "non-Western", more community-driven approach to sustainable tourism has appeal because it accepts and respects the host society in its own contexts and circumstances. A modern and efficiency-driven approach – often caricaturized as "international" and "Western" – tends to marginalize local situations, and the strategies may not be appropriate and relevant. Tourism development strategies for a small village in Italy cannot be replicated in a village in Taiwan, for instance. This chapter however explains why this approach should be embraced with caution.

A "truly" local or indigenous approach to tourism is hard to find. Social, cultural and economic diversity has diminished across the global tourism industry because tourism is a product and perpetuator of globalization. To participate in the global tourism industry, countries must largely embrace international tourism-related institutions and practices, such as passports and border controls, maintaining safety standards for air travels, and embracing English as the *lingua franca*. Widespread modern cross-border travels are possible because they are facilitated by common technologies, standards, systems and procedures. Best practices are shared internationally; destinations develop similar attractions (e.g. observation towers, themed-parks, contemporary art museums), host similar events and festivals (e.g. film festivals, marathons, heritage food events) and sell almost identical souvenirs (e.g. T-shirts, chocolates, trinkets) (Ooi, 2011). The lines between so-called Western and non-Western approaches are blurred. Regardless, putting the local community first is considered a necessary step to a more sustainable tourism. Respecting social, cultural, political and economic differences between destinations, local communities and ways of doing business is part of the localization strategy that underpins common approaches to sustainable tourism development globally. In this context, sustainable tourism encapsulates the entanglements of global and local practices. This chapter focuses on four internationally-common sustainable tourism approaches that are also locally embraced: (1) the triple bottom line; (2) public-private partnerships; (3) redesigning the market; and (4) community-led initiatives.

This chapter argues and will show that these four common approaches deal with a more fundamental problem embedded in global tourism. Despite its entanglements with society, tourism is still an industry that uses the market for economic exchange, so as to price goods and services, and to provide incentives to buy and sell experiences, goods and services. The capitalist market however has two moral limits. This does not mean that the market is immoral, it just means that there are inherent limitations to how the market maximises or enhances the welfare of society. These four sustainable tourism approaches attempt to mitigate these two moral limits, through varying methods and with different results. They have to be adapted into the local context and circumstance, and address these moral limits to some extent. While laudable, caution is however still needed because Asian adaptation may not be better because local interventions may further aggravate the moral limitations of markets. The following sections will unpack this argument.

10.2 The Moral Limits of the Market

The market is a human-made social economic institution (North, 1991). It serves important functions in modern society; it distributes and allows for the convenient exchange of goods and services. The market brings great benefits and welfare to society. Compared to bartering, transactions in the modern market are straight forward and efficient. The market facilitates exchange between individuals who may not necessarily know each other (Fligstein, 2002; North, 1991; Roth, 2015). Money is the common denominator that enables us to trade and to acquire products and services seamlessly. However markets that use money as a medium of exchange have at least two moral limits (Sidelsky & Skidelsky, 2015; Simmel, 1978). Let me elaborate.

10.2.1 Moral Limit 1: Price and Impact on Non-Economic Values

> I recall an awkward encounter when I visited a Jain temple in Delhi. I was told not to bring animal products and money into the temple. The priest is also not supposed to touch money. So in my respectful manner, I left my leather wallet and belt in the locker outside. At the end of the temple tour by the priest, while still in the temple, he demanded a tip and chided me for not having my wallet with me. I sheepishly stepped out of the temple to collect my wallet, and went back in to give him the so-called tip. That encounter was awkward.

The use of money as a means for universal exchange has consequences. It has become a common denominator that allows economic exchange on – arguably – everything. Money has created a market that we have come to recognize today (North, 1991; Simmel, 1978). There are many advantages. Money liberates the individual and provides accessibility to almost all goods and services. Money enhances personal liberty and individual freedom but it is also responsible for weakening personal relations (Simmel, 1978, p. 295). Instead of having to build trust and closer relations between persons to facilitate bartering, money is used. This means of exchange is efficient and effective (North, 1991; Roth, 2015; Williamson, 1998). Tourism today is made possible because people can travel to places without knowing their hosts personally. Visitors have access to experiences and attractions in exotic places.

But some things are not supposed to be priced because they are sacred, revered or supposedly priceless. These are repugnant transactions (Roth, 2015). My experience with the Jain priest is an example of how I have misunderstood the guest-host relationship. Possibly because visitors did not give him satisfactory amount of money in the donation box placed just outside the temple, he demanded that each visitor gives him the money directly even though he is not supposed to touch money. By so doing, did I receive a diluted Jain temple experience? Or worse, did money and tourism corrupt the priest?

It is generally accepted that certain things are not for sale, and they should not be priced. Another example is voting in a democratic system; votes are not supposed to be for sale. In tourism, tourists are sometimes reminded that they do not have the right to visit a destination; it is a privilege to be able to visit. For instance, because of over tourism, super popular destinations around the world face strong backlashes

(Burgen, 2018). In the island of Crete, before the early 2020s COVID-19 pandemic, many residents were fed up with tourists. Activists and artists vandalized walls by stating that they welcome refugees but not tourists (Fig. 10.1). This is an assertion and a reminder that money cannot buy everything.

There are many other activities and places that tourists are not welcomed. For instance, how much should a Chinese family charge tourists to join in their annual traditional reunion family dinner on the eve of the lunar new year? Is it appropriate to bring visitors to observe private weddings or to observe grieving families at funeral parlours in Malaysia? Should we shrug off the lucrative child-sex exploitation tourist business in Cambodia? The market is able to price all services, experiences and products but some face strong social and moral resistance. Repugnant tourist activities and transactions are not supported by many in the community, and are not sustainable.

Similarly, pricing the priceless may transform and denigrate the product, service and experience. For example, "buying authenticity" is an oxymoron. MacCannell (1992) describes that as "staged authenticity", and has become a prevalent practice in cultural and heritage tourism. In the context of sustainable tourism, host cultures and societies are touristified as communities are transformed by what tourists want and willing to pay (Ooi, 2019b). A new social and economic hierarchy emerges in the host community. This is problematic as the society aims to please the constant flows of temporary visitors rather than the residents who live there, especially residents are infinitely more socially, culturally, politically and emotionally vested in the place than fleeting visitors. Moral limit 1 of the market points to how economic exchange transforms products, services and experiences in ways that denigrate and even destroy the intrinsic values of what are being bought.

Fig. 10.1 REFUGEES WELCOME TOURISTS GO HOME, a political graffiti in Rethymno, Greece. (Source: Image by Tomisti, 2020. This image is licensed under the Creative Commons Attribution-Share Alike 4.0 International license)

10.2.2 Moral Limit 2: Accessibility to and Distribution of Benefits

In 2017, I was at a wedding dinner in Australia. I told an elderly lady sitting next to me that I was from Singapore. She started telling me of her two visits to the island-state. She was disappointed in her most recent trip because she could not re-experience old Singapore. When she was first there in the 1970s, Singapore River was polluted but full of life. She remembered the many sweaty coolies working along the banks, boats carrying goods, and derelict shophouses lining the river (Fig. 10.2). In her recent trip, she saw a sanitized and gentrified Singapore River. Today, the river is clean, the only boats there ferry tourists on cruises, and the shops have become fancy eating and drinking places. She reminisced and complained about the more modern Singapore. I told her that I used to live in a derelict shophouse in Singapore. My childhood experience was not at all romantic. Proper sanitation, good lighting and other modern comforts in the public housing flat I later lived in are appreciated by my family and I.

Slum tourism is a relatively new phenomenon but consuming poverty is not (Steinbrink, 2012). There are many slums in Asia and tourists can go on slum tours (Dyson, 2012; Tzanelli, 2018). Dyson (2012) finds that visitors who visited Dharavi, Mumbai, developed more sympathetic and positive attitudes towards the slum. Slum tourism is considered authentic, and offers a local experience. It commodifies poverty (Freire-Medeiros, 2009). Slum tourism however does not help the many residents living in horrid conditions who face adverse poverty. There is a market for such tourist experiences but the market benefits do not go to the slum dwellers. In a

Fig. 10.2 Singapore River (around 1980) was polluted, filled with *tongkangs* or tugboats and staffed by manual dock workers: Exotic and promoted to tourists then. (Source: Singapore Tourist Promotion Board Collection, courtesy of National Archives of Singapore)

perverse manner, improving the conditions in these places may make it less desirable for visitors. The market does not necessarily distribute profits to the people who need them most. This goes against the social equity tenet of sustainable tourism.

It was mentioned earlier that the market is to enhance the welfare of society by providing the mechanisms for the effective and efficient exchange of goods and services. People would have access to things that they would not otherwise have. However the market does not necessarily distribute the benefits or profits from the market to many. The market may enrich a small group of businesses while the wider society and the environment suffer. For example, many places of worship, cultural institutions and nature parks attract visitors but they may not get the tourist dollars because visitor fees are not collected. In economic terms, there is market failure when the disadvantages are not priced into the product or service.

And related to how benefits and costs are distributed through the market, accessibility to goods and services is largely based on people's ability to pay in the market exchange, rather than based on a person's needs. For instance, a wealthy person can spend and buy many houses, while a poor person may have to be homeless. Criticisms of how tourists have driven rental prices up in popular destinations alludes to this moral shortcoming of the market (Wachsmuth & Weisler, 2018). Residents are pushed to the sidelines even though they live in their cities, and many poorer residents could not afford to reside in neighborhoods that are closed to their workplaces. Displacing the local community through tourist market forces is morally reprehensible, and does not contribute to supporting the community. Moral limit 2 of the market points to how the market fails to distribute benefits of market exchange equitably, and to those who need them more.

10.3 Four Approaches Towards Sustainable Tourism

The market offers many advantages and play an important role in society. Market activities are not necessarily immoral. The market is a way of enhancing the welfare of society by distributing wealth and benefits to many. The market mechanisms however have also generated limits to how that can be done. To reiterate, moral limit 1 points to how economic exchanges transform many products, services and/or experiences in ways that denigrate and even destroy their intrinsic values. Moral limit 2 refers to how the market distribute the benefits of market exchange in unequitable ways. Accessibility to goods and services is based on people's ability to pay rather than their needs, and thus the benefits of the market do not necessarily always go to deserving parties.

Popular sustainable tourism practices, as will be elaborated in this section, will show that these approaches address and try to mitigate the moral limits of the market. Different countries have different social, cultural, political and economic structures, and their sustainable tourism strategies will reflect this. However, can the lessons from Asia be used in other places to bring about better results?

There are at least four broad and interrelated sustainable tourism models or approaches. The first - the Triple Bottom Line - has been adopted by many tourism businesses, as they aim to be more sustainable. Their strategy is based on stakeholder theory and operated by measuring three bottom lines – profits, people and planet. The second model is often initiated by public authorities. They are responsible for providing public goods and services, such as building infrastructure, supporting cultural institutions and maintaining wilderness. These authorities look after the welfare of the community and the environment but their expertise may fall short or they have limited resources. Public-private partnerships are one way out. These partnerships involve the public and private sectors in bringing about a more economically, socially and environmentally sustainable model of community and economic development. The third sustainable tourism approach deals with the regulation and redesigning of tourism product markets. Industry structures can be reorganized, and differentiated pricing can be introduced to bring about more equitable results. And finally, tourism development would be more sustainable if the local perspective is given primacy because locals understand their environment and community more than anyone else; tourism businesses and planners should let the community drive development. Such tourism developments will be community-led, and they involve tapping into the expertise of residents who have the local knowledge and who are vested in ensuring the success of the projects.

10.3.1 Stakeholder Theory and the Triple Bottom Line

Freeman's stakeholder framework is the bedrock of sustainable development and sustainable tourism (Budeanu et al., 2016). It advocates a holistic understanding of how different aspects of society work together, and that different stakeholders – industry, workers, residents, civil society, the environment – are intertwined. Their diverse needs and interests must be served, albeit through negotiation and collaboration (Angelo & Maria, 2010; Ooi, 2013). The focus on diverse stakeholders addresses the previous dearth of concern by many businesses for the environment and community. The lack of engagement with the local community is irresponsible and these businesses will be resisted and rejected. Hotels and airlines will have uncomfortable customers if residents protest and tourists told to "Keep Out," such as in Barcelona and Venice before the COVID-19 pandemic. Front line workers must be treated well if these businesses are to provide quality services. From the stakeholder perspective, it is necessary to take into consideration the needs and agendas of different constituents in society. This is easier said than done. There are many scholars who have identified the challenges and difficulties in communication, cooperation, collaboration and support (Garcia & Cater, 2020; Ooi, 2020). Tourism businesses must be responsible, and engage in social and environmental responsibility; they need to integrate the myriad of stakeholder perspectives and needs in their planning, implementation and evaluation of corporate social responsibility (CSR) activities (Budeanu, 2009; Font & Lynes, 2018).

However the stakeholder framework offers a set of principles with limited guidance on the operationalization of stakeholder needs and interests. While people can agree that everyone's interests is important and must be respected, how would that actually translate into feasible practice? And for sustainable business activities to be considered effective, it is essential that results can be documented and not just speculated. One popular way of operationalizing the stakeholder framework is through an accounting framework of the Triple Bottom Line (TBL) – profits, people and planet (Ringham & Miles, 2018). In a balance sheet, the economic bottom line is the easiest to quantify as that is an original purpose of the accounting framework. But from the sustainability perspective, it is also important to measure the firm's contribution to the community and to the environment. There are now TBL mechanisms to do so. For example since 2013, Singapore Airlines releases an annual sustainability report. The airlines stopped using plastic straw on flights from September 2019, and in that same year, its staff canteen has become eco-friendlier by eliminating polystyrene foam and installing a machine to convert food and canteen waste into refuse-derived fuel (Singapore Airlines, 2020). And during the COVID-19 pandemic, it redeployed cabin crew to support the Singaporean community, taking up roles in healthcare, transport and social service sectors (Singapore Airlines, 2020). TBL focuses the minds of management, albeit selectively on specific economic, social and environmental tasks, issues and/or causes.

Each community has its own set of contexts and circumstances that TBL can be adapted into. The social and environmental causes that firms adopt in their three bottom lines should reflect the local situation and those relevant to the community. A hotel in Cambodia may present their TBL differently from one in Japan. The TBL approach has allowed firms to choose the most relevant, and their favorite causes to support.

Tacitly, the stakeholder framework and the TBL address the moral limits of the market by focusing on bringing about and distributing community and environmental "profits" more equitably, and also to avoid repugnant transactions. Through consultation and collaboration, the industry would be more sensitive to presenting and commercializing culture, heritage and the environment. They may not be allowed to commodify certain aspects of society. With support for and from residents and civil society, these tourism businesses should be more welcomed. The triple bottom lines help mitigate negative impacts and address the two moral limits of the market.

Challenges however remain when TBL is localized or "Asianized". Many tourism companies promote a more sustainable form of tourism but commerce, environment and community interests do not necessarily overlap. The balance between the different stakeholders is often influenced by those with more resources to push for their agendas (Liu, 2003; Ooi, 2013). A more localized practice of TPL will reflect or even perpetuate existing social hierarchies in society. Being respectful of the local situation and circumstance is central, and any Asian TBL practices that are effective and efficient or less effective and inefficient reflect the local context that may not be transferable. More generally, localized TBL practices are more likely to bring about more sustainable tourism practices if the principles and goals are conscientiously pursued with a strong business and political will, and not be sidetracked by other irrelevant agendas.

10.3.2 Public-Private Partnerships

Complementing the stakeholder approach and TPL, is the idea of public-private partnerships or PPP. The state has the responsibility to ensure the well-being of the population and the environment. There are many public goods, such as infrastructure and natural parks that are important to both residents and visitors. Developing these public goods is expensive, and the public service may not have the expertise to build, operate or maintain them. Public authorities may even hinder sustainable tourism development because of power struggles, the lack of competence and failure to do proper local consultation (Ruhanen, 2013). Collaborating with the private sector may help. For instance, environmental activists are experts and are good at protecting a wilderness parks; a business on the other hand may have the resources and have experiences in managing the financials and in management. The government may develop a wilderness conservation project that engages the private sector and in consultation with environmental groups, to bring about a public-private partnership that benefits all. In forming a partnership with the private sector in general, common public goods, such as in social services, nature conservation, education and cultural services will benefit from the strengths of different complementing groups (Wong et al., 2012).

PPP has become popular in tourism development (Jamal & Getz, 1995; Mariani & Kylänen, 2014; Vernon et al., 2005). Such an approach focuses minds on the complementary expertise of various stakeholders and on their common goals and objectives. Ideally, by cooperating and collaborating, joint benefits for industry, community and the environment can be realized. Many tourist attractions are public goods (e.g. parks, places of worship, beaches, cultural institutions). With the commercial expertise of businesses and the competences of the public sector in serving the people, local solutions can be found to provide public tourism services that are effective, efficient and even profitable. Progress can be measured and managed, such as through TPL (Andersson & Getz, 2009; Castellani & Sala, 2010; Zapata & Hall, 2012). For example, Haw Par Villa, a public heritage sculpture park in Singapore, is operated by a private company. The private company has promised that admission to the park stays free. Special events, sale of souvenirs, hosting flea markets, providing guided tours and operating food outlets should make the park commercially viable even without an entrance fee (Lin, 2015). Similarly the Singapore Tourism Board, a statutory board, has been corporatized and is run like a business. They set regulations, provide public resources to direct business development, and support tourism operators, and at the same time, engages with local cultural institutions, grassroot organizations and the mass media (Ooi, 2018). While keeping the local Asian context intact, this approach breaks walls and silos, promoting a whole-of-destination approach to tourism development that removes red-tapes and providing supporting regulations on new projects, shares business risks among different parties, and jointly brings about social, environmental and economic viability. Singapore is not unique. State-owned tourism enterprises in other Asian countries, like China, use the same set of principles to bring about societal and environmental welfare through enhanced coordinated efforts across sectors, through good management, and through the mobilization of financial and business resources (Cheng et al., 2018).

Relations embedded in PPP may however be unequal. In Asia, like in many other continents, influential businesses and/or authoritarian political partners may dictate PPP projects. Local social and environmental causes are appropriated by businesses and politicians to further their own selfish goals (Iossa & Martimort, 2016; Lai & Ooi, 2015). Nepotism, corruption and dictatorships in many Asian countries make a mockery of such partnerships, as social and environmental interests are acknowledged only in name. This may aggravate the second moral limit of the market – only a small group of people benefit from the PPP. These considerations should not detract us from the principles of engaging stakeholders with complementary skills. Singapore is a good Asian example because of its strong formal institutions. As a reminder, PPP can be adopted to various local Asian contexts, and good Asian practices are universally accepted ones – sensitive to local needs, and respect for transparency, accountability and the rule of law.

10.3.3 Redesigning the Market

While capitalism and the free market have been severely criticized for the propagation of social economic inequalities in modern society, the market can also be the solution to these challenges. Markets can be designed for specific purposes. The COVID-19 pandemic showed that tourism is an economic driver that can be curtailed. Public health and saving lives are more important than travels. And many governments provided economic support for businesses and workers in tourism and hospitality. There are many lessons from the pandemic, and one of them is that the state still plays an important role in the market. The market can be managed, regulated and even destroyed. It is thus possible to also manage the moral limits of the market through new market designs.

Following moral limit 1, there are things that cannot be priced but can still be bartered through a well-designed market mechanism. The kidney exchange is the classic example of how many countries allow for the organ to be exchanged but not sold (Roth, 2015). A kidney is a donation even though economic resources are needed for an exchange to take place. To ensure that there is a sufficient amount of kidneys in the exchange, loved ones of potential organ recipients would donate one of their kidneys to the system. And the exchange will be matched with other potential donors and recipients. This is a sophisticated bartering system. In tourism, Couch Surfing (www.couchsurfing.com) is designed as a market for bartering couch spaces between strangers (and potential new friends) (Germann Molz, 2013).

Similarly, Willing Workers on Organic Farms or WWOOF uses the bartering market to attract tourist-workers to further the organic farming movement (Deville et al., 2016). WWOOF is a work exchange network, and participants spend their so-called holidays helping out in organic farming work in exchange for board and lodging. Tourist-workers and farm work providers engage and create non-commercial tourism experiences that are considered deeper and more engaging.

Markets can also be regulated and modified to manage market failures. For example, the carbon emission market attempts to slow and then reverse climate change (Narassimhan et al., 2018; Nordhaus, 2019; Randalls, 2017). But regulating the market and correcting prices may be insufficient. For instance, carbon pricing is supposed to reduce aviation travel; it has unfortunately not (Markham et al., 2018). Regardless providing incentives and disincentives, and disallowing certain market activities, are mechanisms through which markets can be redesigned.

Complementing designed market mechanisms, taxing profits is a common strategy to address the moral limit of the market 2. Taxes can be levied and increased for highly profitable businesses, and then spent on community initiatives. The revenue distribution aspects of taxes address market failures. More broadly the universal basic income and negative income tax concepts embrace the same income redistribution aim (Tondani, 2009). For the visitor economy, a visitor tax option would serve the same purpose of spreading the economic benefits to more people (Arguea & Hawkins, 2015; Burns, 2010; Nepal & Nepal, 2019). Asian countries like Japan, India and Malaysia are already collecting some form of taxes from visitors. Bhutan is (in)famous for its high tourist tax, and has successfully controlled the number of visitors to the mountain kingdom and promote its brand of ecotourism (Gurung & Seeland, 2008).

To reiterate, the market economically segregates who can buy from the exchange, the market also shapes who benefit from the selling. The market system has created a class of entrepreneurs, marketing and salespersons who can frame and package culture and nature into profitable products. They - fortunately or unfortunately - also know how to work around any redesigned market system. Businesses have appropriated social and environmental responsibility cause into their profit-motive. In a study on greener hotels in Malaysia for example, Noor and Kumar (2014) find that it is necessary to engage greener guests in environmentally friendly activities to enhance the green experience. It has to be a "product". But the desire to commodify environmentalism has created artificial products, with the paradoxical goal of producing green experiences, alluding to moral limit 1 of the market.

The market does not readily distribute the economic benefits of tourism fairly to the wider community. But markets can be twitched, regulated and redesigned to prohibit repugnant transactions, and to distribute market benefits more widely. Is there an Asian way of redesigning the market? Most Asian (or otherwise) destinations are already doing so in their own ways. Tourism is acknowledged as an integral part of the social and environment development of society. Many Asian destinations have tweaked their tourism market to ensure that visitor revenues go to their host society. Each state has to regulate the market and to distribute the benefits. The role of an Asian state in the market and how welfare is distributed reflect the local practices, circumstances and situation. Unfortunately a redesigned market does not ensure a more transparent and more equitable manner for the benefits to be distributed. Local politics matter. Redesigned markets may still face many of the same moral limits as the more laissez faire ones.

10.3.4 Community-Led Tourism: Learning from the Local

Respecting different stakeholders is central in sustainable tourism practices, and TBL forces businesses to pay attention to the community and the environment. PPP taps into the complementary resources and expertise of businesses and the public sector to bring about public benefits to residents, the environment, visitors and also businesses. The visitor economy is regulated, and its market can be redesigned to bring about desired visitor and business behavior. As already pointed out earlier, these three approaches have been adopted by many Asian tourism businesses and Asian authorities. Their strategies entail some forms of interpretation and adaptation to local conditions and circumstance (Puriri & McIntosh, 2019). There is no research on whether Asian societies are better at implementing these strategies. TBL, PPP and redesigned markets are good frameworks but can be easily subverted by local (and foreign) business and political interests. Attempts at adapting and localizing these models may be ineffective or inefficient. And these internationally-recognized and accepted methods of doing sustainable tourism can also be considered another form of colonization and an imposition of global ideas from the West onto the rest (Tarulevicz & Ooi, 2019; Timothy, 2019). The prevalence of these methods has not reduced the serious social challenges in the current economic and market system, including the concentration of wealth in a small number of people, and that our consumption has become the driver of growth that resulted in the unsustainable exploitation of natural resources (Cave & Dredge, 2020).

Following stakeholder theory, another approach to sustainable tourism is to take local stakeholders even more seriously than the above-mentioned approaches. Sustainable tourism strategies should be developed from the ground-up and be community-driven (Muganda et al., 2013; Sofield, 1993). Local communities know their culture, heritage and environment, and have created opportunities for themselves to thrive, and have found solutions to the challenges they face. The community should be consulted extensively, and should lead the development (Okazaki, 2008). A more ground-up approach offers alternative ways of doing local economic, social and environmental activities. Cave and Dredge (2020) suggest that lessons be learned from the Global South and indigenous communities. Local practices are not commodified for tourist consumption but instead residents find their own local ways to do tourism. Consequently there will be less economic leakage, more local control and thus enhance socio-economic equity (Nyaupane et al., 2006). For example, Sin and Minca (2014) examine an Elephant Camp in Thailand, and how traditional ways of life are passed from generation to generation, and how visitors volunteer and engage with a simpler way of life and caring for the elephants over a week or so. Such an approach is community-specific and community-led.

Furthering this line of argument, more researchers and practitioners are advocating regenerative tourism (Ateljevic, 2020; Cave & Dredge, 2020; Pollock, 2019). This view advocates that tourism should be first a resource for community and environmental development (Pollock, 2019). It turns tourism's primary focus on a set of economic activities to being a means for developing the community and to give back to the environment. Traditional and tested local practices often treat the environment respectfully and establish a sustainable future for the community. For instance, in the village of Sirubari, Nepal, residents lead their tourism development with the support of the government (Thapa, 2010). The participation and sense of ownership of the project are seen as necessary for this village-driven tourism project to succeed. The village's Tourism Development and Management Committee assign visitors to hosts on a rotational basis. Members operate and manage their tourism services and facilities, and receive direct economic benefits from tourists (Thapa, 2010). Residents are in the best position to decide on the destination's capacity and capability, as well as, are also sensitive to and responsible to local social, political and cultural norms and practices. The considerations embedded in TPL and PPP are inevitably incapsulated in such community-led tourism development.

So if there is such a thing as sustainable tourism from an Asian perspective, it is most likely to be found in such a community-driven approach. After studying 10 Asian case studies, Nair and Hamzah (2015) propose a nine-step process to developing a community-based tourism project. It starts with assessing the community needs and readiness for tourism, educating and preparing the community for tourism and establishing local champions and supporters. This systematic approach points to the importance of local context, circumstance and support in devising a community-led initiative. But this also suggests that any specific Asian experience may not be transferable to other Asian and non-Asian context. Village experiences may also not be suitable for scaling up elsewhere.

Translating the good principles and values of sustainable tourism is challenging. In moving away from any romanticized view of the local, there are dangers and challenges that homegrown practices are entangled in local politics, struggles and challenges. Any community-driven sustainable tourism strategies can be exploited to perpetuate local inequalities, exploitations and autocracy (Nguyen et al., 2021; Ooi, 2019a). In the earlier mentioned Elephant Camp in Thailand, traditions are staged and corruption and self-interest are infused into the business (Sin & Minca, 2014). There may also be a local warped sense of sustainability. When conservationist Jane Goodall visited Singapore, she was stunned by a suggestion that wildlife in the city-state should be sent to and be conserved in the local zoo (Wong, 2019).

Views on sustainability differ across countries and cultures. Many domestic Asian visitors may not appreciate sustainable tourism activities and facilities in the same way as visitors from Europe and America (Le, 2012). In this context, community-driven tourism has its merits but the reality and the practice are more nuanced and complex. Local ways of doing tourism may actually aggravate the moral limits of the market. Sustainable tourism entails values, and "universal" values may clash with local ones. We have seen that value-driven visitors have ganged up to boycott certain destinations or tourist products. Such attempts starve certain places or products from the benefits of the tourist market. For instance, in 2019 Sultan Hassanal Bolkiah of Brunei passed Islamic criminal laws that allow for the stoning of offenders to death for gay sex and adultery in his country (Holson & Rueb, 2019). Celebrities such as Elton John, Ellen DeGeneres and George Clooney and big global companies rallied behind the boycott of nine luxurious hotels owned by the Sultan, one of the richest men in the world. It remains unclear if there is any economic impact on the Sultan. So, if we are to consume, we might as well bring about some good too but are we being ethnocentric (Ooi, 2021)?

10.4 Limits to Local Alternatives That Bring About a More Sustainable Form of Tourism?

The Table 10.1 compares the different sustainable tourism approaches, and summarises the discussion. The tourism industry has been resilient in responding to changing consumer demands. The desire for tourism to be more responsible and sustainable has created changes in travel and the visitor economy. Stakeholder theory is used as a guide to introduce TBL to tourism businesses. PPP is developed to engage the private sector in providing more efficient, effective and sustainable public tourism services and products. Markets are redesigned and regulated to ensure that the benefits of the industry are better distributed, and that repugnant transactions are avoided. Respect for and initiatives from the grassroots and community are encouraged and promoted in sustainable and community-driven tourism projects. All these mitigate the potential moral limits of the market.

Tourism is not sustainable if it is not sensitive to aspects of culture and nature that are put up for tourist consumption. As in the first moral limit of the market, local practices and behaviour may change when their culture and nature are priced. Tourism is also not sustainable when many local stakeholders and the environment do not benefit from the industry, and instead are inconvenienced or even destroyed. This is the second limit of the market. Are there Asian approaches to addressing these moral limits, and thus offer lessons for other parts of the world in sustainable tourism?

The direct answer is that many of these sustainable tourism practices are context- and circumstance-specific. Tourism is a global phenomenon, and any society that engages with it needs to largely embrace internationally-accepted institutions, structures, regulations, technologies, practices and norms, such as border control, health and safety standards, currency exchange facilities and means of communication. As alluded to in this chapter, the decentralization of economic control and the celebration of the local often ignore the importance of outside or global influences in communities. Common sustainable tourism approaches – TBL, PPP, redesigned

Table 10.1 Comparing the four sustainable tourism approaches

	Triple bottom lines	Public-private partnerships	Market designs	Community-led development
Principle and approach	Companies account for and measure their profits, and their social and environmental impacts.	Bring private and public sectors together so as to serve the needs of industry, community and environment.	Redesigned market mechanisms to shape business, visitor and resident behavior.	Community-led tourism initiatives and activities that respect the local situation and environment.
Who takes initiatives and the main mechanisms	Businesses and organizations devise an expanded accounting framework that incorporates their contributions to the environment and the community.	Policy makers and regulators devise schemes that require or encourage private sector involvement in delivering public services and goods. The partnerships ensure that the interests and agendas of different stakeholders are included and aligned.	Regulators and policy makers redesign markets to influence business, visitor and resident behavior. Market mechanisms aim to reduce market failures and to distribute the benefits from the market more equitably.	Members of the community lead or work with businesses and regulators. Local community goals and agendas should shape tourism development strategies.
Addressing moral limit 1	Repugnant transactions should be avoided.	Repugnant transactions should be avoided. Businesses and the community can generate new acceptable economic, social and environmental values.	Repugnant commercial transactions are prohibited. Transactions of sacred and priceless services can be bartered or non-commercially transacted.	Communities will decide from their own sentiments, practices and norms to allow what can and cannot be offered to visitors.
Addressing moral limit 2	Benefits are measured and distributed to the community and environment, albeit only selectively.	Because of aligned interests of the public and private partners, the benefits from the market are broadly distributed to the business, community, environment.	Markets are redesigned through regulations and taxes, ensuring that market benefits are shared more widely.	Local communities have established ways to support themselves and distribute welfare to their members. Tourism benefits will be distributed in a similar manner.

(continued)

Table 10.1 (continued)

	Triple bottom lines	Public-private partnerships	Market designs	Community-led development
Main limitations of approach	Selective issues, and social and environmental causes are appropriated solely for marketing and public relations purposes. Getting stakeholder cooperation is challenging and may not be forthcoming.	Partnerships may not be equal, and the PPP project may be appropriated by a more powerful partner.	A perfectly redesigned market remains a dream. The redesigned market may not be appropriate for all tourism activities, and the redesigned market may not eliminate inequity and injustices.	Local politics and entrenched local corruption may drive the community-led initiatives.
Asian context	TPL is used across the world, and the Asian context is reflected in the selected social and environmental causes in the people and planet bottom lines.	Policy makers have adopted PPP within their economic, political and social circumstances. There is no single Asian way of doing partnerships, and any partnership reflect or emerge from local circumstances.	The role of the state in the market is debated globally. Any redesigned market reflects the ideological position of the country, as whether the economy should be more regulated or more freewheeling.	Any community-led tourism strategy will reflect the community's social and cultural embeddedness. That can be a boon or a bane.

markets and community-led initiatives – account for both the global and local, and aim to make an international industry more responsible to local concerns and issues.

There are many celebrated sustainable tourism examples, and their successes should not be discounted. This chapter however does not take a romantic view of the community. Local practices and way of doing things may not be the best way forward even if they have been around for a long time. Shifting economic control from multinationals to corrupt local chiefs, for instance, does not entail a more sustainable economy that will protect the environment and the community. Economic exchanges based on social hierarchies and personal relations may work under a small-scale context, and they may just merely perpetuate the inequality and inequity of the system. So-called global standards – such as transparency, accountability and the rule of law – as assumed in various sustainable tourism approaches matter. While we do not want to be ethnocentric, being culturally relativistic has its own perils (Ooi, 2019a, b).

So can Asia offer alternatives to doing better sustainable tourism? The challenges of tourism are often found globally but the impact and the solutions are local. The

Asian sustainable tourism solutions straddle between global issues and local solutions, like in all places. These solutions entail respecting specific situations to find local answers, and the process must be transparent, accountable and respectful of the rule of law, so as to bring about better equity and a wider sharing of benefits from tourism. These solutions must aim to mitigate the moral limits of the market, not aggravate them.

References

Andersson, T. D., & Getz, D. (2009). Tourism as a mixed industry: Differences between private, public and not-for-profit festivals. *Tourism Management, 30*(6), 847–856. https://doi.org/10.1016/j.tourman.2008.12.008

Angelo, P., & Maria, C. (2010). Analysing tourism stakeholders networks. *Tourism Review, 65*(4), 17–30. Retrieved from http://dx.doi.org/10.1108/16605371011093845

Arguea, N. M., & Hawkins, R. R. (2015). The rate elasticity of Florida tourist development (aka bed) taxes. *Applied Economics, 47*(18), 1823–1832. https://doi.org/10.1080/00036846.2014.1000519

Ateljevic, I. (2020). Transforming the (tourism) world for good and (re)generating the potential 'new normal'. *Tourism Geographies, 22*(3), 467–475. https://doi.org/10.1080/14616688.2020.1759134

Budeanu, A. (2009). Environmental supply chain management in tourism: The case of large tour operators. *Journal of Cleaner Production, 17*(16), 1385–1392. https://doi.org/10.1016/j.jclepro.2009.06.010

Budeanu, A., Miller, G., Moscardo, G., & Ooi, C.-S. (2016). Sustainable tourism, progress, challenges and opportunities: An introduction. *Journal of Cleaner Production, 111*, 285–294. https://doi.org/10.1016/j.jclepro.2015.10.027

Burgen, S. (2018, June 25). "Tourists go home, refugees welcome": Why Barcelona chose migrants over visitors. *The Guardian*. Retrieved from https://www.theguardian.com/cities/2018/jun/25/tourists-go-home-refugees-welcome-why-barcelona-chose-migrants-over-visitors

Burns, S. (2010). Local authorities, funding tourism services and tourist taxes. *Local Economy: The Journal of the Local Economy Policy Unit, 25*(1), 47–57. https://doi.org/10.1080/02690940903545398

Castellani, V., & Sala, S. (2010). Sustainable performance index for tourism policy development. *Tourism Management, 31*(6), 871–880. https://doi.org/10.1016/j.tourman.2009.10.001

Cave, J., & Dredge, D. (2020). Regenerative tourism needs diverse economic practices. *Tourism Geographies, 22*(3), 503–513. https://doi.org/10.1080/14616688.2020.1768434

Chambers, D., & Buzinde, C. (2015). Tourism and decolonisation: Locating research and self. *Annals of Tourism Research, 51*, 1–16. https://doi.org/10.1016/j.annals.2014.12.002

Cheng, Z., Yang, Z., Gao, H., Tao, H., & Xu, M. (2018). Does PPP matter to sustainable tourism development? An analysis of the spatial effect of the tourism PPP policy in China. *Sustainability, 10*(11), 4058. https://doi.org/10.3390/su10114058

Deville, A., Wearing, S., & McDonald, M. (2016). WWOOFing in Australia: Ideas and lessons for a de-commodified sustainability tourism. *Journal of Sustainable Tourism, 24*(1), 91–113. https://doi.org/10.1080/09669582.2015.1049607

Dyson, P. (2012). Slum tourism: Representing and interpreting 'reality' in Dharavi, Mumbai. *Tourism Geographies, 14*(2), 254–274. https://doi.org/10.1080/14616688.2011.609900

Fennell, D. A. (2018). *Tourism ethics* (2nd ed.). Channel View Publications.

Fligstein, N. (2002). *The architecture of markets: An economic sociology of twenty-first-century capitalist societies*. Princeton University Press.

Font, X., & Lynes, J. (2018). Corporate social responsibility in tourism and hospitality. *Journal of Sustainable Tourism, 26*(7), 1027–1042. https://doi.org/10.1080/09669582.2018.1488856

Freire-Medeiros, B. (2009). The favela and its touristic transits. *Geoforum, 40*(4), 580–588. https://doi.org/10.1016/j.geoforum.2008.10.007

Garcia, O., & Cater, C. (2020). Life below water; challenges for tourism partnerships in achieving ocean literacy. *Journal of Sustainable Tourism*, 1–20. https://doi.org/10.1080/09669582.2020.1850747

Germann Molz, J. (2013). Social networking technologies and the moral economy of alternative tourism: The case of couchsurfing.org. *Annals of Tourism Research, 43*, 210–230. https://doi.org/10.1016/j.annals.2013.08.001

Gurung, D. B., & Seeland, K. (2008). Ecotourism in Bhutan. *Annals of Tourism Research, 35*(2), 489–508. https://doi.org/10.1016/j.annals.2008.02.004

Hales, R., Dredge, D., Higgins-Desbiolles, F., & Jamal, T. (2018). Academic activism in tourism studies: Critical narratives from four researchers. *Tourism Analysis, 23*(2), 189–199. https://doi.org/10.3727/108354218X15210313504544

Holson, L. M., & Rueb, E. S. (2019, April 3). Brunei hotel boycott gathers steam as anti-gay law goes into effect. *The New York Times*. Retrieved from https://www.nytimes.com/2019/04/03/world/asia/brunei-hotel-boycotts.html

Iossa, E., & Martimort, D. (2016). Corruption in PPPs, incentives and contract incompleteness. *International Journal of Industrial Organization, 44*, 85–100. https://doi.org/10.1016/j.ijindorg.2015.10.007

Jamal, T. (2019). *Justice and ethics in tourism*. Routledge.

Jamal, T. B., & Getz, D. (1995). Collaboration theory and community tourism planning. *Annals of Tourism Research, 22*(1), 186–204. https://doi.org/10.1016/0160-7383(94)00067-3

Lai, S., & Ooi, C.-S. (2015). Branded as a World Heritage city: The politics afterwards. *Place Branding and Public Diplomacy, 11*(4), 276–292. https://doi.org/10.1057/pb.2015.12

Le, T. (2012). *Sustainable tourism, a balancing act*. Retrieved June 10, 2021, from https://www.reportingasean.net/sustainable-tourism-a-balancing-act/

Lin, M. (2015, September 27). Haw Par Villa looks set for another makeover. *The Straits Times*. Retrieved from http://str.sg/Z2qw

Liu, Z. (2003). Sustainable tourism development: A critique. *Journal of Sustainable Tourism, 11*(6), 459–475. https://doi.org/10.1080/09669580308667216

MacCannell, D. (1992). *Empty meeting grounds: The tourist papers*. Routledge.

Mariani, M. M., & Kylänen, M. (2014). The relevance of public-private partnerships in coopetition: Empirical evidence from the tourism sector. *International Journal of Business Environment, 6*(1), 106–125.

Markham, F., Young, M., Reis, A., & Higham, J. (2018). Does carbon pricing reduce air travel? Evidence from the Australian 'Clean Energy Future' policy, July 2012 to June 2014. *Journal of Transport Geography, 70*, 206–214. https://doi.org/10.1016/j.jtrangeo.2018.06.008

Mietzner, A., & Storch, A. (2019). *Language and tourism in postcolonial settings* (A. Mietzner & A. Storch, Eds.). Channel View Publications. https://doi.org/10.21832/MIETZN6782.

Muganda, M., Sirima, A., & Ezra, P. M. (2013). The role of local communities in tourism development: Grassroots perspectives from Tanzania. *Journal of Human Ecology, 41*(1), 53–66. https://doi.org/10.1080/09709274.2013.11906553

Nair, V., & Hamzah, A. (2015). Successful community-based tourism approaches for rural destinations: The Asia Pacific experience. *Worldwide Hospitality and Tourism Themes, 7*(5), 429–439. https://doi.org/10.1108/WHATT-06-2015-0023

Narassimhan, E., Gallagher, K. S., Koester, S., & Alejo, J. R. (2018). Carbon pricing in practice: A review of existing emissions trading systems. *Climate Policy, 18*(8), 967–991. https://doi.org/10.1080/14693062.2018.1467827

Nepal, R., & Nepal, S. K. (2019). Managing overtourism through economic taxation: Policy lessons from five countries. *Tourism Geographies*, 1–22. https://doi.org/10.1080/14616688.2019.1669070

Nguyen, D. T. N., D'Hauteserre, A.-M., & Serrao-Neumann, S. (2021). Intrinsic barriers to and opportunities for community empowerment in community-based tourism development in Thai Nguyen province, Vietnam. *Journal of Sustainable Tourism*, 1–19. https://doi.org/10.1080/09669582.2021.1884689

Noor, N. A. M., & Kumar, D. (2014). ECO friendly 'activities' vs ECO friendly 'attitude': Travelers intention to choose green hotels in Malaysia. *World Applied Sciences Journal, 30*(4), 506–513. https://doi.org/10.5829/idosi.wasj.2014.30.04.14062

Nordhaus, W. (2019). Climate change: The ultimate challenge for economics. *American Economic Review, 109*(6), 1991–2014. https://doi.org/10.1257/aer.109.6.1991

North, D. C. (1991). Institutions. *Journal of Economic Perspectives, 5*(1), 97–112. https://doi.org/10.1257/jep.5.1.97

Nyaupane, G. P., Morais, D. B., & Dowler, L. (2006). The role of community involvement and number/type of visitors on tourism impacts: A controlled comparison of Annapurna, Nepal and Northwest Yunnan, China. *Tourism Management, 27*(6), 1373–1385. https://doi.org/10.1016/j.tourman.2005.12.013

Okazaki, E. (2008). A community-based tourism model: Its conception and use. *Journal of Sustainable Tourism, 16*(5), 511–529. https://doi.org/10.1080/09669580802159594

Ooi, C.-S. (2011). Branding and the accreditation approach: Singapore. In N. J. Morgan, A. Pritchard, & R. Pride (Eds.), *Destination brands: Managing place reputation* (pp. 185–196). Elsevier.

Ooi, C.-S. (2013). Tourism policy challenges: Balancing acts, co-operative stakeholders and maintaining authenticity. In M. Smith & G. Richards (Eds.), *Routledge handbook of cultural tourism* (pp. 67–74). Routledge.

Ooi, C.-S. (2018). Global city for the arts: Weaving tourism into cultural policy. In T. Chong (Ed.), *The state and the arts in Singapore* (pp. 165–179). World Scientific. https://doi.org/10.1142/9789813236899_0008

Ooi, C.-S. (2019a). Asian tourists and cultural complexity: Implications for practice and the Asianisation of tourism scholarship. *Tourism Management Perspectives, 31*, 14–23. https://doi.org/10.1016/j.tmp.2019.03.007

Ooi, C.-S. (2019b). The changing role of tourism policy in Singapore's cultural development: From explicit to insidious. *Tourism Culture & Communication, 19*(4), 231–242. https://doi.org/10.3727/194341419X15542140077648

Ooi, C.-S. (2020). Sensitive and sensible tourism development. In C.-S. Ooi & A. Hardy (Eds.), *Tourism in Tasmania* (pp. 9–22). Forty South. Retrieved from https://www.utas.edu.au/__data/assets/pdf_file/0011/1283366/book-tourism-in-tasmania.pdf

Ooi, C.-S. (2021). Gay tourism: A celebration and appropriation of queer difference. In O. Vorobjovas-Pinta (Ed.), *Gay tourism: New perspectives* (pp. 15–33). Channel View Publications.

Pollock, A. (2019). *Regenerative tourism: The natural maturation of sustainability*. Retrieved March 11, 2021, from https://medium.com/activate-the-future/regenerative-tourism-the-natural-maturation-of-sustainability-26e6507d0fcb

Puriri, A., & McIntosh, A. (2019). A cultural framework for Māori tourism: Values and processes of a Whānau tourism business development. *Journal of the Royal Society of New Zealand, 49*(sup1), 89–103. https://doi.org/10.1080/03036758.2019.1656260

Randalls, S. (2017). Assembling climate expertise: Carbon markets, neoliberalism and science. In V. Higgins & W. Larner (Eds.), *Assembling neoliberalism* (pp. 67–85). Palgrave Macmillan US. https://doi.org/10.1057/978-1-137-58204-1_4

Ringham, K., & Miles, S. (2018). The boundary of corporate social responsibility reporting: The case of the airline industry. *Journal of Sustainable Tourism*, 1–20. https://doi.org/10.1080/09669582.2017.1423317

Rio+20 United Nations Conference on Sustainable Development. (2012). *The future we want*. Rio. Retrieved from https://webunwto.s3-eu-west-1.amazonaws.com/2019-07/rio20outcomedocument.pdf

Roth, A. E. (2015). *Who gets what and why: The hidden world of matchmaking and market design*. William Collins.

Ruhanen, L. (2013). Local government: Facilitator or inhibitor of sustainable tourism development? *Journal of Sustainable Tourism, 21*(1), 80–98. https://doi.org/10.1080/09669582.2012.680463

Sidelsky, E., & Skidelsky, R. (2015). The moral limits of markets. In E. Skidelsky & R. Skidelsky (Eds.), *Are markets moral?* (pp. 77–102). Palgrave Macmillan. https://doi.org/10.2491/jjsth1970.6.153

Simmel, G. (1978). *The philosophy of money*. Routledge & Kegan Paul.

Sin, H. L., & Minca, C. (2014). Touring responsibility: The trouble with 'going local' in community-based tourism in Thailand. *Geoforum, 51*, 96–106. https://doi.org/10.1016/j.geoforum.2013.10.004

Singapore Airlines. (2020). *Sustainability report FY2019–20*. Singapore.

Sofield, T. H. B. (1993). Indigenous tourism development. *Annals of Tourism Research, 20*(4), 729–750. https://doi.org/10.1016/0160-7383(93)90094-J

Steinbrink, M. (2012). 'We did the slum!' – Urban poverty tourism in historical perspective. *Tourism Geographies, 14*(2), 213–234. https://doi.org/10.1080/14616688.2012.633216

Tarulevicz, N., & Ooi, C. (2019). Food safety and tourism in Singapore: Between microbial Russian roulette and Michelin stars. *Tourism Geographies*. https://doi.org/10.1080/14616688.2019.1654540

Thapa, K. (2010). *Village tourism development & management in Nepal: A case study of Sirubari Village*. Retrieved June 8, 2021, from https://ecoclub.com/education/articles/488-sirubari-village-tourism-nepal

Timothy, D. (2019). *Handbook of globalisation and tourism* (D. J. Timothy, Ed.). Edward Elgar Publishing. https://doi.org/10.4337/9781786431295.

Tondani, D. (2009). Universal basic income and negative income tax: Two different ways of thinking redistribution. *The Journal of Socio-Economics, 38*(2), 246–255. https://doi.org/10.1016/j.socec.2008.10.006

Tzanelli, R. (2018). Slum tourism: A review of state-of-the-art scholarship. *Tourism Culture & Communication, 18*(2), 149–155. https://doi.org/10.3727/109830418X15230353469528

Vernon, J., Essex, S., Pinder, D., & Curry, K. (2005). Collaborative policymaking. *Annals of Tourism Research, 32*(2), 325–345. https://doi.org/10.1016/j.annals.2004.06.005

Wachsmuth, D., & Weisler, A. (2018). Airbnb and the rent gap: Gentrification through the sharing economy. *Environment and Planning A: Economy and Space, 50*(6), 1147–1170. https://doi.org/10.1177/0308518X18778038

Williamson, O. E. (1998). Transaction cost economics: How it works; where it is headed. *De Economist, 146*, 23–58. https://doi.org/10.1023/A:1003263908567

Wong, E. P. Y., de Lacy, T., & Jiang, M. (2012). Climate change adaptation in tourism in the South Pacific—Potential contribution of public–private partnerships. *Tourism Management Perspectives, 4*, 136–144. https://doi.org/10.1016/j.tmp.2012.08.001

Wong, P. T. (2019, November 27). Shocking that Singaporeans ask for wildlife to be "returned" to the zoo, says Jane Goodall. *Today*. Retrieved from https://www.todayonline.com/singapore/shocking-that-singaporeans-ask-wildlife-be-returned-zoo-says-jane-goodall

Zapata, M. J., & Hall, C. M. (2012). Public–private collaboration in the tourism sector: Balancing legitimacy and effectiveness in local tourism partnerships. The Spanish case. *Journal of Policy Research in Tourism, Leisure and Events, 4*(1), 61–83. https://doi.org/10.1080/19407963.2011.634069

Can-Seng Ooi is an anthropologist/sociologist. He is also Professor of Cultural and Heritage Tourism at the School of Social Sciences, University of Tasmania. His research career, in and outside the university system, spans over three decades. Singapore, Denmark, Australia and China are some of the countries he has conducted investigations. Besides tourism studies, he has contributed significantly to theories and understanding of art worlds, cross-cultural management, the experience economy, and place branding. His personal website is www.cansengooi.com.

Index

A
Access to recreation, 10, 66, 76
Accountability, 20, 21, 187, 193
Angkor Wat, 168, 173
Anxieties, 83, 87, 90, 91, 94
Asian tourism, 2, 7–10, 12, 13, 189
Asian values, 20, 34, 35
Attachments, 66, 68, 75
Authenticity, 66, 94, 130, 132, 181

B
Bali, 12, 123, 124, 128, 142, 143, 145, 148, 150–152, 154, 155
Bayanihan, 32–34
Belt and Road Initiative (BRI), 169, 172
Boracay wetlands, 9, 25, 27–33
Borneo, 10, 69, 70
Bumiputra policy, 86

C
Cambodia, 7, 12, 13, 164–173, 181, 185
Cambodian Ministry of Tourism, 173
Cambodian Tourism Development Strategic Plan, 168
China, 7, 8, 11, 23, 33, 40, 82, 83, 85–88, 91, 94, 102, 103, 111, 114, 115, 149, 168–172, 187
China Ready initiative, 169
Chinese consumer, 172, 173
Chinese investments, 169–171
Chinese tourism, 115
Chinese tourists, 10, 11, 75, 83–89, 91–95, 169, 172
Chinese visitor, 10, 82–95, 169, 170
Civil society, 32, 167, 177, 178, 184, 185
Collaborations, 9, 20, 24–26, 33, 34, 44, 111, 113, 114, 184, 185
Community, 5, 9–11, 13, 20, 22, 23, 28, 29, 32, 34, 42, 46, 47, 66, 68, 82, 83, 87, 90, 95, 104, 107, 111, 112, 115, 141–145, 152, 155, 156, 177–179, 181, 183–186, 188, 192, 193
Community based tourism (CBT), 10, 41–53, 67, 124
Community-led tourism, 13, 189, 190, 193
Community participation, 10, 39–59, 111, 112, 167
Conviviality, 131
Corporate social responsibility (CSR), 9, 19–25, 27, 29–35, 184
Corruption, 82, 187, 190, 193
COVID-19, 2, 7, 9, 11, 12, 102, 122–134, 141, 142, 144, 145, 148, 149, 151–156, 169
COVID-19 pandemic, 2, 12, 33, 40, 42, 70, 86, 107, 115, 122, 123, 125, 126, 129–131, 142, 145, 147, 150, 151, 154, 155, 165, 168, 173, 181, 184, 185, 187
Crisis management, 149

D

Destination, 2, 3, 7–13, 20, 23, 24, 41, 49, 56, 58, 59, 65–70, 72, 76–78, 83, 85, 88, 90, 92, 94, 102, 104–106, 112–115, 124, 126–131, 133, 141–145, 150, 151, 155, 156, 168, 169, 172, 179, 180, 183, 188, 190, 191
Destination image, 58, 85, 86
Destination management organization (DMO), 11, 102, 105–108, 113, 115
Discourse, 11, 21, 88, 91, 92, 123–126, 129–134
Discourse analysis, 124, 134
Discrimination, 82, 84, 86, 88–94
Diversification, 12, 103, 128, 165–167, 170, 171

E

Economic dimensions, 5, 49–50, 56, 58, 141
Ecotourism, 27, 41, 106, 124, 164, 165, 168, 188
Emerging destinations, 115
Energy Development Corporation (EDC), 25, 29–33
Environmental dimensions, 5, 10, 51–52, 57, 58, 84
Environmental sustainability, 12, 27, 51, 55, 58, 109–111, 115, 129, 131–133, 140
Ethnic harmony, 88–91, 93
Ethnic tourism, 7

F

Families, 9, 20, 22, 25, 29, 30, 32–34, 43, 44, 46, 49, 73, 75, 83, 89, 90, 92, 181, 182
Filipino values, 33
Focus group, 66, 71
Forestry, 11, 103, 104, 106–112, 114, 115, 141
Foucauldian discourse analysis, 125

G

Genhe, 11, 101–116
Globalization, 178, 179
Green development, 109

H

Health and hygiene protocols, 11, 12, 123, 128, 129, 131, 133
History, 7, 23, 112, 115, 145, 150

Homestays, 7, 10, 39–59, 171
Homestay sustainability conceptual framework, 10, 48–53, 58
Horizontal coordination, 35
Hospitality industry, 12, 104, 141, 155
Host communities, 10, 22, 41, 65–78, 82, 90, 91, 178, 181
Host-guest relations, 11, 84, 93–95

I

Indicators, 10, 40, 49–53, 56, 57, 66, 72, 77, 78, 102, 111, 113, 114, 130, 140, 149
Indonesia, 9, 11, 12, 22, 34, 40, 45, 83, 122–126, 129–132, 134, 140–156
Indonesian tourism, 11, 12, 122–134, 140, 141, 145, 149–151, 155
Industrial transition, 11, 102, 115
Inner Mongolia, 11, 102, 106, 107
Institutional dimensions, 4, 5, 41, 50–51, 55–58
Interpretive, 71, 87
Interviews, 25, 66, 71, 87, 116, 142, 151, 152
Intrinsic values, 13, 181, 183

L

Lesson-drawing, 25, 27
Local communities, 2, 5, 10–13, 24, 39–59, 76, 82, 84, 85, 93, 94, 105, 124, 132, 141, 143, 144, 150, 152, 164–167, 170–173, 178, 179, 183, 184, 189, 192
Local wisdom, 130, 132, 134

M

Malaysia, 7, 10, 34, 40, 41, 43–47, 49, 50, 52, 53, 58, 59, 66, 70, 77, 82–95, 140, 145, 181, 188
Marine parks, 10, 66, 70, 75–77
Market redesign, 187–189, 191–193
Meanings, 66, 68, 69, 71–73, 76, 77, 88, 125, 132, 165
Miso Walai Village Homestay, 41, 45–53
Moral limits, 13, 177–194
Multiculturalism, 86, 88–89
Multi-dimensional perspectives, 41
Mutual understandings, 84–86

Index

N
Nepotism, 187
New normal, 11, 12, 122–134, 141, 142, 149, 151–153, 155, 156
Non-governmental organization (NGO), 42, 164, 167

O
Outbound tourism, 83, 102

P
Philippines, 9, 20, 22–25, 28, 32–35, 140
Place branding, 113
Places, 10, 20, 21, 66–69, 71, 72, 75–78, 82, 83, 88, 92, 94, 103, 125, 127–129, 142, 145, 151, 180–183, 186, 187, 191, 194
Pole of Cold, 108
Post-COVID-19 tourism, 129, 132, 133
Poverty alleviation, 5, 42, 67, 102, 168
Power-relations, 125
Prices, 40, 45, 76, 140, 172, 179–181, 183, 188
Public and private partnerships, 9, 20, 32, 179, 184, 186, 187, 192

Q
Q-methodology, 66, 71
Qualitative, 10, 66, 71, 77, 142
Quality tourism, 11, 67, 69, 123, 126, 129–132

R
Re-aligning business processes, 12, 153, 155
Recovery strategies, 12, 152–155
Reflections, 91–92, 140–156
Reformulation, 140–156
Regenerative tourism, 82, 190
Regional tourism, 106, 114, 128, 141
Responding to new business opportunities, 12, 153, 155
Restructuring the business, 12, 153, 155
Retargeting the market, 12, 153–155
Revenue leakages, 13, 49, 164, 172
Rule of law, 187, 193, 194

S
Sense of place, 10, 65–78
Siem Reap, 168, 173
Sihanoukville, 168–170, 172

Silence, 10, 11, 82, 84, 91–93
Social distancing, 8, 11, 123, 126–128, 131, 145, 150, 153
Social enterprises, 12, 13, 21, 164–168, 170, 171
Social entrepreneurship, 164, 166, 172
Social equity, 6, 42, 58, 124
Social justice, 30, 66
Social learning, 9, 20, 24–27, 29–35
Social media, 83, 85, 91, 93, 94, 154
Social sustainability, 10, 11, 65–78, 83–85, 88, 93–95, 111–112, 115, 124, 131, 143
Socio-cultural perspective, 52, 57–58
Stakeholders, 4–12, 20, 22, 24, 26, 29, 30, 32, 33, 35, 50, 51, 53, 55–59, 66, 67, 94, 101–116, 122, 123, 125, 127–132, 143, 144, 149–151, 154–156, 166, 171, 172, 184–187, 189, 191–193
Survival strategies, 149
Sustainability, 2, 5, 6, 8–13, 19–35, 39–59, 65–69, 72, 76–78, 81–95, 102, 103, 106–108, 111, 113–114, 122–134, 141, 143, 144, 149, 156, 164–167, 185, 190
Sustainable development, 2–6, 10, 27, 41, 42, 66, 70, 102, 111, 123, 143, 164, 165, 167–170, 177, 178, 184
Sustainable livelihoods, 12, 42, 164, 166
Sustainable tourism, 1–13, 23, 41–43, 46, 48, 50, 53, 56, 58, 66, 68, 77, 82, 101–116, 123, 124, 126, 131–134, 141–144, 149–151, 155, 156, 164–173, 177–194
Sustainable tourism development, 5, 9, 11, 12, 20, 41, 102, 103, 106, 108, 114, 124, 141, 144, 154, 155, 164–173, 179, 186

T
The Greater Khingan Range, 102, 106, 107
Top-down policy, 109
Tourism, 2–13, 19–25, 32, 34, 35, 40–47, 49–52, 57–59, 65–68, 70, 71, 76–78, 82–86, 88, 91–94, 102–107, 109, 110, 112–115, 122–134, 140–145, 147–152, 154–156, 164–173, 178–182, 184–194
Tourism-based social enterprise (TSE), 170, 171
Tourism boycotts, 191
Tourism developments, 7, 10–12, 40, 42, 51, 66–68, 76–78, 84, 94, 102, 104, 115, 123, 124, 130, 132, 142–144, 164–168, 171, 179, 184, 186, 190, 192
Tourism in Indonesia, 122, 141, 142
Tourism recovery, 77, 130

Tourism research, 2, 12, 105, 155, 164
Tourism sustainability, 2, 5, 8–11, 13, 41,
    104–106, 113, 122–134, 140–156
Tourism villages, 128, 130
Tourist bubbles, 83, 90, 93
Tourist walls, 10, 11, 81–95
Transparency, 20, 21, 35, 47, 187, 193
Travel reviews, 83, 84
Triple-bottom-line, 20, 21, 102, 108, 114, 141,
    179, 184, 185

V
Visitor employed photography
    (VEP), 71

W
Well-being, 42, 66, 68, 72,
    78, 186
Western traditions, 21, 34